EDMUND BURKE

ON THE
AMERICAN REVOLUTION
Selected Speeches and Letters

Edited by
ELLIOTT ROBERT BARKAN

Second Edition with
NEW PREFACE

PETER SMITH
Gloucester, Massachusetts
1972

ON THE AMERICAN REVOLUTION

Introduction, compilation and headnotes
copyright © 1966 by Elliott Robert Barkan

Second edition, with new Preface
copyright © 1972 by Elliott Robert Barkan

International Standard Book Number: 0-8446-0045-8
Library of Congress Catalog Card Number: 72-76994

Printed in the United States of America

ON THE
AMERICAN
REVOLUTION

Contents

TEXT

INTRODUCTION
by
ELLIOTT R. BARKAN

ALTHOUGH Edmund Burke (1729–1797) has long been recognized as one of England's greatest orators and political philosophers, exhaustive investigations of his life and ideas have yielded more questions than satisfying answers. The questions range from his definition of natural law to the consistency of his views on the French and American Revolutions. This edition attempts to shed more light on only one aspect of Burke's life and thought: the American Revolution.

It is my contention that Burke developed a sophisticated and complex political philosophy during the earlier half of his life— one to which he consistently adhered, one against which he measured all issues. His repudiation of the French Revolution following his support of American resistance to Great Britain was not, consequently, hypocritical but a logical step in view of the dramatically contrasting nature of those two momentous events. An outline of the major points of his political thought, though scarcely doing justice to his genius, will help throw more light on the motives for his behavior during that era of the American Revolution.

I

Burke was reared in his father's religion, Anglicanism, but his mother, a Roman Catholic, nevertheless helped to instill in him a deep belief in the existence of God. He therefore maintained that it was God who had ordained government as a necessary instrument to curb man's excesses in order that he might know true liberty and the fulfillment of his true natural, civil rights, which may be summed up as the right to a decent life for oneself and one's family.[1]

---

[1] Alfred Cobban, *Edmund Burke and The Revolt Against the Eighteenth Century*, 2nd ed. (London, 1960), p. 52; Peter J. Stanlis, *Burke and the Natural Law*, (Ann Arbor, 1958), pp. 23, 68, 71, 160-61; Burke

His respect for Christianity, the English Common Law, and the classical tradition, particularly Cicero and Aquinas, led him to conclude that God had also established a universal natural law that bound all men and represented reason, justice, equity, and the ethical teachings of Jesus Christ.[2]

Furthermore, impressed by Montesquieu's writings, Burke maintained that the particular form of each government as well as the laws of each society ought to reflect the customs, composition, and character of the people subject to them.[3]

Imbued, in addition, with the particular principles of the English Common Law and constitutional development, Burke developed a bitter hostility to abstract, *a priori* schemes for any polity because by their very nature they were inflexible and consequently would be outmoded at the outset.[4]

He was, therefore, opposed to radical innovations in politics, for the Common Law was a lesson in the success of political evolution. He never believed, though, that preserving the *status quo*, much less any regression, was the best policy, for he understood that if a state were to survive it must adapt to new and unforeseen circumstances.[5] He maintained instead that a statesman's most important criteria in matters of government policy were prudence and expediency.[6]

Moreover, since government was entrusted to statesmen by the people who created it and by God who demanded it as a

to Richard Shackleton, July 26, 1744, *The Correspondence of Edmund Burke*, Thomas Copeland ed., (4 vols., Cambridge, 1958 —). Unless otherwise noted, all letters may be found in this collection, hereafter cited as *Corr.*

[2] Philip Magnus, *Edmund Burke, A Life*, (London, 1939), 125-27; John C. Weston, "Edmund Burke's View of History," *Review of Politics*, XXIII (1961), pp. 218-19; *Works* [see below, p. xxvii], VI, 323, 326-27, 332.

[3] John Morley, *Burke* (New York, 1879), p. 48, 82; Stanlis, p. 304, n25; *Works*, I, 395.

[4] Weston, pp. 212-13, 220, 223-24; *PH*, XXVII, 283; Carl B. Cone, *Burke and The Nature of Politics; The Age of The American Revolution* (Lexington, 1957), pp. 21-22.

[5] Even during the French Revolution Burke never became reactionary. See Weston, pp. 217-18: F.L. Lucas, *The Art of Living: Four Eighteenth Century Minds* (London, 1959), p. 173: J.G.A. Pocock, "Burke and the Ancient Constitution; A Problem in the History of Ideas," *Historical Journal*, III (1960), 125, 132-33, 142.

[6] Stanlis, p. 120: Howard B. White, "Edmund Burke on Political Theory and Practice," *Social Research*, XVII (1950), pp. 126-27.

necessary institution, it was a trust best conferred on the most responsible class, the aristocracy.[7]

These conclusions in general led Burke to venerate the Settlement of 1689 as the culmination of England's political evolution. Her limited monarchy and parliamentary structure most successfully preserved the vital institutions of society, the church, the constitution, the law, and property, protected the liberties of the people, and adjusted to the inevitable changes that confront every government.[8] Born an Irishman, Edmund Burke, in his heart, became an English Whig in the best tradition of 1689.

* * * *

At the age of twenty-one, two years after graduating from Trinity College, Dublin, Burke decided to try his fortunes in London. Although the years between 1750—when he arrived in England—and 1757—when he began writing *The Annual Register*—have often been called his "missing years," it is apparent that this was a period during which much of his political philosophy developed and matured. In 1757 he revised extensively his cousin William's work, *An Account of European Settlements in America*, in which he expressed his earliest views on America. With regard to Britain's trade policy, Burke declared, as most Englishmen did then, that "the only points at which our restrictions should aim" were colonial importation of foreign manufactured goods and those colonial manufactured goods also produced in England. "These purposes ought not [however] to be compassed by absolute prohibitions and penalties, which would be unpolitical and unjust. . . ."[9]

But America represented much more to Burke than one part of an imperial commercial system; it was a land occupied by fellow countrymen, men who could exploit the infinite opportunities she proffered. "In no part of the world are the ordinary sort so independent, or possess so many of the conveniences of life. . . ."[10] He seemed to feel America beckoning him, too, and

[7] Edmund and William Burke, *An Account of European Settlements in America* 2 vols., 6th ed. (London, 1777), II, 267. Cited hereafter as *Account. Works*, VI, 473: *PH* [see below, p. xxvii], XVI, 376: Cobban, pp. 47, 70: Cone, pp. 44, 180, 221.

[8] See above, Note 4.

[9] *Account*, II, 182-83.

[10] *Ibid.*, pp. 167, 262: B. to John Noble, February 21, 1775.

more than once pondered the idea of emigrating. In 1761 he sought, unsuccessfully though, the position of Agent for New York.[11]

During these years, England's injustices against Ireland also troubled him. His wrath against the Popery Laws[12] had never subsided, and he now, in the early 1760's, attempted to translate that anger into a *Tract on the Popery Laws in Ireland.* Although it was never completed, the ideas embodied in the existing fragments are an important link in the life-long chain of Burke's political thought.

In support of the repeal of the Popery Laws, he declared that the law was made for the good of the people, and, therefore, the ultimate consent of the people, actual or implied, was "absolutely essential to its validity."

A law against the majority of the people is in substance a law against the people itself. . . . It is not particular injustice, but general oppression. . . .

It followed, then, that if an act were repugnant to a large part of the population and their approbation denied to that act, it had no authority; for no body of men have a right to make what laws they please, or [to legislate upon the presumption] that laws derive any authority from their institution merely and independently of the quality of the subject matter."[13]

He concluded with a warning that the real danger to a state lies in its people being "justly discontent" and/or believing "that no change can be for their advantage."[14] Burke would soon return to these same ideas, even to the same phrases, as he pleaded for justice, reason, and equity in Britain's policy towards the colonies in North America.

II

On July 11, 1765, with the assistance of his cousin William, Burke obtained the position of private secretary to the Marquis of Rockingham, the leader of the last of the Old Whigs (of the

[11] B. to Shackleton, August 10, 1757: B. to Charles O'Hara, July 10, 1761: B. to Gen. Charles Lee, February 1, 1774.

[12] These were enacted by Parliament during the reigns of William III and Anne and severely curtailed Irish political and religious freedoms.

[13] The three quotes are in his *Works*, VI, 320-22.

[14] *Ibid.*, pp. 351, 356.

Pelham–Newcastle factions) and recently appointed by George III to form a ministry. Five months later, to increase Burke's usefulness, his cousin arranged for him to receive a pocket borough seat in Parliament. Burke was now thirty-seven and a Member of Parliament.

The major issue confronting the ministry at this time was the explosive question of the repeal of the Stamp Act. Burke actively supported the repeal movement[15] and, as Rockingham's secretary, played a major role in the latter's effort to initiate a merchant petition supporting the ministry's position. He viewed the issue as critical for the preservation of liberty in the empire. In fact, he declared that "the liberties (or what shadows of Liberty there are) of Ireland have been saved in America."[16]

Burke based his evaluation of the controversy on two primary considerations: the rights and the sovereignty of Parliament. He was convinced that Parliament had the *right* of taxation, as the superintending legislature of the empire, but that the exercise of it had been inexpedient and imprudent. The colonies were almost purely of commercial value to England, and her recent series of commercial legislation, capped by the Currency and Stamp Acts, seemed deliberately intended to paralyze the colonial economy. Yet he denied American claims that they were exempt from taxation because of their charters and/or because they were unrepresented. If either argument were tenable, he retorted, then most English towns and "nine-tenths" of England could likewise claim exemption.[17]

But the more pressing question was that of Parliament's sovereignty. He felt himself to be so committed to the Settlement of 1689 and the resulting concept of parliamentary supremacy that he could not accept the validity of any argument questioning that principle. If power were misused, the flaw was in the persons of the ministry, not in the structure of the political system. Furthermore, although he thought of the empire as one composed of individual parts, each with *privileges* and local jurisdiction, he steadfastly believed that all *rights* and powers ultimately resided with Parliament. He was convinced that

[15] B. to O'Hara, December 31, 1765.
[16] *Ibid.*
[17] *Annual Register*, 1765, pp. 18-19, 22-26, 33-37; *Corr.* p. 242n; B. to William Dowdeswell, circa January 8, 1767.

surrendering any of them would undermine Parliament's authority and sovereignty and, consequently, the solidarity of the empire.[18]

His views on imperial relations were not unique; they amounted to a call for repeal but without compromising Parliament's position. The solution arrived at by the Rockingham ministry combined repeal with a Declaratory Act, a product of principle and expediency—expediency because few Englishmen would have supported the repeal without some reaffirmation of Parliament's supremacy.[19]

* * * *

Burke had little time after the repeal passed in March to acquire further experience near the ministerial level of the government, for King George intensely disliked the Old Whigs and wasted little time in arranging their political demise. In early July, 1766, he finally convinced William Pitt to form a new ministry and rewarded him with the title Earl of Chatham. Burke went to Chatham seeking a position but with the stipulation that he could resign if Rockingham went into Opposition. In so doing, he linked his fortunes to Rockingham's, for Chatham refused his request, and Burke remained out of power with the Marquis for sixteen years.[20] This turn of events set the stage for all of Burke's later political behavior with regard to America.

As a Rockingham (as members of that faction were called), Burke played an active role in the tournament of factional politics that characterized English public affairs in the 1760's. His motives were typical of the Opposition. Unremittingly they sought issues that would enable them to undermine the ministry, rally the

[18] Cone, pp. 23, 43, 168, 250-52: *Works*, I, 390-91, 398: *FBCorr.* [see below, p. xxvii], IV, 486-92.

[19] George Guttridge, *English Whiggism and The American Revolution*, (Berkeley, 1942), p. 61; Rockingham to Joseph Harrison, October 2, 1768, and R. to George Dempster, September 13, 1774, in George Thomas, Earl of Albermarle, *Memoirs of The Marquis of Rockingham and His Contemporaries*, (2 vols., London, 1852), I, 79, II, 252-57, respectively. Cited hereafter as *Memoirs*.

[20] Several historians have underestimated the strength of Burke's ties to Rockingham, among them Cone, pp. 100ff. See, however, B. to O'Hara, July 28, August 19, post November 11, 1766.

outcasts, and sweep themselves into power. Charles Townshend's Revenue Act of 1767 provided, it seemed, just such an issue.[21] However, American liberties had more than tactical value for Burke and the other Rockinghams; their defense of them had become party policy because of conviction and the need for a consistent American policy. It also helped divert attention from the question of Parliamentary reform, whic was anathema to the Whigs whose strength lay in the inequities of the old system.

However, these were not his principal motives in the 1770's. With the installation of King George's compliant Minister, Lord North, in early 1770, the possibility of mustering sufficient votes to force North's resignation seemed progressively less likely. Consequently, when the American crisis flared anew in 1774, Burke recognized that with the King's support, North's position was nearly impregnable and the crisis' potential political value almost negligible. Yet he was as vociferous in his condemnation as ever, for he was now stirred not so much by political motives as by the conviction that the Ministry's course was one of arbitrary rule and repeated injustice and foreshadowed countless dangers for the empire and the English people.

There is no evidence from these years that Burke either had predicted the impact of the Revenue Act by June, 1767 (although he later claimed to have done so), or had heard any reports of new American disturbances much before September 1, 1768.[22] But once Parliament convened, he initiated an unrelenting assault[23] on the Ministry. His attack centered about three themes, each of which he would further develop and expand in the months following the Boston Tea Party of 1773. First, the effort to impose taxation for revenue upon the colonies was at variance with their temperament and generated distrust.[24] Second, ministerial policy had endangered English liber-

---

[21] Guttridge, pp. 66-70; Rockingham to Burke, July 17, 1769.

[22] See pp. 1-4; Burke to O'Hara, July 4, 1767, September 1, 1768.

[23] See below, pp. 1-4, for example.

[24] One extraordinary passage from our second selection below expresses this view perfectly:

The Americans have made a discovery, or think they have made one, that we mean to oppress them; we have made a discovery, or think we have made one, that they intend to rise in rebellion against us. Our severity has increased their ill behavior. We know not how to advance; they know not how to retreat.

See p. 5; also pp. 4, 11-12; *Cav.* I, 550; *Works*, I, 356.

ties in America and might ultimately do the same in England itself.[25] Third, the solution lay neither in American representation in Parliament nor in any circumspection of the latter's sovereignty but rather in a return to the tranquil times that existed prior to 1764, when Parliament refrained from taxing and the colonies from disobeying.[26]

Burke evidently did not speak during the debates on the repeal of Townshend's Revenue Act, but on November 13, 1770, he needled the ministry once more for the American debacle and the hollow remnant of its program, the symbolic tea tax.

As you, however, still keep up the duty upon tea, in order to preserve the right of taxation, they forbid the introduction of tea, in order to deny that right.[27]

III

In the following years, the early 1770's, Burke shifted his attention to Indian and domestic affairs. He was alarmed over ministerial behavior but he was almost panicky over the "apathy," "indifference," and "insensibility" of the public response to political affairs.[28] His plan for arousing England called for the secession of the Old Whigs from Parliament. Rockingham, however, was unenthusiastic; two years later, when Burke again proposed it, Lord Germain and William Dowdeswell, Commons leader of the Rockinghams, also dissented.[29] Not until 1776 when all else had failed would the party adopt Burke's scheme. By that time, his concern for domestic and imperial affairs had convinced him that in the American cause lay the cause of English liberties.

And yet Edmund Burke did not fully comprehend the movement towards American independence with which his name has

[25] *Cav.*, I, pp. 198-99: *Works*, I, 368, 395: below, pp. 12-14.
[26] *Works*, I, p. 403.
[27] See p. 23.
[28] B. to O'Hara, December 31, 1770; April 2, 1771; June 1, September 30, 1772: B. to Rockingham, February 16, 1771.
[29] B. to O'Hara, July 14, 1771; Rockingham to B., October 24/27; Dowdeswell to B., B. to John Cruger, June 30; B. to William Dowdeswell, October 27, November 6/7; Rockingham to B., October 24/27; Dowdeswell to B., November 8; B. to Rockingham, November 11; Duke of Richmond to B., November 15; B. to Richmond, post November 15; Rockingham to B., November 20, 1772.

long been associated. From 1770 to 1775, Burke served as the agent in England for the New York Assembly, and, because of the conservatism that prevailed in the high circles of New York politics, this tie only widened the discrepancy between his low-keyed estimate of America and the reality of persisting discontent.[30] When at last the pressure of events forced the facts upon him, he was slow to accept them; for he had fixed his conception of imperial relationships just as Americans were altering their own.

His love for the British Constitution and empire had blurred his perception and seemed to leave him one or two steps behind events. His insight on occasion was remarkably acute, but well after 1774 he still did not grasp that the dispute *had* already gone beyond the issue of the right of taxation, even beyond English liberties, that Americans had outgrown the regulatory system, and that their adherence to constitutional principles exceeded even his own estimate. Perhaps he lagged because of the nature of his sources of information; perhaps he did not notice the shift in the thought of an increasing number of Americans in the direction of abstract, universal rights because of his desire to see the struggle as one over particular *English* liberties; and perhaps he could not accept American proposals for a federation-type empire because those particular schemes would have strengthened the crown at the expense of Parliament.[31]

Illusory then had been his own plan in his 1769 pamphlet, *Observations on a Late Publication Intituled "The Present State of the Nation,"* to go back to the relationship existing before 1763 when the colonies were untaxed—and submissive. And he lived on in that illusion until mid-1775 and the news of Lexington and Concord. Only then would he begin to understand that Americans were demanding rights, no longer privileges. And furthermore, although he had for some time described the issue as one over tyranny, he did not ever seem to shake off the notion that it was tyranny over English colonists rather than a new people. Hence, his immortal speech in 1774 on American taxa-

---

[30] *Corr.*, II, 215. This subject was studied by Ross Hoffman, in his work, *Edmund Burke, New York Agent*, (Phila., 1956).

[31] Regarding English liberties see B. to John Cruger, April 16, 1773. The American schemes are perhaps best represented by John Adams, in his essay entitled *Novanglus*.

tion was a monumental triumph of oratory but wholly inadequate for the needs of the moment.[32]

* * * *

In view of the fact that a month prior to this speech Burke had shifted the focus of his attacks to the question of the injustices of the proposed penal laws,[33] his speech on American Taxation, given exactly one year before the Battle of Lexington, seems almost out of place; for he here concentrated not on the quickly spreading fire of public indignation and parliamentary vengeance but on the tea tax, which had been lost in the flames of general constitutional debate and punitive legislation. Burke's speech shows his awareness that the colonists were questioning Parliament's rights. But in asserting that quenching the spark would kill the fire, he revealed his misjudgment of the intensity and extent of the conflagration, both in England and America.

Nevertheless, four of his many conclusions are particularly noteworthy. First, he destroyed any existing justification for the tea tax. Second, he emphasized that Americans were challenging Parliament's power and, if no conciliation were made, would soon "cast your sovereignty in your face, [for] nobody will be argued into slavery."[34] Third, he declared that the tea tax was the root of the controversy and if it were repealed and the penal laws tabled, all would be resolved. Fourth, although he continued to speak of "*privileges* which the colonies ought to enjoy *under* Parliament's rights" (italics are mine), one sees the seeds of the federalist scheme that he was to develop more fully in late 1775. He was gradually coming to recognize the imperial relationship as one in which Parliament's authority was distinguishable from that of local jurisdiction, which was more or less a permanent *privilege*. Parliament, he stated, "ought never to intrude into the place of others, whilst they are equal

[32] See below, pp. 25-69. *Works*, I, 430 ff: B. to James Delancey, June 9, 1771, December 4, 1771: B. to Committee of Correspondence of New York (CCNY), April 6, 1774. Compare above with B. to O'Hara, August 16, 1775; B. to Count Patrick Darcy, October 5, 1775; B. to Dr. William Robertson, June 9, 1777.

[33] His major speeches in 1774 on America are listed below, p. xxviii.

[34] See p. 65.

to the common ends of their institution;" yet its powers must remain (theoretically) boundless in order to cope with any eventuality.[35]

Perhaps the greatest shortcoming of the speech (aside from the omission of any promise of revenue) lay in Burke's unrealistic optimism that an indignant and proud people would make such concessions and that an aroused and suspecting people would accept them as sufficient.

*   *   *   *

The months that followed the famous address were trying ones. Burke despaired of England's retaining the American colonies much longer. The mother country had upset the constitutional equilibrium by disregarding colonial rights and protests and had conferred arbitrary power on royal officials: clearly acts of provocation.[36] In the late summer and fall of 1774 he attempted to initiate a merchant petition supporting the repeal of the punitive laws.[37] At the same time he stood for Parliament in England's second city, Bristol. His election not only increased his prestige but also opened new channels for early news from America through his new friend, Richard Champion, a leading Bristol manufacturer. The merchant petition, however, failed to materialize; and although he remained puzzled about the reasons for the failure, he did realize that time had strengthened North's position and that Rockingham would not soon be returning to office on a wave of mercantile discontent.[38] Consequently, when the situation would deteriorate in 1775, Burke would emphasize the need for an "Effective Minority," one that could achieve the only success still possible, not the fall of the ministry but a modification of its policy.

[35] See pp. 64-67. It should here be emphasized that Burke's federalism did not call for any strengthening of royal power as did, for example, John Adams'.

[36] *FB Corr.*, IV, 490: Rockingham to B., January 30, 1774.

[37] Boston Port Act, the Massachusetts Government Act, and the Administration of Justice Act, primarily.

[38] Charles Ritcheson, *British Politics and The American Revolution* (Norman, Okla., 1954), pp. 180-81; Hoffman, p. 167; B. to Champion, January 10; B. to Rockingham; January 12; Rockingham to B., February 9, 1775.

IV

By early 1775, Burke had received new information on America and he warned his colleagues that the colonies were being pushed into a justifiable rebellion.[39] He ridiculed North's plan of conciliation as "obscure and insidious," designed to divide the colonies, perhaps by winning over New York and thereby breaching their united front.[40]

The colonies are to be held in durance by troops, fleets and armies, until singly and separately they shall do—what? Until they shall offer to contribute to a service which they cannot know, in a proportion which they cannot guess, on a standard which they are so far from being able to ascertain, that Parliament which is to hold it, has not ventured to hint what it is they expect. They are to be prisoners of war, unless they consent to a ransom, by bidding at an auction against each other and against themselves.[41]

Yet the New England Restraining Bill he considered by far the most odious of England's punitive legislation, for it was designed to preserve Great Britain's authority by economic suffocation of her dominions. In fact, he declared, it was a treatment one independent nation dealt another.[42] When, soon after the bill's passage, its provisions were extended to include the southern colonies as well, Burke lamented that:

I have been a strenous advocate for the superiority of this country— but I confess I grow less zealous when I see the use which is made of it. I love firm Government; but I hate tyranny which comes to the aid of a weak one.[43]

He had not, however, passively resigned the initiative to the ministry during February and March. On the 22nd of March Burke presented his first speech on Conciliation.[44] His central argument asserts that the penal and tax laws had clashed with

[39] Gen. Charles Lee to B., December 16, Benjamin Franklin to B., December 19, 1774, *FB Corr.*; Rockingham to B., January 7/8; B. to Citizens of Bristol, January 20; B. to CCNY, March 14, 1775. In addition, see above n. 29, and *PH*, XVIII, 172-73.

[40] *PH*, XVIII, 320, 335-37: B. to John Noble, February 21; B. to James DeLancey, March 14, 1775; below, pp. 114-118.

[41] *PH*, XVIII, 336.

[42] *Ibid.*, 304-05, 389-92, 458-61: *FB Corr.*, IV, 470-74: B. to Champion, March 9, 1775.

[43] B. to Champion, March 9, 1775.

[44] *Memoirs*, II, 267: Rockingham to B., February 13, 1775.

the American spirit of freedom and that breaking that spirit in
order to enforce those laws would only destroy the force that
had made the colonies' prosperity possible, a matter of far
greater importance to England than the trivial revenue derived
from taxes. He called upon Parliament to repeal obnoxious legislation dealing with the colonies and to leave the task of taxing
the colonists to their own assemblies. Yet he offered no broader
federalist scheme than he did in 1774; nor did he concede any
separation of taxation from Parliament's general legislative
authority or rights. He still did not believe that any major concessions were warranted in order to achieve a reconciliation.[45]
Consequently, although his speech revealed a deeper understanding of America, it demonstrated no greater appreciation
of the true nature of the issues in question.

It was left for his brother, Richard, however, to express the
inner feelings that had then inspired Burke's oratory.

In short, by what I can learn, he has done himself infinite credit—I
know that he has discharged his conscience of a load that was on it.
I do not use the word conscience, other than in its ordinary accepta-
tion; believe me America was not on his mind as a Politician, it hung
on his conscience as a being accountable for his actions and his conduct.[46]

*   *   *   *

The next seven months were depressing. Burke was ill over
two months and his numerous schemes, his "one last effort to
give peace to" England,[47] all proved abortive. The Remonstrance
from New York met with an unyielding Commons; a third petitioning movement in England remained inert; Rockingham
turned a deaf ear to his pleas for a more "Effective Minority";
and the Duke of Richmond listened, somewhat aghast, to his
ludicrous plan for a revolt by the Irish Parliament against
British policy. Furthermore, he finally discovered that the diminution of merchant support was due, on the one hand, to the
decline in American-held debts and, on the other, to the open-

[45] Below, pp. 93-94, 95-96; "I do not know that the colonists have in
any general way, or in any cool hour, gone much beyond the demand
of immunity in relation to taxes," below p. 112. Also B. to Francis
Maseres (1776).
[46] Richard Burke to Champion, March 22, 1776.
[47] B. to Rockingham, August 17, 1775.

ing of new markets and the expectation of huge profits from military contracts.[48]

Nevertheless, Burke still had one trump card, one last play in his deadly serious effort to "avert the heavy calamaties that are impending . . . and, if possible, to keep the poor, giddy, thoughtless people of our Country from plunging headlong into this pious war."[49] On November 16, 1775, he delivered a second speech on Conciliation.

Five fears figured prominently in his preparation of the speech: the intervention of France, the growth of royal power, the danger of standing armies, the danger of arbitrary laws, the decline of trade, and the dismemberment of the empire. They had convinced him of the inadequacy of simply removing offensive legislation; his solution now to the practically insolvable crisis was a fully federated empire. Adamant in his belief that "the cause of the quarrel was taxation, [and that] that being removed the rest would not be difficult,"[50] Burke proposed that Parliament surrender the power of taxation to the colonies. Yet he once more reaffirmed his adherence to the Declaratory Act by asserting that its essential objective would not be weakened by his scheme; for Parliament was sovereign over America, and sovereignty, being an element of great complexity, did not necessarily have to reside in its entirety in any particular part of a society. Consequently, he claimed, such a step would not be detrimental to Parliament's power in other spheres and, hence, not to the Declaratory Act either. Indeed, he strenuously opposed any suggestion for repealing that Act, as any such move would seriously undermine Parliament's prestige.

The speech itself is significant in revealing Burke's realization that Parliament could not retain all her powers and still

[48] On New York see *PH*, XVIII, 643-44, 650-55; B. to CCNY, July 7, 1775; Hoffman, 157-59, 177-86. On the petitioning movement and his new realizations, see B. to O'Hara, August 17; B. to Rockingham, September 14; B. to Count Darcy, October 5, 1775; Ritcheson, pp. 220-22. On Rockingham and Richmond, see B. to Rockingham, August 22/23; Rockingham to B., September 11, 24; B. to Richmond, September 26, 1775; and B. to Rockingham, October 1, 1775. See also, B. to O'Hara, circa May 28; B. to Champion, June 28, July 19, 1775; *Corr.*, III, 161 n. 5, 172n., 173n., 179.

[49] B. to Rockingham, August 22/23, 1775.

[50] Below, p. 133.

hold the empire intact. In fact, despite his denial, his proposal was also to a degree an acknowledgement of the futility of the Declaratory Act.

But the speech was a failure, not only because the scheme never would have satisfied the Americans, who were now more angry and incensed over a wider variety of issues, but also because he had again asked his countrymen to swallow their pride and patriotism and submit to a people they considered no better than rabble. They chose rather to wage an inglorious war to an ignominious end.

V

1776 was another year of pessimism and despair. Distraught over America's inevitable reaction to the Prohibitory Act and over England's inexplicable apathy in the face of a disintegrating empire, Burke became as dogmatically fixed on the need for concessions as he had formerly been on the danger of them.[51] The shift emerges with particular clarity in his correspondence, and a striking example is the juxtaposition of two letters to Richard Champion, dated January 1, 1775, and March 19, 1776, respectively.

As for my American measures, they have one thing to recommend them: a certain Unity of Colour, which has stood wearing for upwards of nine years, and which every day appears more and more fresh. It is indeed dyed in Grain.

Those who wished to quiet America by concession thought it best to make that concession at the least possible diminution of the reputation and authority of this Country. This was the principle of those who acted in a responsible situation for that measure of 1766. In this possibly they were wrong.

He and his fellow Old Whigs were torn in their loyalties and affections between their mother country and English colonials whom they believed had been provoked to resistance and driven to independence. They saw little good resulting from victory by either side, only much evil.

---

[51] B. to Rockingham, May 3; B. to Champion, May 30, 1776. With regard to his earlier "obstinate perseverance," see below p. 71. John Brooke, who is compiling Burke's speeches in England has also come to this same conclusion, viz. that Burke adhered to the same ideas from, at the latest, his entry into Parliament until 1775. Letter to the author, April 27, 1964.

I do not know how to wish success to those whose Victory is to separate us from a large and noble part of our Empire. Still less do I wish success to injustice, oppression, and absurdity. . . .[52]

The news of Washington's defeat on Long Island was depressing; and the Rockinghams, anticipating a more inflexible government policy, prepared for one last appeal—and then secession from Parliament. The day was November 6, 1776.[53] Public pressure, though, soon necessitated some form of official explanation, and Burke responded with his Addresses to the King and to the North American Colonists and his Letter to the Sheriffs of Bristol. However, fear of the probable ramifications resulting from the extreme position outlined in the first two prompted the Rockinghams to permit only the third to be published at that time.[54]

In a sense, the three essays are an account of the broad spectrum of political thought spanned by Burke since 1765. Yet the primary objective of these tracts was not to recount history but to convince the King and England of the dangerous nature of the ministry's policy and the validity of the Rockinghams' motives for secession. Americans were assured that more numerous advantages awaited them *in* the empire and that there existed a party *in* Parliament struggling for the recognition of American rights.

One thing in particular was at last now clear to Burke. Circumstances had so changed that the Declaratory Act had become outmoded and a diminution of Parliament's authority unavoidable, for

when the dispute had gone to these last extremeties . . . the concessions which had satisfied in the beginning could satisfy no longer, because the violation of tacit faith required explicit security.[55]

[52] B. to Shackleton, August 11, 1776; also, B. to Duke of Portland and to Earl of Charlemont, both June 4; and B. to Rockingham, July 4, 1776.

[53] B. to Champion, October 10; Chas. Fox to B., Rockingham to B., both October 13, 1776; *Corr.*, III, 302; *Works*, II, 375-76; Guttridge, pp. 89-91.

[54] On this view see Burke's letter to Rockingham, January 6, 1777. Another possibility is mentioned by Thomas Copeland, a foremost Burke authority. He notes that Burke "did not *often* publish his own writings unless" he considered them to be of first rate quality and importance. Letter to the author, December 14, 1964.

[55] See below, p. 198.

And so he declared to the colonists that his party wished only that America and England could be united by the ties of common counsel, commerce, and defense. "Other subordination in you we require none. . . . [A]s long as it is our happiness to be joined with you in the bonds of fraternal charity and freedom, with an open and flowing commerce between us, one principle of enmity and friendship pervading, and one right of war and peace directing the strength of the whole empire," that empire would be invincible.[56]

For that remained his major concern: the welfare of the empire. Fears pervaded these essays, fears of French and Spanish intervention, diminishing imperial trade, growing royal power, public apathy, blind chauvinism, and especially the impact of arbitrary government in America on English liberties at home. The soldiers who enforced that government could not

so transform themselves, merely by crossing the sea as to behold with love and reverence, and submit with profound obedience to, the very same things in Great Britain which in America they have been taught to despise. . . .[57]

An independent and friendly America, he concluded, would be far more desirable than a broken, hostile people whose resistance had precipitated international war, monarchial domination, and suppression of liberties.

It was in protest against all that had occurred, against all that they feared would occur, and against the total ineffectiveness of their role in Parliament that the Rockinghams seceded from Parliament and for the justification of which Burke had written these three pieces.

* * * *

The Old Whigs were, however, too few in numbers and too disorganized to be effective. By February, they suspected it; by April they knew it.[58] On the 16th of that month, Burke returned to the Commons. The rest of the year was a period of fluctuation, from depths of dejection and defeatism, such as following the news of the Battle of Brandywine, to heights of joy and optimism, such as appeared when rumors of a Burgoyne defeat

[56] See below, pp. 163-164.
[57] Below, p. 158. See also, *PH*, XVIII, 1395; *FB Corr.*, IV, 509-13.
[58] *Memoirs*, II, 304, 309.

in September—before Saratoga—flew through London in late November.[59]

On Thursday, November 27, Chatham and Rockingham, buoyant and reconciled, arranged to lay before both Houses on Tuesday next a motion for an inquiry into the State of the Nation.

On Monday, rumors of further defeat threw London into turmoil. Burke gloated and informed Champion that

> I do not know how a total defeat of the King's Troops could be received with a more general gloom than has this day overspread the City. . . . The true value of victorys in the American War seems to be a little better understood.[60]

The following day, December 2, he returned to the scheme that had preoccupied him now for several years. He told the Commons that

> if we have a government in America, it is founded upon conquest; since they set up their independence, and as they enjoy the right *de facto* and we alone *de jure*, we must and ought to treat with them on the terms of a **foederal union.** (emphasis is mine)[61]

The next day, Germain announced that Burgoyne had indeed surrendered at Saratoga.

The story does not end here, for Burke did not yet recognize American independence. He continued to speak of reconciliation, even of subordinating them as much "as we can . . . with their consent."[62] But by April, 1778, little hope remained. Only a Franco-American alliance against England seemed certain. America, the Rockinghams had concluded, was irretrievable. On the 10th of April, Thomas Powy moved that the Carlisle Commission be empowered to recognize American independence, and Burke gave "his hearty approbation of the motion.[63]

Thereafter Burke gave scant attention to American affairs.

[59] B. to Rockingham, January 6; B. to Fox, October 8; B. to William Baker, October 12; B. to Rockingham, November 5; B. to Champion, November 1; B. to Baker, November 9, 1777; *Memoirs*, II, 316-17, 319-20, 321ff; Ritcheson, pp. 231-32.

[60] B. to Champion, December 1, 1777; *Corr.*, III, 396, 397, 406; *Works*, VI, 400 *Memoirs*, II, 319-20, 324-25; *Lloyd's Evening Post*, December 1, 1777.

[61] *PH*, XIX, 515-17; also Rockingham to B., December 3; and B. to Champion, December [7], 1777, [I think it more likely to have been written on the third].

[62] *PH*, XIX, 560.

[63] *Ibid.*, p. 1088.

He experienced only a sense of helpless resignation when con-
templating them. Only the formation of a coalition of European
powers against England aroused in him some concern for the
safety of the English naval and merchant fleets; but most often
he expressed his concern with little or no show of emotion.[64]
His time was soon fully taken with other matters, such as the
East India Company, Irish and Catholic affairs, the Gordon
Riots, the Bristol election, administrative reforms, and Warren
Hastings. With regard to America, he remained convinced that
the North ministry was the "constant obstruction to all settlement."[65] He wished only for a prompt, non-vindictive peace, a
revival of Anglo-American trade, and, in June, 1788, some compensation to American Loyalists.[66] One year later the French
Revolution began and the American Revolution remained only
a memory.

V I

This narrative of Edmund Burke's actions during the American crisis is the tale of an Anglicized Irishman with strong
moral convictions about the importance of reason, justice, and
equity and with a deep involvement in eighteenth-century English factional intrigue. Only if we keep in mind how strongly
his principles influenced his actions as well as his political
interests, can we begin to understand his conduct. His attitudes
were complex. As a politican, he knew that America was a useful weapon in the constant factional warfare. As an Irishman,
he was sensitive to the oppression of colonial peoples by a
mother country. As a Whig, he dreaded the possibility that the
conflict might strengthen the crown at the expense of Parliament, weaken the imperial commercial structure, and endanger
English liberties.[67]

Until 1774 he viewed the colonies as being predominantly of
commercial value and therefore argued that Parliament ought
not to tax for revenue but should retain the right to do so. From
1774 until 1778 he gradually developed a scheme for a federal
structure of the empire, but not until November 1775, did he

[64] B. to the Duke of Portland, [ante October 24, 1781]: also B. to
Champion, August 23; B. to Garrett Nagle, August 25; B. to Richard
Burke, November 20, 1778; B. to John Lee, July 26; B. to Rockingham,
August 8, 1779.

[65] B. to Champion, August 13, 1779.

[66] See below, pp. 211-220.

[67] See below, especially, p. 208.

yield his conviction that Parliament always possessed the *right* to tax and the colonies merely the *privilege*. Finally, after April 10, 1778, Burke was unreservedly in favor of American independence.

Interestingly enough, in his very multiplicity of feelings lies the explanation of Burke's astigmatism with regard to America. He attempted to sustain concurrently both the rights and liberties of the colonists and the supremacy of Parliament. He could reconcile them as long as the issue was clearly one of English liberties and institutions. Long after many Americans had abandoned this view, however, he still adhered to it, for he saw the colonists only as Englishmen-across-the-sea and not as a truly new people, with a unique environment, temperament, and set of prejudices.[68] These were a people who started out by resisting an invasion of ancient privileges but had ended by defending the abstract, natural rights of all men. Burke erred in his estimation of the distinctiveness of the emerging American character; he missed that transition of American thought in the mid-1770's; he failed to appreciate the force of the abstractions summed up in the Declaration of Independence. As a result, Edmund Burke never fully understood the American Revolution.

ACKNOWLEDGEMENTS

I would like to thank all those whose interest and generous assistance has enabled me to assemble this edition. Bernard Bailyn, Harvard University; Thomas Copeland, University of Massachusetts; John Brooke, Central Library, Sheffield, England; Solomon Lutnick, Queens College; Leverett Norman, City College; Gayle Barkan and Leah Weisburd; Pace College, for a grant to complete this manuscript; and the editors of the American Perspectives Series, William Leuchtenburg and Bernard Wishy, whose advice was invaluable.

I would like to dedicate this edition of Burke to my wife, Esther, companion in all things and in all ways.

---

[68] Besides the earlier examples of this sentiment, above note 11, see also B. to James Ogelthorpe, June 2, 1777; B. to Benjamin Franklin, February 22, and B. to Henry Laurens, March 27, 1782. Despite numerous references to the American Spirit, his English conservatism, and perhaps also 3000 miles of ocean, obstructed any really clear conception of the developing American character.

Bibliography of Burke's Speeches and Writings on America

Historians differ on whether the Historical Article of the *Annual Register*, which Burke began in 1757, was still written by him after the 1764 edition.[1] I have based my conclusion that he did on a comparison of the 1765 edition with his views in *An Account of the European Settlements in America* (1757), *A Tract on the Popery Laws in Ireland* (1761–64, unfinished), his correspondence, and his speeches in Parliament (see below for enumeration) and, in addition, on the facts that the publication of that edition was delayed until June 27, 1766, because of an "Accident unforseeable and unpreventable" (*London Chronicle*, XX, 572) and that Burke was seriously ill following his exhausting efforts to bring about the repeal of the Stamp Act (March, 1766). The point of his authorship is significant because there are therein some very interesting observations on American affairs (pp. 18–34).[2]

Hereinafter and in the introduction and text also, the following four abbreviations will be used. Thomas C. Hansard, *The Parliamentary History of England from the Earliest Period to the Year 1803*, (36 vols., London, 1813–14): *PH*; *Sir Henry Cavendish's Debates of the House of Commons, During the Thirteenth Parliament of Great Britain*, John Wright, ed., (2 vols., London, 1841–42): *Cav.*; Charles William, Fifth Earl of Fitzwilliam, and Lt. Gen. Richard Bourke, *The Correspondence of the Rt. Hon. Edmund Burke*, (4 vols., London, 1844): *FBCorr.*; and *The Writings and Speeches of Edmund Burke*, (6 vols., Boston, 1906): *Works*.

[1] See particularly Thomas Copeland, "Edmund Burke's Authorship of the Book Reviews in the Annual Register, for the years 1758-70," (unpublished dissertation, Yale University, 1933); Copeland, *Our Eminent Friend Edmund Burke: Six Essays*, (London, 1950); and letter from Copeland to author, April 15, 1964, in which Prof. Copeland restated the fact that differences still persist.

[2] See B. to O'Hara, March 1, 4, 1766; Copeland, *Our Eminent Friend, Edmund Burke*, pp. 98, 101, 106-07, 115-17; *Corr.*, I, 239.

Below is a list of Burke's speeches on America. Newspaper sources for a number of these speeches may be found in the introduction to the individual selections of this edition. The quality of those sources is touched upon in the Note on the Contents, but I hope to go into that question in greater detail in the near future.

1766–1770: *A Short Account of a Late Short Administration* (1766), *Works*, I, 265-268; *Cav.*, I, 37-40, 198-200; *Observations on a Late Publication Entituled, "The Present State of the Nation,"* (February, 1769), *Works*, I, 269-432; *Cav.*, I, 398-99; *PH*, XVI, 672-76, 720-26; *Thoughts on the Cause of the Present Discontent* (April, 1770), *Works*, I, 433-537; *Cav.*, I, 549-51; II, 14-37, 46-50.

1774: *PH*, XVII, 1160, 1161-62, 1183-85; *Works*, II, 5-79; *PH*, XVII, 1314-15, 1391, 1392, 1393; XVIII, 44-45, 57, 71-73; *FBCorr.*, IV, 482—notes for a speech probably given in early May—and 486-92— notes for another speech probably given in early June.

1775: *PH*, XVIII, 172-73, 233, 262-64, 304-05, 320, 335-37, 389-92, 458-61; *Works*, II, 99-186; *PH*, XVIII, 643-44, 963-82.

1776: *PH*, XVIII, 1441-45; *Works*, II, 187-245.

1777: *Works*, VI, 149-97; *PH*, XIX, 515-17, 537-39, 560, 1088.

1780–88: Bristol, September 6, 1780, *Works*, VI, 365-424; PH, XXII, 354-56 (May, 1781); *PH*, XXII, 1035-41 (February, 1782); *PH*, XXIII, 466-69, (February, 1783); *PH*, XXIII, 611-14, (March, 1783)[3]; *PH*, XXVII, 614-15, (June, 1788).

[3] Many portions of Hansard were taken from John Almon's *The Parliamentary Register*, which was taken over by John Debrett in 1781; but certainly not all of it came from that source. In the case of this and the last selections, Debrett's versions appear to be more complete and, therefore, although I have given Hansard here, the texts of these two speeches come from Debrett as is noted in the introduction to each of them.

A Note on the Contents

Every edition of Burke's writings and speeches on America has included the same material, e.g. those that Burke himself published in pamphlet form. As far as I know, only one editor has hitherto attempted to broaden the standard presentation but only to the extent of including a summary of Burke's Second Speech on Conciliation. The difficulty of comprehensiveness lies in the fact that Burke wrote out few of his speeches; he used notes, most of which are either undated and/or illegible. At the present time, an effort is being made in England to assemble all of his speeches in several volumes that would supplement those containing his correspondence. This ambitious project, though, will take several years. Nevertheless, until then, I believe it would be useful to students of the period to have at their disposal a fuller selection of Burke's speeches on America than those yet published.

Since no copies of his notes are available in this country, I have turned to newspaper and private accounts primarily. Thomas C. Hansard's *The Parliamentary History of England from the Earliest Period to the Year 1803*, (Vols. 16-27), is the best known. For many years, however, scholars have been quite skeptical about the accuracy of Hansard's reporting, especially where Burke was involved.[1] Yet a close analysis of it reveals its superiority in many instances over all available newspaper reports, such as those in *Lloyd's Evening Post, The London Packet, The Morning Post, St. James' Chronicle, The Kentish Gazette, The London Magazine, The Gentlemen's Magazine*, and at times even over John Almon's *The Parliamentary Register*. Consequently, I have drawn many of the speeches from Hansard, as well as from Sir Henry Cavendish, Almon, and Debrett. In a few instances *Gentleman's Magazine* and newspapers are used.

It is true that as a result we are forced in places to sacrifice some of Burke's brilliance and eloquence, although most of

---

[1] A very influential—yet very limited—article on this was that by H.V.F. Somerset, "Burke's Eloquence and Hansard's Reports," *English Historical Review*, XLV (1930), 110-14.

those qualities is already lost, but we do retain in those accounts his important political ideas, too many of which have been neglected by historians. Finally, it has also been necessary to omit portions of those works, and others completely, which are readily available in their entirety in most collections, in order to allow for the inclusion of other speeches with which too few students of the period are familiar. I trust they will find that those omissions have in no very significant way materially weakened the purpose of this edition: to present a more complete picture of Burke's views on America during the period of the Revolution in a form as close to the original as we now have available. The only other modification has been the modernization of punctuation for the benefit of today's reader.

Preface to the Second Edition

When this volume was originally being compiled American military involvement in Southeast Asia was roughly at the same kind of stage as the British efforts to enforce the 1774 penal acts against the North American colonies. The problem of dissent in a nation stumbling into a distant war had not yet reemerged, and the remarkable modernity of Burke's dissenting role during the critical decade before the American Revolution eluded me. What had begun as an opportunistic political tactic became a matter of deep conviction by the mid 1770's. In the draft of his Address to the King (1777), Burke expressed his paramount conviction that "we cannot permit ourselves to countenance, by the appearance of a silent assent, proceedings fatal to the liberty and unity of the empire (p. 161, below).

His anxieties would not at all have been misplaced in America of the 1960's. He was preoccupied with the ministers' efforts to commit Parliament to policies without its prior consent and Parliament's loss of influence in that policy making, the real possibility of intervention by another of the great powers, the excessive concern with prestige and dignity in ministerial decisions regarding America, their increasing tendency to overreact to outbursts there, the haphazard arrangements for the peace commission, and the danger to English liberties in an increasingly grave threat from militant M.P.s and a growing military establishment. Moreover, he stressed that existing policy, based on improvisation and pride rather than facts and common sense, gave no assurance of a satisfactory outcome in any manner: "I can well conceive a country completely overrun, and miserably wasted, without approaching in the least to settlement" (p. 181).

When the crisis of the 1770's began, Burke unceasingly urged moderation and magnanimity upon his colleagues in Parliament at the risk of greater harrassment and even political suicide. In 1774 he strenuously denied that similar opposition to the Stamp Act had encouraged American resistence at that time (p. 55). As the situation deteriorated and all protest appeared in vain, he at last prevailed upon Rockingham and his followers to escalate their protest and secede from Parliament, a virtually unprecedented act of protest. The secession marked the apex of Burke's dissent and his strongest effort to redirect English policy.

Burke reserved his most explicit defense of the right of dissent for his address to the king and his letter to the sheriffs of Bristol. He contended that the throne could not "stand secure upon principles of unconstitutional submission and passive obedience" (p. 159). He feared that arbitrary powers were accumulating in the hands of the ministry by first being applied overseas where Englishmen were less cognizant of them (p. 178). He also observed that those most militant against America were equally hostile toward "those neighbours of theirs whose only crime is that they have charitably and humanely wished them to entertain more reasonable sentiments, and not always to sacrifice their interest to their passion" (p. 185). He added that such rage at dissenters stemmed from the uncertainty among the majority as to whether they were really in the right (p. 185), for although they already had the nation and its purse committed to the war, they demanded unanimity as well. However, "frenzy does not become a slighter distemper on account of the number of those who may be infected with it." Not only would such unanimity yield no fruitful results but, on the contrary, Americans ought to know that a party existed "to whom they could always look for support," for it would suggest the possibility of moderation and compromise (p. 186).

"I am charged with being an American" and have been told that my dissent encouraged rebellion, he remarked (p.

190). In words now famous he replied, "*general* rebellions
and revolts of a whole people never were *encouraged*, now or
at any time. They are always *provoked*." And even if it were
true that such actions might encourage resistence,

Does anybody seriously maintain that, charged with my share of the
public councils, I am obliged not to resist projects which I think
mischievous lest men who suffer should be encouraged to resist? ...
Is it then a rule that no man in this nation shall open his mouth in
favour of the colonies, shall defend their rights, or complain of their
sufferings? Or, when war finally breaks out, no man shall express his
desires of peace? ... Even looking no further than ourselves, can it
be true loyalty to any government or true patriotism toward any
country to degrade their solemn councils into servile drawing rooms,
to flatter their pride and passions rather than to enlighten their
reason ... ? By such acquiescence great kings and mighty nations
have been undone... (p. 187)

Whatever the earlier sentiments may have been, once at
war, all citizens must unite. This unpalatable position Burke
strenuously rejected. "On the principle of this argument,
the more mischiefs we suffer from any administration, the
more our trust in it is to be confirmed. Let them but once
get us into a war, and then their power is safe, and an Act
of oblivion passed for all their misconduct" (p. 188). Across
200 years Burke's words admonish us that if the preservation of liberty depends upon eternal vigilence, so too does it
depend upon preserving the right of dissent.

                                                    E.R.B.

San Bernardino, California

April 9, 1971

SPEECH BEFORE
THE HOUSE OF COMMONS
IN SUPPORT OF WILLIAM
DOWDESWELL'S AMENDMENT TO
THE ADDRESS OF THANKS

NOVEMBER 18, 1768[1]

News of disturbances in America in reaction to the Townshend Acts reached England in late August, 1768. As soon as Parliament reconvened in November, Burke and the Rockinghams prepared to attack the ministry's policies. Burke seized his opportunity when Dowdeswell proposed an amendment to the Address relating to American affairs.

I RISE with a particular awe upon the present occasion. It is, Sir, a great crisis of the tranquillity of this country, and of the subjection and obedience of America. There are two very extraordinary facts that well deserve the consideration of this House. With regard to America, the honourable seconder of the Address[2] has made a discovery of a deep-laid plan; he has found out that all the disturbances now existing in America have been regularly created by ministerial mismanagement; and for this we are to thank his Majesty! He has discovered that an act of parliament was passed for the purpose of raising discontent: to shew America, as well as Great Britain, how discontent was to be raised. And, according to the honourable gentleman, it has shown them both. This, Sir, is a subject, so far as America is concerned, upon which I should think it a crime to remain silent. The honourable gentleman has attributed the present disorders in America to the repeal of the Stamp act. Sir, the repeal of that act was a wise, a deliberate measure of this House, so far as this House was

---

[1] *Cav.*, I, 37-40.
[2] Hans Stanley.

concerned. You had commercial opinions of all kinds, from the greatest philosopher down to the shoemaker. It was a call of the merchants of England upon an affair of the first magnitude. It was the correction of a former mistake. I am astonished that the gentlemen who brought about that act can sit in silence upon the condemnation of this measure, a measure upon which they have founded their characters—if they have any characters at all. We have now at the head of the law a nobleman whose authority has been cited in America. This, indeed, is encouragement; well may they have gone such lengths! Another high authority has been quoted, that of a great statesman. These two distinguished men pleaded, for a long time, the cause of the Americans; but they have changed their opinions. Sir, these changes of opinion are what will undo this country. How can the Americans be sure that the persons who vote for them to-day will vote for them to-morrow? As for the amendment pleasing Mr. Otis, or displeasing the noble lord, of that I know nothing; the former may, perhaps, hold opinions that would scatter firebrands and death. Nothing can possibly tend more to estrange America from the mother country than the opinion that there is no person in Great Britain steady, but that the people in the lump are ready to change. It is our bounden duty to show her that there are some who are steady.

Let us take a brief review of the state of that country from the time of the repeal of the Stamp act. When the Stamp act was repealed, there was peace in America and trade flowed in its usual channels. The very next year—such was the fashion of throwing our own burthens upon the shoulders of others—we began to hanker after an American revenue. The very next session after you had determined upon that measure, many persons began to think that we should let down something of our haughty dignity for the sake of the peace and prosperity of this country. When they had the peace, they began to pine and whine for their dignity, for some little revenue that should give them back their dignity. A person of the first rate abilities,[3] of ten thousand talents, who had a desire to please everybody, the next year, in order to please other respectable persons, produced a plan of taxation for America. He never gave as the reason that those duties were intended as a test of America. The reasons he gave were that it was in order to establish a police in America—to strengthen and fortify

[3] Charles Townshend, Chancellor of Exchequer.

the government of America. With regard to my own conduct, when this proposition was made to the House, I expressed the little opinion I had; and I shall prove a true prophet. I said that you would never see a single shilling from America. I reminded you that it was not by votes and angry resolutions of this House, but by a slow and steady conduct, that the Americans were to be reconciled to us.[4] I have heard no reason to induce me to change my opinion; and I am sure no honest man ought to change his opinion without reason. But, Sir, to grace the declamation of the day and please the ear of the House, dangerous truths were produced, which ought to have lain hid in the Cabinet. These taxes, or regulations—it is indifferent to me which they are called—were intended to distress the manufacturers of Great Britain. We resumed an act altogether similar to the Stamp act. It must throw the people of America into despair when they reflect that the very men are in the King's council who were the proposers of it.

Sir, as to Governor Bernard,[5] though, no doubt, an exceedingly good man, he has one great fault, a love of controversy. When the repeal of the Stamp act went over to America, the parties proceeded to controversies, trying who should give the smartest repartee and the liveliest answer, who should show himself the best writer. As to the letter of the noble Secretary of State,[6] such an order to a Governor was an annihilation of the assembly; and when the assembly was dissolved, an usurped assembly met. Was it wise, Sir, to bring troops into that government? and with regard to quartering them after the assembly was dissolved, who was to provide for them? They entered into an open town. And there is the whole transaction; there is the whole merit of the administration. While you have your troops in one place, you will want them in another. There is no such thing as governing the whole body of the people, contrary to their inclinations. It is not votes and resolutions, it is not arms that govern a people.

Another part of the Speech from the throne relates to foreign affairs. When I heard that speech first read, I did not know who was the author of it. It was intended, it would seem, to come as near "your true no-meaning" as possible; and it certainly has attained its object. It is like penning a whisper; though words may

---

[4] This editor has been unable to find any record of the speech to which Burke is here refering.

[5] Francis Bernard, Governor of Massachusetts.

[6] Lord Hillsborough, Secretary of State for the Colonies.

be heard, they cannot be understood. And, as far as regards the public, the less those words are understood by them, the greater chance they have of being admired and of gaining for ministers an unanimous approbation of their measures.

The honourable seconder of the Address has adverted to two circumstances. First, we are informed that the colonies of America are desirous of withdrawing themselves from their dependence on Great Britain; next, that his Majesty is determined to support the dignity of his Crown. Here, Sir, we tell the world that his Majesty is determined to support the dignity of his Crown; and then, to show how unable he is to do so, we also tell it that the colonies of America are going to throw off their subjection to us.

His Majesty hints at an attempt that may be made, derogatory to the honour and dignity of his Crown, and at the vigilance with which he shall watch over the general interests of Europe. Here we have, first an attempt, then assurances; but there is no retrospect. Now, I should be glad to know, Sir, to what this attempt refers; what remonstrances have been made relating to it; and what has been the vigilance here spoken of. Is Corsica an instance of it? I have not heard of a single step that has been taken by ministers, in consequence of the accession of that island to France. . . . The King of Sardinia is driven into a corner. What is Genoa better than a privileged city of France? These things are a great shame to the nation. I shall vote for the amendment proposed by my honourable friend. The compliments of a parliament, like its actions, ought to be grave and wise. An inquiry should not be prevented by the lullaby of the Address upon the soft, downy breast of administration. If it be said that the Opposition aim at the situations, and not the measures, of the ministry, that hits none of us. If our hearts do not echo this representation of the abilities of our ministers, we shall be highly blameable in voting for the Address. Let the world judge, whether it best becomes us to be the humble addressing representatives of a free people or an avenging Parliament.

2

SPEECH BEFORE
THE HOUSE OF COMMONS
IN SUPPORT OF GOVERNOR
POWNALL'S MOTION FOR THE
REPEAL OF THE AMERICAN
REVENUE ACT OF 1767[1]

APRIL 19, 1769

Debates over American affairs had continued throughout the winter of 1768–69, during which Burke spoke several times. He made several exceptionally incisive remarks in this speech supporting Thomas Pownall's motion to repeal Townshend's Revenue Act of 1767, the source of the present controversy.

I AM not at all surprised that the honourable gentleman should dislike the propositions because they are acceptable to the people. I look upon them with a degree of languor approaching to despondency. Absurdity itself never devised such a plan of taxation as the one proposed in 1767. The then chancellor of the exchequer was driven upon it, having promised to bring forward some plan; and he fancied we should consider the slight duties on certain articles as insignificant. With regard to the administration, I never relaxed my opposition to them, but I had reason to repent it. Every revenue act we make concerning the colonies touches the whole American system. This act of the seventh of the king was an act of expediency. The Americans have made a discovery, or think they have made one, that we mean to oppress them; we have made a discovery, or think we have made one, that they intend to rise in rebellion against us. Our severity has increased their ill behaviour. We know not how to advance; they know not how to retreat. This is my opinion of our situa-

---

[1] *Cav.*, I, 398-99.

tion, with regard to America; and he is a bold man, who can say what measures we ought to take. If the question was whether we should repeal or whether we should enforce the act in question, I have no hesitation in saying, repeal. But we cannot, the gentlemen say, repeal it during the present session; it is part of a complicated commercial system. The question, therefore, is whether, when you cannot repeal it, you ought to agitate it. If we dismiss the question without holding out the hope of reviving it, it will go out to America that so long as they will not withdraw their declaration, so long we will never repeal our acts of parliament. Some party must give way, and there is a willingness in that country to meet us. If the disposition of that country is alienated from us, the law cannot be executed. You put on a hard, frowning, iron countenance. You suspend your own government in order to execute your laws upon America. Why these strong debates when it is not in your power to remedy the evil? The disposition of the administration, with regard to America, must have some change. Why go on with the parade of parliamentary debates, which is poison, gall, and bitterness to the Americans? The more eloquence we display, the further we deviate from wisdom. What is done must be done silently, and in the closet. There is the prejudice of party in this affair. I would be to the Americans personally a friend, to their power an eternal enemy; but I would rather never agitate or stir that question. I hope that when they see the unfortunate end of every measure, they will come to a better feeling. A man of a good and moderate temper, a thousand to one would be a wise proposer. I never thought America should be beat backwards and forwards, as the tennis ball of faction. To propose plans of government from this side of the House would not, in general, be wise; an ill temper might be generated, which would pass from this House to America, and we should be mutually inflaming one another.

3

SPEECH INTRODUCING A
MOTION FOR AN ENQUIRY
INTO THE CAUSES OF THE
LATE DISORDERS IN AMERICA[1]

MAY 9, 1770

The Rockinghams had refrained from offering a clearcut alternative policy for American affairs, contenting themselves with attacking the ministry. They felt that North's repeal of all the duties but those on tea (March, 1770) and the ministry's policy in general were insufficient. As the session drew to a close, they decided to forebear no longer and Burke delivered the following speech, expressing his and the Rockingham position on American affairs in the 1760's. Burke explains all this in the opening portion of the speech. He began by asking that several papers relating to America be read. Among them were Hillsborough's letters of April 21 and 22, 1768, and of May 13, 1769; the King's Speeches of March 10, November 8, 1768, May 9, 1769, and January 9, 1770; and the House resolutions of February 8, 1769, relating to 35 Henry VIII (The complete list is on Cav., I, 14.). After they were all read, he went on.

I REALLY am sorry, Sir, for the trouble I have been obliged to give the House and the still greater trouble and delay that I shall give them in commenting upon these papers. I feel this as strongly as anybody, both on my own account and that of others. At a time when the session is almost spent, and gentlemen are naturally anxious to retire to their recreations, something overrules the inclination and makes me wish to try the patience of the House a little longer. Our attendance here should be regulated not by the almanack but by duty. We should feel that nothing but the accomplishment of the public business gives us a

---

[1] *Cav.*, II, 14-25.

title to repose; that so long as the happiness of the country or the
dignity of government is at stake, no circumstances of toil or
trouble, no motives of pleasure or repose, should call our minds,
for one moment, from the consideration of matters so arduous
in their nature, so pressing in point of time.

I am now going to bring before you the affairs of America. If
you do not find in those words motives to give me your diligent
attention, nothing that I can say will induce you. If I have not
done this before, the House, I trust, will clear me. I have been
three years silent upon American affairs. But when I say silent, I
do not mean to affirm that when measures with regard to the
colonies have been brought before the House, we have not freely,
fully, and boldly given our assent or dissent to them; but no vexatious proceedings, no enquiries, with a view to obstruct government in their plan of operations, have been taken on this side the
House. Our former silence, however, obliges us to speak now. I
postponed my motion from day to day, in the hope that those who,
on the first day of the session, involved the House in a promise to
the Throne, would have helped us a little at the last, and thrown
some light upon the mode in which we could best perform it. That
hope was passed away. I was induced, Sir, to wait for another
reason. I felt that any proposition in the shape of censure ought
to be brought forward with a great deal of deliberation; that its
propiety depended upon its evident necessity; that every thing
that tended to throw the least imputation on any individuals
should as much as possible be avoided; that no blame should be
cast whilst there remained the smallest prospect of amendment.
That hope is vanished, every particle of it. The ministers who advised his Majesty to call your serious attention to the state of his
government in America, and who induced you to promise that no
endeavours should be wanted on your part to make effectual provisions against the unwarrantable measures carried on in the
colonies, have proved to you by their conduct that they think you
ought to do nothing of the kind; that the royal recommendation
ought to have no weight and your promise no sanction.

In this situation even I, Sir, shall, I hope, be excused for ven-
turing to bring this great matter before the House. I have a series
of resolutions in my hand; but I will cheerfully throw them away,
trample upon them, if others will take it up. The reason I move
in it is, for my own particular part, from the sense I feel of the
grievance, and the opinion I entertain, that parliament ought not

to be bankrupt in every one of its promises. I do it from a conviction that it involves the immediate salvation of the whole empire—crumbling, I know not how; one part tottering, another
humbling, I know not how; confusion in every part of your dominions. But when I say this, let me not be mistaken; let it not be
supposed that I am going to propose any plan to this House.
Whatever my conduct with regard to America has been, it has
been universal. You, Sir, have a good memory, and may remember
my words on a former occasion.[2] My opinion is that America cannot be governed here; that the detail of her military and civil
affairs cannot be administered in a house of parliament; that,
with regard to interior measures, the profoundest deliberations of
cabinet wisdom would shrivel into folly, if once blown upon by the
rude breath of a popular assembly. Their designs are not at all the
same. The characteristic of parliament is to establish general
laws, to give general powers and large grants of public money,
It is the part of administration to use those powers with judgment, to employ those supplies with effect, and to conduct the
whole body, civil and military, with order, with economy, with
system, in every way that can tend to force them to their true
service, and, what is all in all, by a proper choice of men. This I
consider the sum total of government, upon this subject. Upon a
large and complicated scene of action, with an ocean of three thousand miles between you and America, the wisest man living can do
nothing if there is not a well-ordered plan of government at home;
nor can such plan be proceeded with without intelligent and effective men to carry it into execution. You must depend upon your
administration. The trust is a great one, but it is a trust that is
necessary, until you are beaten out of it by every abuse. For my
part, I am free to declare that it is not every little trifling accident
that may happen, that it is not every rumour you find in a newspaper, that it is not every letter of alarm from a governor, that it
is not every angry voice of an assembly, that it is not every
mutiny in the constituency, that is not every mutiny of your
troops—all these little accidents are to be passed by. You are not
to call for a peevish cavil from the House of Parliament. This I
am free to declare. I do not know any thing that would do you
more mischief than, upon every accident of this kind, to lay it to
the fault of government. This concession, Sir, will clear the way

[2] See preceding speech.

for the resolutions I am about to propose. Let my motions be rejected with disdain. If they are so, I am not to quarrel with any particular defect of government; I am not to quarrel with any little lapses of humanity. I disdain to proceed upon such ground. If I do not lay before you such a series, such a concatenation of inconsistencies as never before were exceeded, then let my motions be rejected with disdain. I may venture to say, it is a thousand times more astonishing that we subsist at all under such a system, than that we have subsisted at all under an arrangement of confusion.

You will forgive me, Sir, if I carry you a few years back. When in 1766 the stamp act was repealed, there were great divisions upon the wisdom of the measure. Many were of opinion that the wounds that had been inflicted by it in America should, from the unreasonable and violent conduct of many persons there, from the weakness of government there, and the inflamed and perhaps improper notions of liberty entertained there, be left open a little longer. Others thought that those wounds could not be closed too soon. Parliament did wisely in passing the declaratory law. Then they were of opinion that, the question of right being laid aside, it came to the question of expedience; that the true policy was not to exercise that right in the taxation of America. Such, whether right or wrong, whether the majority or the minority, were the prevailing opinions in this House. It was called for by the hear! hear! hear! of gentlemen on both sides. The consequence was immediate peace and quiet.

In 1767, a change having taken place in the ministry, another spirit began to prevail: the spirit of taking advantage of the Americans, not through internal revenue but through commerce. A third opinion arose and became prevalent. This country, it was said, had lost some portion of its dignity. This fretted certain gentlemen exceedingly; and the then chancellor of the exchequer[3] gave it as his opinion that a revenue must be obtained out of America, and a bill for that purpose was accordingly brought in. The preamble of it was framed upon two principles. The ostensible part was to find a support independent of the people there. In the next place, it was to serve as a test, whereby the recognition of our right to tax them was to be ascertained. The firmness of this country, its dignity, and all its power were to be exerted. The

[3] Charles Townshend.

Americans were to shew themselves to this House, and this House
was to shew itself to the Americans: to discover the true character of each and which could hold out the longest. To gain over
the colonists, it was made, with the ayes of all the House, an
uncommercial act, the duties being to be laid on our own manufactures; and to please the friends of taxation, the collection was
to be levied in the colonies. The substance of the whole act was to
draw from the Americans a recognition of our right. If that came
to be opposed, then you were to pursue a series of strong measures until you had obtained your object. Accordingly, Sir, upon
this new voyage in search of a revenue on which you set out, your
bottom was rotten; you had laid in no provisions; you had taken
no expedient to provide against the climate. You went naked. The
wind began to blow; the storm which had subsided, in consequence of the repeal of the stamp act, was revived by this new
measure. No step was taken to reconcile it to the minds of the
Americans. In the preamble, the assemblies thought they read
their own annihilation. Here, said the gentlemen opposite, is a
foundation laid for a revenue in America, without affecting the
prejudices of the people; here is a foundation laid for establishing
for ever our government there, in such a manner as not only to
secure obedience to this law, but to all other laws! Sir, what you
heard with pleasure, the colonies heard with confusion and dis-
may. The stamp act was to go to the pay of the army; but this
struck at the root of their assemblies. An ill temper began to
spread. The assemblies came to resolutions; the boldness of the
lower and upper assembly manifested itself. Two combinations
were raised up against you: one, aimed at the trade of this country, engaging not to import our manufactures; another, establishing the authority in one of their assemblies. These were dangerous
measures. The administration at home had hardly passed this act
before they began to discover, from its consequences, that they
had acted unwisely. The parliament separated but with a determination not to change their plan of conduct. Had the government consented to repeal the act when a proposition to that effect
was made in this House, they would not have been exposed to
the humiliating circumstances that have since taken place.

I now come, Sir, to the letter of Lord Hillsborough to [Governor]
Bernard, of the 22nd of April 1768, directing him to require the
assembly of Massachusetts Bay to rescind the resolution made
against the authority of this country. An impression prevailed

that the assembly would take no notice of it but treat it with contempt. If they should do this, the governor was empowered immediately to dissolve it. As soon as the circular reached the other colonies, they saw in it a direct attempt to call upon them for a disavowal of what the assembly of Massachusetts Bay had done. They received it with great alarm, as going to break up the combinations. I agree, that to dissolve the assembly was an act to which the Crown was entirely competent; but there is no right that may not terminate in a wrong, if it is not guided by discretion. If you thought proper to send an unconditional order to dissolve, it behoved you, before you committed the government to a measure which you could not easily recede from, to provide against the consequences. Had you, Mr. Speaker, with those talents which you exercised so wisely for your clients, been consulted, would you not have asked Governor Bernard, "What do you know of the temper of this assembly?" You would have asked that question. You would have asked, "What kind of influence have you among them? What influence have you with the leading interests in the country? Would a new assembly be more tractable than the old one? What is your plan of management? Could you contrive to govern without any assembly at all?" Sir Fletcher Norton, I know you would have asked those questions. You are not to commit the government to any measure unless you are sure you can carry it through. However, the letter did go abroad; the assembly did take notice of it; they took notice of it with a vengeance; the question for rescinding the resolution was rejected by ninety-two to fourteen; the governor did dissolve; the combinations were fortified and strengthened; all America was in a flame. They saw, as they thought, an act virtually setting aside all their assemblies, a general suspension of all legislation. No hint was given that they would be resumed. They believed there was an end of the free British mode of governing America.

All these things had an alarming effect on the minds of the people; it became a trial who should yield first. At length, the disorder grew to such a height that the government brought out the grand resource, the military. In vulgar merriment, they entered the town of Boston with all the parade of a capitulation. Taking the whole together, there was nothing to be seen on the face of it but a determination to over-rule all constitutional authority in America and to set up in its place a standing army. As soon as the troops entered, the governor declared his authority to be at an end. After this, the people became ungovernable. A town meeting was held, at which it was proposed to summon a convention, and circular letters were sent to all the other towns, inviting them to send delegates. These letters were framed in the very teeth of the army. They were dispatched from one end of America to the other and fastened the bond of union ten times stronger. The origin of all these disorders was the circular letter.

Never did an administration appear so mean, so contemptible, as the British government at this moment. Finding the no effect of some of their measures, and the small effect of others, they next came forward with addresses to the Throne, respecting the riots and disturbances in the town of Boston; and, upon this plan, there was brought before you—I really know not what to call it— a proposition to revive an obsolete act of Henry VIII., passed in the dotage of his understanding and the last year of his reign, and combining a strong portion of ancient ferociousness with modern effeminacy.[4] It was brought here without a father, without any one to own it. Two honourable gentlemen called out, Who is the father of this? The House would not inquire who it came from. They took this little foundling, this Œdipus, this riddle. They laid it upon your table, and you accepted it. One would have imagined, after they had gone through all these violent letters and plans, that they were about to annihilate these rebellious subjects, that they were proceeding forthwith to crush these disobedient people. They were going to do nothing of the kind. On the contrary, they were, at this very time, launching a measure of absolute, unconditional, entire submission to them.

Having taken a view of their plans of force, I shall beg leave to state to the House what they did and what was the effect produced in America. The detail is a melancholy one. The first thing was to suspend the assembly of New York for not obeying the act enjoining them to provide quarters for the troops. This produced resolutions, in which the assembly maintained that they were self-originated, that they held their power from the law of nature, that the colony had an internal legislature of its own, which could not be suspended or annulled by any authority of the Crown. This resolution is in full vigour; your act of parliaments is in none at all. The reason you gave for the measure was that by punishing one colony you should terrify all. The assembly at Bos-

---

[4] See below, pp. 14-15.

ton refused. Was that suspended? No. The Bostonians resolved that quartering the troops was a high insult and a proof that the military power was master of the whole legislative; yet that assembly remains undissolved. This was your first measure for the maintenance of your dignity. Sir, you have lost every thing. You have not kept a single rag of your authority to cover you. The assembly of Virginia resolved that the sole right of imposing taxes on the colony was, legally and constitutionally, vested in them. The assembly of New York resolved that no tax, under any name or denomination, could be imposed upon the colony but of their free gift. Your assertion of the right brought on their denial; your attempts to put down combinations made combinations spring up in every colony. Your right of taxation, your right of destroying combinations, your right of proroguing their assemblies, has been directly opposed by the people of America, in all its parts. Every measure you have taken has been met by a contrary measure. Your acts have not been listened to. They deny your right to send out an army to them. They have resolved that the establishment of a standing army is an invasion of the rights of the people. Let them pass resolutions against the army if they will; but, Sir, they have taken an active part against the army. You withdrew one-half of it; they have driven out the other half. You sent it to protect the civil government; and when it arrived, there was no civil government to protect. Here, then, all is gone! I can name no one instrument of government that is not levelled with the ground and trampled under foot. You have neither military nor civil power from the senseless manner in which you exercised them. A government without wisdom never will be without woe. All is shaken to the foundation by the entire absence of common sense.

I have forgotten one thing—the act of the 35th of Henry VIII. What, Sir, has been done, in consequence of your address to his Majesty to direct the Governor of Massachusetts Bay to procure information touching all treasons, or misprisions of treason, committed since December 1769, in order that the offenders might be brought to this country to be tried by a special commission, pursuant to the provisions of that statute? When the proposition was first started in this House, I looked upon it with horror. While you considered it in the light of an act that was to awe and terrify, I looked upon it as one that conceived all sorts of horrible things, but as one that was never intended to be put in execution.

Of all follies in a government, the worst thing it can do is to render the severity of its punishments ridiculous. This *genitor cum fulmine*—what did you do in consequence of your strong resolutions? Whom have you caused to be apprehended? What examinations have been taken? Have you had any answers from your agents in America? Sir, they cannot answer. They lie in this distressful dilemma; and we along with them. If there has been treason, why have you not acted boldly? If there has been treason, he is next to the traitor who winks at it. What did you send the army to Boston for? To support the civil government? The noble secretary at war told you last night, you had no civil government to support. Then you ought not to have sent it. If, under the authority of legal magistrates, the troops could not act against illegal proceedings, they were put in a worse condition than the rest of the King's subjects. Like this old act of Henry VIII., you sent them to America to be insulted and trampled upon. You order away two of the regiments; and the other two are turned out of the town in disgrace. Not that their being so turned out reflects any disgrace upon the officers. They could not risk a rebellion and a civil war. I speak of the ignominy attached to those who put them in that situation, and to the House of Commons that thanked ministers for what they had done. The noble lord tells us these troops are not to go there again. Were they wanted there originally? Are they wanted now? By the entire removal of your government the town is become quiet. So much for the new plan of dignity you set out upon! The idle, the unfighting subjects of England in America forced you to try your strength with them. Every act of authority exerted by you has been treated with contempt and attended with the disgrace of your forces. Go on, Sir! trust to the same hands! Confide in them again! that your wise resolutions, your laws, and your troops, may, in the same ignominious way, be again defeated!

I have done, Sir, with their plan of vigour and am going to open their plan of lenity. But before I do so, permit me to say that a plan of lenity requires to be as artfully conducted as any plan of force whatever. As plans of force require to be carried on with as little appearance of activity as possible, so plans of lenity require to be carried on with as little show of fear. It was several times suggested, that it would be a wise thing to repeal these obnoxious acts. The answer was, "Never! We will not give them an iota; we will not give them a peppercorn; we shall shortly have them at our feet; there will soon be submission on their side, and authority on ours." The Speech from the Throne and your address breathed nothing else. The Crown talked big; the parliament thanked the Crown grossly. "It is the only way," said the gentlemen opposite, "to bring about peace: we will persevere; we will support your Majesty in all your measures." That, too, was the language of the last session. Not a breath escaped; not the slightest intimation was given that there was to be an entire submission. Whilst our atmosphere blazed with lightning in every quarter, in America all was mild. The letter of Lord Hillsborough to the governors in America, written on the 13th of May, five days after the close of the session, after reciting the substance of the King's Speech, went on to say, "I can take upon me to assure you, notwithstanding insinuations to the contrary from men with factious and seditious views, that his Majesty's present administration have at no time entertained a design to propose to parliament to lay any further taxes upon America for the purpose of raising a revenue; and that it is at present their intention to propose, the next session of parliament, to take off the duties upon glass, paper, and colors, upon consideration of such duties having been laid contrary to the true principles of commerce." And for what reason? What new discovery had they made at the end of three years? In this letter the ministers read their creed and sign the thirty-nine articles of their American faith. They tell them what they have done, what they are doing, and what they intend to do. They kneel to be kicked, and they are kicked. They beg the Americans to receive their submission, and are afraid they will not accept it. The letter goes on to say, "these have always been, and still are, the sentiments of his Majesty's present servants, and by which their conduct, in respect to America, has been governed: and his Majesty relies upon your prudence and fidelity for such an explanation of his measures." To remove the fears of the assembly of Virginia, lest the sentiments, which had been "always those of the King's ministers," might be hereafter counteracted, the governor, Lord Botetourt, on the 7th of November, thus addressed them— "It may possibly be objected, that, as his Majesty's present administration are not immortal"—the noble lord knew the materials of which the government is composed, that they are here today and gone to-morrow—"their successors may be inclined to attempt to undo what the present ministers shall have attempted to perform; and to that objection I can give but this answer—

that it is my firm opinion that the plan will never be departed from; and so determined am I for ever to abide by it, that I will be content to be declared infamous if I do not, to the last hour of my life, at all times, in all places, and upon all occasions, exert every power with which I either now or ever shall be legally invested in order to obtain and maintain for the continent of America that satisfaction which I have been authorized to promise this day by the confidential servants of our gracious Sovereign, who, to my certain knowledge, rates his honour so high that he would rather part with his Crown than preserve it by deceit." The word of the Crown, you see, is pledged. Mr. Speaker of the House of Commons, to what is the King's word pledged? Have we been sent here to see the business of parliament settled by the King's confidential servants? Why, Sir, what we were to do with these duties was communicated to the assembly of Virginia before it was communicated to us. Why was the word of the King, why was the word of his confidential servants, so pledged, but to influence parliament? There would have been no impropriety in saying what they intended to move. But to assure the colonies that an act would be repealed because the British government intended it, was making this House a mere instrument. And how did the assembly of Virginia understand it? See, Sir, whom they blame for laying on taxes, whom they praise for taking them off! "We are sure," say they, "our most gracious Sovereign, under whatever changes may happen in his confidential servants, will remain immutable in the ways of truth and justice, and that he is incapable of deceiving his faithful subjects." In Ireland, it was disputed whether money-bills could originate with the Crown. In America, you see they can. "We esteem your lordship's information not only as warranted, but even sanctified by the royal word." I really cannot read this without emotion. His Majesty is made the sole mover of every measure of relief; he is to receive all the thanks for removing public burthens and parliament all the odium of laying them on. Was it fitting that we should not be let into the secret of your intention? Was it fitting that the first intimation of what we were to do with these duties should come from the other side of the Atlantic? If a repeal, upon commercial principles, of the duties imposed by the bill of 1767 was necessary, why did you not repeal as soon as you had discovered your error? It is too late for you to appear in triumph, with the British parliament begging at the door of an American assembly. The ministers told them the duties were to be repealed because they went upon un-commercial principles. The people of America were not such fools as you took them to be. They laughed at this most miserable of all pretences. Is the folly of laying duties on your own manufactures a new discovery? Was it not known before the year 1770? Had you no insight into this? Was it never talked of in debate? Sir, the folly was as well-known when you laid them on, as it was when you meanly promised a repeal. You subjected the principles of commerce to considerations of policy in order to establish a civil government. That was your pretence. Upon that pretence the act was passed; and upon that pretence it was supported for three years together. To tell them, therefore, that it was to be repealed upon commercial principles was an assertion too gross for the sober understanding of an American assembly and, until of late, too insulting to be listened to with patience by a British House of Commons.

But, if this House is to come into these measures of repeal, the dignity of parliament should be preserved in doing the act. The first point of dignity, in doing what is just, is to do it speedily; the next, that it should be seen to be your own voluntary deed. Now, Sir, as far as the Speech from the Throne goes, nothing at all of this is intimated. You declare against the repeal of the act. To whom, then, has the grace come? To his Majesty's ministers and confidential servants. They promulgate in America what it is intended we should do before we are allowed to think of it. Surely, the least they could have done was to leave your judgment free. Suppose you should think proper to levy a tax upon America— would not the people have reason to look upon the King's word as forfeited? Parliament is not free. The ministers are bound up; the King is bound; the parliament is bound. Why did you make the covenant in America? What good have you got by it? The com-bination they have entered into against your manufactures I am not so much afraid of. The combination I dread is of a more formidable nature. Nothing destroys the trade of a country so much as the universal aversion of one people to another. One is a mere combination upon paper; the other a combination of the heart.

I have now, Sir, gone through the several points to which I was anxious to draw your attention. I have shewn that every power you possessed has been lost by the very measures you took to maintain them, until your conduct is laughed at from one end of

America to the other. Every step you have taken to quiet the
people there has made them behave ten thousand times worse. I am
at last come to the power of parliament. We consented, for the
reasons the ministers thought fit to give us, to repeal five-sixths
of the act of 1767. Upon the paltry pretext of commercial principles, we repealed the duty on paper, our own paper; the duty on
glass, our own glass; the duty on painters' colours, a miserable
idea! Sir, the ministers do with us just what they please. We were
told, that by agreeing to this we should strengthen government in
America and restore peace there. If I had been of that opinion,
I, for one, would have readily acquiesced. Restore parliament to
its native dignity, and you will then restore peace in America.
When they see you have honour and dignity and power enough to
put down their systems of fraud and violence, they will believe
you can bring back tranquillity and happiness. But, if they see
you going on in the same blind course of subserviency, they will
then say that the government which is not conducted by wisdom
cannot be supported by any authority whatever—that the British
parliament that attempts to prop up a building made of rotten
materials will pull it down upon its own head. Whenever the attention of the House has been called to this subject, we on this side
have been told that it would be improper, at such a moment, to
weaken the government in America. Can that government be
weaker than it now is? Can it, in any way, be restored? Yes, Sir;
when it is something less than it now is. "But, if we consent to an
inquiry, we may lose some of our powers!" What powers have
you to lose? Sir, it is an unhappy practice when ministers, by
their weakness, precipitate a country into difficulties and then
urge those difficulties as a reason why you should not inquire.
I will give them credit for all the success; I will give them credit
for all that has been right in their plans; the rest I will leave to
parliament. If you find the destruction that has come upon you
is the effect of a blow from heaven, then it will be the business
of parliament to awake. The condition of your troops bids you
awake; your Sovereign bids you awake; your own honour bids you
awake; and yet you do nothing, absolutely nothing. You promised
a remedy; you have provided none. If America is ill governed, it
is your duty to censure the government; if well-governed, to support it. I have now, Sir, discharged the great load that weighed
upon my mind, and shall sit down with moving the following
resolutions:

1. "That in several of his Majesty's colonies in North America, Disorders have of late prevailed, prejudicial to the trade and commerce of this kingdom, and destructive to the peace and prosperity of the said colonies.

2. "That a principal cause of the Disorders which have lately prevailed in North America hath arisen from the ill-judged and inconsistent Instructions given, from time to time, by persons in administration to the governors of some of the provinces in North America.

3. "That the directing the Dissolution of the Assemblies of North America, upon their refusal to comply with certain propositions, operated as a menace injurious to the deliberative capacity of these Assemblies, and tended to excite Discontents and to produce unjustifiable Combinations.

4. "That the Assemblies of North America having been dissolved for not disavowing or discountenancing certain Combinations, and the suffering new Assemblies to sit without disavowing or discountenancing the said Combinations, was a proceeding full of inconsistency and tending to lower, in the minds of his Majesty's subjects in America, all opinion of the wisdom and firmness of his Majesty's councils.

5. "That it is unwarrantable, of dangerous consequence, and an high breach of the privilege of this House, to promise to the Assemblies in North America the interposition or influence of his Majesty, or of his confidential servants, with this House, in any manner which may tend to create an opinion in those Assemblies that such interposition or influence must necessarily bring on a repeal of any duties or taxes laid, or to be laid, by authority of parliament.

6. "That it is highly derogatory from his Majesty's honour, and from the freedom of parliamentary deliberation, to pledge the faith of the Crown to the said Assemblies for the repealing or laying on, or continuing, or not laying on, any taxes or duties whatsoever.

7. "That to give assurances in his Majesty's name, distinguishing certain principles of taxation, and disclaiming an intention to propose any taxes within the said description, in order to establish and justify unwarrantable distinctions, has a tendency further to disturb the minds of his Majesty's subjects in America, and weaken the authority of lawful government.

8. "That to lay before this House suggestions of treason, or

misprisions of treason, subsisting in America, in order to bring this House into a plan for the repressing and punishing such supposed treasons or misprisions of treason, when in reality no such treasons or misprisions of treason did subsist, or if they did subsist, no measures whatsoever have been taken, or appear to have been intended, for apprehending and punishing the persons concerned in the same, is an audacious insult on the dignity of parliament, and, in its consequences, tends either to bring a reflection on the wisdom and justice of parliament, or to encourage treasons and and treasonable practices, by neglecting to carry into execution measures recommended by parliament."

4

AN EXCERPT FROM A SPEECH
BEFORE THE HOUSE OF COMMONS
DURING THE DEBATE ON THE
ADDRESS OF THANKS[1]

NOVEMBER 13, 1770

Burke had received news from America during the summer and fall which indicated that many Americans were critical of the retention of the tea tax and determined not to give up their efforts to force Parliament to repeal that symbol of its authority. On the day Parliament reconvened, Burke expressed his general dissatisfaction with British foreign policy and at one point spoke about America. He was not aware that nearly all American merchants had accepted the repeal as sufficient and were eager to resume trade with England. (The greatest portion of the speech contains Burke's defense of his May 8, 1769 motion for an inquiry into the riots at St. George's Fields and a bitter, lengthy attack on the King's Speech, especially that small part wherein the King threatened retaliation against Spain because of the Governor of "Buenos Ayres'" attack on the Falkland Island. His comments on America were, according to Cavendish, his concluding remarks.) This excerpt is on Cav., II, 50.

O NE WORD on the subject of America. The affairs of the colonies make me tremble. The ministry cry victory, as if they had gained some great triumph. In my opinion, Sir, the resistance of the Americans, hardened almost to rebellion, is not half so insolent as what is told us from the Throne. They have consented, it seems, to relax their agreement not to import our manufactures, and will now admit such goods to enter as you impose no duties upon. You have repealed about nine-tenths of those duties, upon

---

[1] *Cav.*, II, 46-50; *London Museum*, III, 45-48; *Gentleman's Magazine*, XLI, 52-54.

commercial principles; they have relaxed nine-tenths of their prohibition, upon commercial principles. As you, however, still keep
up the duty upon tea, in order to preserve the right of taxation,
they forbid the introduction of tea, in order to deny that right.
This is the mighty matter upon which we are to cry victory. No
gentleman remembers me to have said one word by way of encour-
aging such proceedings. I abhor and detest them. I am astonished
that they should have held out so long. I think there is a tremendous spirit prevailing in that country; landed interest there is
none, or very little. When I find these people pressing everything
for two years together, I cannot look upon such a spirit without
terror. The matter of triumph, on our part, is no more than this—
that some of the provinces have at length condescended to admit
the importation of our manufactures. In this they have imitated
the example of a great monarch. Whenever the King of Prussia
finds any of the commodities of his territories prohibited, he pro-
hibits in return. If you lay a duty upon them, he lays a duty upon
yours. America has done precisely the same. I speak of the state
of America, as I have spoken of peace and war. I have nothing to
recommend with regard to it. The spirit you have there roused is
not a useful spirit at a time of war. Do you remember the ships?
do you remember the money? do you remember the vast prepara-
tions they made during the last war? Do you think that is a country from which you can now pour upon the enemy with hands,
hearts, and purses? America never wanted more the assistance of
a sober, systematical government than she does at this moment.
Before you go to war, consider what circumstances you stand in
with regard to the colonies, with regard to Ireland, with regard
to your own people. . . .[2]

[2] Both John Almon's *London Museum* and *The Gentleman's Magazine*
have accounts and arrangements of the speech quite different from
Cavendish's but very similar to each other—although all three are in
substance about the same. Nevertheless, in this particular case it is
worthwhile adding here Almon's version, which is more thorough than
The Gentleman's Magazine's. Both are reprinted in *PH*, XVI, 1044-47,
1066-71.

　　Sir; to me the noble lord seems to tread close in the footsteps of
his fellow-labourers in the ministerial vineyard and to crow over us
with the same reason that they triumph over the Americans. As the
injured colonists have begun to import, they conclude that their
point is gained and they cry out victory! But what ground have
they for this exultation? The colonists have all along continued true

to their grand original principle. As the ministers were not satisfied with the Declaratory Act, but reduced to practice a right which should have been deemed only speculative; as they imposed taxes upon certain articles of commerce, the colonists discontinued the importation of these articles. As the ministers, in their great wisdom, chose to repeal every new tax but that on tea, the colonists chose to keep pace with them in their scheme of reconciliation and to recommence the importation of the articles which were again freed of taxes. But as the ministers thought proper, for the sake of preserving the right of taxation, to continue the duty on tea, the colonists, in order to deny this right, thought proper to continue their associations for the non-importation of tea. In short, they have invariably regulated their conduct by that of the ministry. As administration rose in its pretensions, America rose. As administration relaxed, America relaxed. Nor has any advantage been yet gained over them. Though the loss of their trade, the loss of their affections and allegiance, has been hazarded, the quarrel is as far as ever from a determination. They have in some measure copied the prudence of the king of Prussia, one of the most politic princes in Europe. When any foreign state lays a tax upon any goods exported out of his territories, what does he do? He immediately lays an equivalent tax upon some commodity exported out of their country. The Americans could not directly take this step, but they did what was tantamount; they entered into a solemn agreement to import none of the taxed goods.

Thus it appears, Sir, from this deduction, that the ministers have no reason to plume themselves upon the termination of the quarrels which they have revived in America, or upon any assistance which they are likely to derive from that quarter. Before the Americans can heartily concur in any measure which it may be necessary for Great Britain to embrace at this juncture, their grievances must be redressed. The same irrefragable arguments, which were applied by my honourable friend to Great Britain, are equally applicable to them and the Irish. Their support must be purchased by the removal of every cause of discontent. This is the only magic, the only charm, which can draw their affection, which can cement and unite the different members of the empire and make it act as if inspired by one soul. Instead, therefore, of charging the Americans with "very unwarrantable practices," and thus threatening them with coercive measures, the minister ought to have immediately proposed the repeal of the Tea Act and to have adopted every other scheme of reconciliation. Thus formed by mutual confidence and attachment into one firm and compact body, we may look our enemies in the face. He who gives any other advice can hardly be an honest, much less a wise counsellor; and the minister who could not see and embrace this truth, is not, by his abilities, entitled to the station which he occupies. For if the Bourbon confederacy be not an object of terror, it is certainly no just object of contempt. He, therefore, who will not strive to exert against it the whole undivided strength of our empire, must either be a foe or a driveller.

5

SPEECH BEFORE
THE HOUSE OF COMMONS
IN SUPPORT OF MR. ROSE FULLER'S
MOTION THAT THE COMMONS
MOVE TO A COMMITTEE OF THE
WHOLE IN ORDER TO DISCUSS THE
THREEPENCE TAX ON TEA[1]

APRIL 19, 1774

The British East India Company had been having financial problems for some time, and by 1773 was on the verge of bankruptcy. Parliament reorganized the government in India and took steps to strengthen the Company's financial position. The Tea Act of 1773 gave the Company a virtual monopoly on the exportation of tea to America. The Company had a tremendous stockpile of tea which this act permitted them to ship to America without having to pay the excise duties levied by the Townshend Revenue Act and retained by North in 1770. This enabled the Company to undersell American merchants. The American reaction was the celebrated Boston Tea Party of December 16, 1773.

Parliament determined to punish Boston and Massachusetts and during the spring of 1774 passed the penal bills (the "Intolerable" Acts) closing the Boston port and placing Massachusetts under General Gage. Burke was still convinced that the tea tax was the source of conflict between England and America and when, during the months that the penal bills were being debated, Rose Fuller moved that the tea tax be repealed, Burke used the opportunity to give his renowned speech on American Taxation.

S IR, I agree with the honourable gentleman[2] who spoke last that this subject is not new in this House. Very disagreeably to this House, very unfortunately to this nation, and to the peace and

---

[1] *Works* II, 5-79.
[2] Charles W. Cornwall, one of the Lords of the Treasury and later Speaker of the House of Commons.

prosperity of this whole empire, no topic has been more familiar to us. For nine long years, session after session, we have been lashed round and round this miserable circle of occasional arguments and temporary expedients. I am sure our heads must turn and our stomachs nauseate with them. We have had them in every shape; we have looked at them in every point of view. Invention is exhausted; reason is fatigued; experience has given judgment; but obstinacy is not yet conquered.

The honourable gentleman has made one endeavour more to diversify the form of this disgusting argument. He has thrown out a speech composed almost entirely of challenges. Challenges are serious things; and as he is a man of prudence as well as resolution, I dare say he has very well weighed those challenges before he delivered them. I had long the happiness to sit at the same side of the House, and to agree with the honourable gentleman on all the American questions. My sentiments, I am sure, are well known to him, and I thought I had been perfectly acquainted with his. Though I find myself mistaken, he will still permit me to use the privilege of an old friendship; he will permit me to apply myself to the House under the sanction of his authority, and, on the various grounds he has measured out, to submit to you the poor opinions which I have formed upon a matter of importance enough to demand the fullest consideration I could bestow upon it. . . .

He desires to know, whether, if we were to repeal this tax, agreeably to the proposition of the honourable gentleman who made the motion, the Americans would not take post on this concession in order to make a new attack on the next body of taxes; and whether they would not call for a repeal of the duty on wine as loudly as they do now for the repeal of the duty on tea? Sir, I can give no security on this subject. But I will do all that I can, and all that can be fairly demanded. . . .

When Parliament repealed the Stamp Act in the year 1766, I affirm, first, that the Americans did *not* in consequence of this measure call upon you to give up the former parliamentary revenue which subsisted in that country, or even any one of the articles which compose it. I affirm, also, that when, departing from the maxims of that repeal, you revived the scheme of taxation and thereby filled the minds of the colonists with new jealousy and all sorts of apprehensions, then it was that they quarrelled with the old taxes as well as the new, then it was, and not till then, that they questioned all the parts of your legislative power; and by the battery of such questions have shaken the solid structure of this empire to its deepest foundations.

Of those two propositions I shall, before I have done, give such convincing, such damning proof, that however the contrary may be whispered in circles or bawled in newspapers, they never more will dare to raise their voices in this House. I speak with great confidence. I have reason for it. The ministers are with me. *They* at least are convinced that the repeal of the Stamp Act had not, and that no repeal can have, the consequences which the honourable gentleman who defends their measures is so much alarmed at. To their conduct I refer him for a conclusive answer to this objection. I carry my proof irresistibly into the very body of both Ministry and Parliament, not on any general reasoning growing out of collateral matter, but on the conduct of the honourable gentleman's ministerial friends on the new revenue itself.

The Act of 1767, which grants this tea duty, sets forth in its preamble that it was expedient to raise a revenue in America for the support of the civil government there, as well as for purposes still more extensive. To this support the Act assigns six branches of duties. About two years after this Act passed, the Ministry, I mean the present Ministry, thought it expedient to repeal five of the duties, and to leave (for reasons best known to themselves) only the sixth standing. Suppose any person, at the time of that repeal, had thus addressed the minister:[3] "Condemning, as you do, the repeal of the Stamp Act, why do you venture to repeal the duties upon glass, paper, and painters' colours? Let your pretence for the repeal be what it will, are you not thoroughly convinced that your concessions will produce not satisfaction but insolence in the Americans, and that the giving up these taxes will necessitate the giving up of all the rest?" This objection was as palpable then as it is now, and it was as good for preserving the five duties as for retaining the sixth. Besides, the minister will recollect that the repeal of the Stamp Act had but just preceded his repeal, and the ill policy of that measure (had it been so impolitic as it has been represented), and the mischiefs it produced, were quite recent. Upon the principles, therefore, of the honourable gentleman, upon the principles of the minister himself, the minister has nothing at all to answer. He stands condemned by himself, and by

[3] Lord North, Chancellor of Exchequer at that time and often referred to by Burke as "the noble lord."

all his associates old and new, as a destroyer, in the first trust of finance, of the revenues; and in the first rank of honour, as a betrayer of the dignity of his country.

Most men, especially great men, do not always know their well-wishers. I come to rescue that noble lord out of the hands of those he calls his friends, and even out of his own. I will do him the justice he is denied at home. He has not been this wicked or imprudent man. He knew that a repeal had no tendency to produce the mischiefs which give so much alarm to his honourable friend. His work was not bad in its principle, but imperfect in its execution; and the motion on your paper presses him only to complete a proper plan, which, by some unfortunate and unaccountable error, he had left unfinished.

I hope, Sir, the honourable gentleman who spoke last is thoroughly satisfied, and satisfied out of the proceedings of Ministry on their own favourite Act, that his fears from a repeal are groundless. If he is not, I leave him, and the noble lord who sits by him, to settle the matter as well as they can together; for if the repeal of American taxes destroys all our government in America—He is the man!—and he is the worst of all the repealers, because he is the last.

But I hear it rung continually in my ears, now and formerly—"the preamble! what will become of the preamble if you repeal this tax?"—I am sorry to be compelled so often to expose the calamities and disgraces of Parliament. The preamble of this law, standing as it now stands, has the lie direct given to it by the provisionary part of the Act, if that can be called provisionary which makes no provision. I should be afraid to express myself in this manner, especially in the face of such a formidable array of ability as is now drawn up before me, composed of the ancient household troops of that side of the House and the new recruits from this, if the matter were not clear and indisputable. Nothing but truth could give me this firmness; but plain truth and clear evidence can be beat down by no ability. The clerk will be so good as to turn to the Act, and to read this favourite preamble:

"Whereas it is expedient *that a revenue should be raised in your Majesty's dominions in America, for making a more* certain *and* adequate *provision for defraying the charge of the* administration of justice, and support of civil government, *in such provinces where it shall be found necessary; and towards* further defraying *the expenses* of defending, protecting, and securing the said dominions."

You have heard this pompous performance. Now where is the revenue which is to do all these mighty things? Five-sixths repealed—abandoned—sunk—gone—lost for ever. Does the poor solitary tea duty support the purposes of this preamble? Is not the supply there stated as effectually abandoned as if the tea duty had perished in the general wreck? Here, Mr. Speaker, is a precious mockery—a preamble without an Act—taxes granted in order to be repealed—and the reasons of the grant still carefully kept up! This is raising a revenue in America! This is preserving dignity in England! If you repeal this tax in compliance with the motion, I readily admit that you lose this fair preamble. Estimate your loss in it. The object of the Act is gone already, and all you suffer is the purging the statute-book of the opprobrium of an empty, absurd, and false recital.

It has been said again and again that the five taxes were repealed on commercial principles. It is so said in the paper in my hand, a paper which I constantly carry about, which I have often used, and shall often use again.[4] What is got by this paltry pretence of commercial principles I know not; for if your government in America is destroyed by the *repeal of taxes*, it is of no consequence upon what ideas the repeal is grounded. Repeal this tax too upon commercial principles if you please. These principles will serve as well now as they did formerly. But you know that, either your objection to a repeal from these supposed consequences has no validity, or that this pretence never could remove it. This commercial motive never was believed by any man, either in America, which this letter is meant to soothe, or in England, which it is meant to deceive. It was impossible it should. Because every man in the least acquainted with the detail of commerce must know that several of the articles on which the tax was repealed were fitter objects of duties than almost any other articles that could possibly be chosen, without comparison more so than the tea that was left taxed, as infinitely less liable to be eluded by contraband. The tax upon red and white lead was of this nature. You have, in this kingdom, an advantage in lead that amounts to a monopoly. When you find yourself in this situation of advantage, you sometimes venture to tax even your own export. You did so soon after the last war, when, upon this principle, you ventured to impose a duty on coals. In all the articles of American contraband trade who ever heard of the smuggling of red lead and

[4] Lord Hillsborough's circular letter.

white lead? You might, therefore, well enough, without danger of contraband and without injury to commerce (if this were the whole consideration) have taxed these commodities. The same may be said of glass. Besides, some of the things taxed were so trivial, that the loss of the objects themselves, and their utter annihilation out of American commerce, would have been comparatively as nothing. But is the article of tea such an object in the trade of England as not to be felt or felt but slightly, like white lead and red lead and painters' colours? Tea is an object of far other importance. Tea is perhaps the most important object, taking it with its necessary connections, of any in the mighty circle of our commerce. If commercial principles had been the true motives to the repeal, or had they been at all attended to, tea would have been the last article we should have left taxed for a subject of controversy.

Sir, it is not a pleasant consideration, but nothing in the world can read so awful and so instructive a lesson, as the conduct of Ministry in this business, upon the mischief of not having large and liberal ideas in the management of great affairs. Never have the servants of the state looked at the whole of your complicated interests in one connected view. They have taken things by bits and scraps, some at one time and one pretence, and some at another, just as they pressed, without any sort of regard to their relations or dependencies. They never had any kind of system right or wrong, but only invented occasionally some miserable tale for the day, in order meanly to sneak out of difficulties into which they had proudly strutted. And they were put to all these shifts and devices, full of meanness and full of mischief, in order to pilfer piecemeal a repeal of an Act, which they had not the generous courage, when they found and felt their error, honourably and fairly to disclaim. By such management, by the irresistible operation of feeble councils, so paltry a sum as the threepence in the eyes of a financier, so insignificant an article as tea in the eyes of a philosopher, have shaken the pillars of a commercial empire that circled the whole globe.

Do you forget that, in the very last year, you stood on the precipice of general bankruptcy? Your danger was indeed great. You were distressed in the affairs of the East India Company; and you well know what sort of things are involved in the comprehensive energy of that significant appellation. I am not called upon to enlarge to you on that danger, which you thought proper yourselves to aggravate and to display to the world with all the parade of indiscreet declamation. The monopoly of the most lucrative trades, and the possession of imperial revenues, had brought you to the verge of beggary and ruin. Such was your representation—such, in some measure, was your case. The vent of ten millions of pounds of this commodity, now locked up by the operation of an injudicious tax and rotting in the warehouses of the company, would have prevented all this distress and all that series of desperate measures which you thought yourselves obliged to take in consequence of it. America would have furnished that vent, which no other part of the world can furnish but America, where tea is next to a necessary of life, and where the demand grows upon the supply. I hope our dear-bought East India committees have done us at least so much good as to let us know that, without a more extensive sale of that article, our East India revenues and acquisitions can have no certain connection with this country. It is through the American trade of tea that your East India conquests are to be prevented from crushing you with their burthen. They are ponderous indeed; and they must have that great country to lean upon, or they tumble upon your head. It is the same folly that has lost you at once the benefit of the West and of the East. This folly has thrown open folding-doors to contraband, and will be the means of giving the profits of the trade of your colonies to every nation but yourselves. Never did a people suffer so much for the empty words of a preamble. It must be given up. For on what principle does it stand? This famous revenue stands at this hour on all the debate, as a description of revenue not as yet known in all the comprehensive (but too comprehensive) vocabulary of finance—*a preambulary tax*. It is indeed a tax of sophistry, a tax of pedantry, a tax of disputation, a tax of war and rebellion, a tax for anything but benefit to the imposers or satisfaction to the subject.

Well, but whatever it is, gentlemen will force the colonists to take the teas. You will force them? Has seven years' struggle been yet able to force them? Oh but it seems "we are in the right. The tax is trifling—in effect it is rather an exoneration than an imposition; three-fourths of the duty formerly payable on teas exported to America is taken off, the place of collection is only shifted, instead of the retention of a shilling from the drawback here it is threepence custom in America." All this, Sir, is very true. But this is the very folly and mischief of the Act. Incredible as it may seem, you know that you have deliberately thrown away a large duty which you held secure and quiet in your hands for the vain hope of getting one three-fourths less, through every hazard, through certain litigation, and possibly through war.

The manner of proceeding in the duties on paper and glass, imposed by the same Act, was exactly in the same spirit. There are heavy excises on those articles when used in England. On export these excises are drawn back.[5] But instead of withholding the drawback, which might have been done with ease, without charge, without possibility of smuggling, and instead of applying the money (money already in your hands) according to your pleasure, you began your operations in finance by flinging away your revenue; you allowed the whole drawback on export, and then you charged the duty (which you had before discharged) payable in the colonies, where it was certain the collection would devour it to the bone, if any revenue were ever suffered to be collected at all. One spirit pervades and animates the whole mass.

Could anything be a subject of more just alarm to America than to see you go out of the plain highroad of finance, and give up your most certain revenues and your clearest interests, merely for the sake of insulting your colonies? No man ever doubted that the commodity of tea could bear an imposition of threepence. But no commodity will bear threepence, or will bear a penny, when the general feelings of men are irritated and two millions of people are resolved not to pay. The feelings of the colonies were formerly the feelings of Great Britain. Theirs were formerly the feelings of Mr. Hampden when called upon for the payment of twenty shillings.[6] Would twenty shillings have ruined Mr. Hampden's fortune? No; but the payment of half twenty shillings, on the principle it was demanded, would have made him a slave. It is the weight of that preamble, of which you are so fond, and not the weight of the duty that the Americans are unable and unwilling to bear.

It is then, Sir, upon the *principle* of this measure, and nothing else, that we are at issue. It is a principle of political expediency.

---

[5] "Drawback" refers to duties on items which are collected and then returned to the importer; today we refer to it as "rebates."

[6] John Hampden, a member of Parliament under Charles I , refused to pay a "Ship Money" levy in 1638 on the grounds that it was unlawful taxation. He lost the case and his trial added to the growing list of grievances against Charles.

Your Act of 1767 asserts that it is expedient to raise a revenue in America; your Act of 1769, which takes away that revenue, contradicts the Act of 1767, and, by something much stronger than words, asserts, that it is not expedient. It is a reflection upon your wisdom to persist in a solemn parliamentary declaration of the expediency of any object for which, at the same time, you make no sort of provision. And pray, Sir, let not this circumstance escape you—it is very material—that the preamble of this Act which we wish to repeal is not *declaratory of a right,* as some gentlemen seem to argue it, it is only a recital of the *expediency* of a certain exercise of a right supposed already to have been asserted; an exercise you are now contending for by ways and means which you confess, though they were obeyed, to be utterly insufficient for their purpose. You are therefore at this moment in the awkward situation of fighting for a phantom; a quiddity; a thing that wants, not only a substance, but even a name for a thing, which is neither abstract right nor profitable enjoyment.

They tell you, Sir, that your dignity is tied to it. I know not how it happens, but this dignity of yours is a terrible encumbrance to you, for it has of late been ever at war with your interest, your equity, and every idea of your policy. Show the thing you contend for to be reason, show it to be common sense; show it to be the means of attaining some useful end, and then I am content to allow it what dignity you please. But what dignity is derived from the perseverance in absurdity is more than ever I could discern. The honourable gentleman has said well—indeed, in most of his *general* observations I agree with him—he says that this subject does not stand as it did formerly. Oh certainly not! Every hour you continue on this ill-chosen ground your difficulties thicken on you; and therefore my conclusion is, remove from a bad position as quickly as you can. The disgrace and the necessity of yielding, both of them, grow upon you every hour of your delay.

But will you repeal the Act, says the honourable gentleman, at this instant when America is in open resistance to your authority and that you have just revived your system of taxation? He thinks he has driven us into a corner. But thus pent up, I am content to meet him; because I enter the lists supported by my old authority, his new friends, the ministers themselves. The honourable gentleman remembers that about five years ago as great disturbances as the present prevailed in America on account of the new taxes. The ministers represented these disturbances as treasonable; and this House thought proper, on that representation, to make a famous address for a revival, and for a new application of a statute of Henry VIII. We besought the king, in that well-considered address, to inquire into treasons, and to bring the supposed traitors from America to Great Britain for trial. His Majesty was pleased graciously to promise a compliance with our request. All the attempts from this side of the House to resist these violences, and to bring about a repeal, were treated with the utmost scorn. An apprehension of the very consequences now stated by the honourable gentleman was then given as a reason for shutting the door against all hope of such an alteration. And so strong was the spirit for supporting the new taxes that the session concluded with the following remarkable declaration. After stating the vigorous measures which had been pursued, the speech from the throne proceeds:

"You have assured me of your firm *support in the* prosecution *of them. Nothing, in my opinion, could be more likely to enable the well-disposed among my subjects in that part of the world effectually to discourage and defeat the designs of the factious and seditious than the hearty concurrence of every branch of the legislature in* maintaining the execution of the laws in every *part of my dominions."*

After this no man dreamt that a repeal under this Ministry could possibly take place. The honourable gentleman knows as well as I that the idea was utterly exploded by those who sway the House. This speech was made on the ninth day of May 1769. Five days after this speech, that is, on the 13th of the same month, the public circular letter, a part of which I am going to read to you, was written by Lord Hillsborough, Secretary of State for the Colonies. After reciting the substance of the king's speech, he goes on thus:

"I can take upon me to assure you, notwithstanding insinuations to the contrary, from men with factious and seditious views, *that his Majesty's* present administration have at no time entertained a design to propose to Parliament to lay any further taxes upon America for the purpose of RAISING A REVENUE; *and that it is at present their intention to propose, the next session of Parliament, to take off the duties upon glass, paper, and colours, upon consideration of such duties* having been laid contrary to the true principles of commerce.

"These have always *been, and* still are, *the sentiments of his*

Majesty's present servants, *and by which their conduct in* respect to America has been governed. . . . "

Here, Sir, is a canonical book of ministerial scripture; the general epistle to the Americans. What does the gentleman say to it? Here a repeal is promised, promised without condition, and while your authority was actually resisted. I pass by the public promise of a peer relative to the repeal of taxes by this House. I pass by the use of the king's name in a matter of supply, that sacred and reserved right of the Commons. I conceal the ridiculous figure of Parliament hurling its thunders at the gigantic rebellion of America, and then five days after prostrate at the feet of those assemblies we affected to despise, begging them, by the intervention of our ministerial sureties, to receive our submission and heartily promising amendment. These might have been serious matters formerly, but we are grown wiser than our fathers. Passing therefore from the constitutional consideration to the mere policy, does not this letter imply that the idea of taxing America for the purpose of revenue is an abominable project, when the Ministry suppose that none but *factious* men, and with seditious views, could charge them with it? does not this letter adopt and sanctify the American distinction of *taxing for a revenue?* does it not formally reject all future taxation on that principle? does it not state the ministerial rejection of such principle of taxation, not as the occasional, but the constant opinion of the king's servants? does it not say (I care not how consistently), but does it not say that their conduct with regard to America has been *always* governed by this policy? It goes a great deal further. These excellent and trusty servants of the king, justly fearful lest they themselves should have lost all credit with the world, bring out the image of their gracious sovereign from the inmost and most sacred shrine and they pawn him as a security for their promises— "*His Majesty* relies on your prudence and fidelity for such an explanation of *his* measures." These sentiments of the minister and these measures of his Majesty can only relate to the principle and practice of taxing for a revenue, and accordingly Lord Botetourt, stating it as such, did, with great propriety, and in the exact spirit of his instructions, endeavour to remove the fears of the Virginian assembly, lest the sentiments, which it seems (unknown to the world) had *always* been those of the ministers, and by which *their* conduct in *respect to America had been governed,* should by some possible revolution, favourable to wicked American taxes, be hereafter counteracted. He addresses them in this manner:

It may possibly be objected that, as his Majesty's present administration are not immortal, *their successors may be inclined to attempt to undo what the present ministers shall have attempted to perform; and to that objection I can give but this answer, that it is my firm opinion that the plan I have stated to you will certainly take place, and that it will never be departed from; and so determined am I for ever to abide by it, that I will be content to be declared infamous, if I do not, to the last hour of my life, at all times, in all places, and upon all occasions, exert every power with which I either am or ever shall be legally invested in order to obtain and* maintain *for the continent of America that* satisfaction *which I have been authorised to promise this day, by the* confidential *servants of our gracious sovereign, who to my certain knowledge rates his honour so high* that he would rather part with his crown than preserve it by deceit.*

A glorious and true character! which (since we suffer his ministers with impunity to answer for his ideas of taxation) we ought to make it our business to enable his Majesty to preserve in all its lustre. Let him have character, since ours is no more! Let some part of government be kept in respect!

This epistle was not the letter of Lord Hillsborough solely, though he held the official pen. It was the letter of the noble lord upon the floor,[7] and of all the king's then ministers, who (with, I think, the exception of two only) are his ministers at this hour. The very first news that a British Parliament heard of what it was to do with the duties which it had given and granted to the king was by the publication of the votes of American assemblies. It was in America that your resolutions were predeclared. It was from thence that we knew to a certainty, how much exactly, and not a scruple more or less, we were to repeal. We were unworthy to be let into the secret of our own conduct. The assemblies had *confidential* communications from his Majesty's *confidential* servants. We were nothing but instruments. Do you, after this, wonder that you have no weight and no respect in the colonies? After this, are you surprised that Parliament is every day and everywhere losing (I feel it with sorrow, I utter it with reluctance) that reverential affection which so endearing a name of authority ought ever to carry with it; that you are obeyed solely from respect to the bayonet; and that this House, the ground and pillar of freedom, is itself held up only by the treacherous underpinning and clumsy buttresses of arbitrary power?

[7] Lord North.

If this dignity, which is to stand in the place of just policy and common sense, had been consulted, there was a time for preserving it, and for reconciling it with any concession. If in the session of 1768, that session of idle terror and empty menaces, you had, as you were often pressed to do, repealed these taxes, then your strong operations would have come justified and enforced, in case your concessions had been returned by outrages. But, preposterously, you began with violence; and before terrors could have any effect, either good or bad, your ministers immediately begged pardon, and promised that repeal to the obstinate Americans which they had refused in an easy, good-natured, complying British Parliament. The assemblies, which had been publicly and avowedly dissolved for *their* contumacy, are called together to receive *your* submission. Your ministerial directors blustered like tragic tyrants here, and then went mumping with a sore leg in America, canting and whining, and complaining of faction, which represented them as friends to a revenue from the colonies. I hope nobody in this House will hereafter have the impudence to defend American taxes in the name of Ministry. The moment they do, with this letter of attorney in my hand, I will tell them, in the authorised terms, they are wretches "with factious and seditious views, enemies to the peace and prosperity of the mother country and the colonies," and subverters "of the mutual affection and confidence on which the glory and safety of the British empire depend."

After this letter, the question is no more on propriety or dignity. They are gone already. The faith of your sovereign is pledged for the political principle. The general declaration in the letter goes to the whole of it. You must therefore either abandon the scheme of taxing, or you must send the ministers tarred and feathered to America who dared to hold out the royal faith for a renunciation of all taxes for revenue. Them you must punish or this faith you must preserve. The preservation of this faith is of more consequence than the duties on *red lead*, or *white lead*, or on broken *glass*, or *atlas-ordinary*, or *demy-fine*, or *blue-royal*, or *bastard*, or *fool's-cap* which you have given up, or the threepence on tea which you retained. The letter went stamped with the public authority of this kingdom. The instructions for the colony government go under no other sanction, and America cannot believe, and will not obey you, if you do not preserve this channel of communication sacred. You are now punishing the colonies for acting on distinctions held out by that very Ministry which is here shining in riches, in favour, and in power, and urging the punishment of the very offence to which they had themselves been the tempters.

Sir, if reasons respecting simply your own commerce, which is your own convenience, were the sole ground of the repeal of the five duties, why does Lord Hillsborough, in disclaiming in the name of the king and Ministry their ever having had an intent to tax for revenue, mention it as the means "of re-establishing the confidence and affection of the colonies"? Is it a way of soothing *others* to assure them that you will take good care of *yourself?* The medium, the only medium, for regaining their affection and confidence is, that you will take off something oppressive to their minds. Sir, the letter strongly enforces that idea; for though the repeal of the taxes is promised on commercial principles, yet the means of counteracting "the insinuations of men with factious and seditious views" is, by a disclaimer of the intention of taxing for revenue, as a constant, invariable sentiment and rule of conduct in the government of America. . . .

[Furthermore,] will the noble lord condescend to tell me why he repealed the taxes on your manufactures sent out to America and not the taxes on the manufactures exported to the Isle of Man?[8] The principle was exactly the same, the objects charged infinitely more extensive, the duties without comparison higher. Why? Why, notwithstanding all his childish pretexts, because the taxes were quietly submitted to in the Isle of Man, and because they raised a flame in America. Your reasons were political, not commercial. The repeal was made, as Lord Hillsborough's letter well expresses it, to regain "the confidence and affection of the colonies, on which the glory and safety of the British empire depend." A wise and just motive surely, if ever there was such. But the mischief and dishonour is that you have not done what you had given the colonies just cause to expect, when your ministers disclaimed the idea of taxes for a revenue. There is nothing simple, nothing manly, nothing ingenuous, open, decisive, or steady in the proceeding, with regard either to the continuance or the repeal of the taxes. The whole has an air of littleness and fraud. The article of tea is slurred over in the circular letter, as it were by accident—nothing is said of a resolution either to keep that tax or to give it up. There is no fair dealing in any part of the transaction.

[8] This refers to the heavy duties approved just before the Townshend Revenue Act was passed.

If you mean to follow your true motive and your public faith, give up your tax on tea for raising a revenue, the principle of which has, in effect, been disclaimed in your name, and which produces you no advantage—no, not a penny. Or, if you choose to go on with a poor pretence instead of a solid reason, and will still adhere to your cant of commerce, you have ten thousand times more strong commercial reasons for giving up this duty on tea than for abandoning the five others that you have already renounced.

The American consumption of teas is annually, I believe, worth £300,000 at the least farthing. If you urge the American violence as a justification of your perseverance in enforcing this tax, you know that you can never answer this plain question—Why did you repeal the others given in the same Act whilst the very same violence subsisted?—But you did not find the violence cease upon that concession. No! because the concession was far short of satisfying the principle which Lord Hillsborough had abjured, or even the pretence on which the repeal of the other taxes was announced; and because, by enabling the East India Company to open a shop for defeating the American resolution not to pay that specific tax, you manifestly showed a hankering after the principle of the Act which you formerly had renounced. Whatever road you take leads to a compliance with this motion. It opens to you at the end of every vista. Your commerce, your policy, your promises, your reasons, your pretences, your consistency, your inconsistency—all jointly oblige you to this repeal.

But still it sticks in our throats—if we go so far, the Americans will go farther. We do not know that. We ought, from experience, rather to presume the contrary. Do we not know for certain that the Americans are going on as fast as possible, whilst we refuse to gratify them? Can they do more, or can they do worse, if we yield this point? I think this concession will rather fix a turnpike to prevent their further progress. It is impossible to answer for bodies of men. But I am sure the natural effect of fidelity, clemency, kindness in governors is peace, goodwill, order, and esteem on the part of the governed. I would certainly, at least, give these fair principles a fair trial, which since the making of this Act to this hour they never have had.

Sir, the honourable gentleman having spoken what he thought necessary upon the narrow part of the subject, I have given him, I hope, a satisfactory answer. He next presses me by a variety of direct challenges and oblique reflections to say something on the historical part. I shall therefore, Sir, open myself fully on that important and delicate subject, not for the sake of telling you a long story (which I know, Mr. Speaker, you are not particularly fond of), but for the sake of the weighty instruction that, I flatter myself, will necessarily result from it. I shall not be longer, if I can help it, than so serious a matter requires.

Permit me then, Sir, to lead your attention very far back, back to the Act of Navigation, the corner-stone of the policy of this country with regard to its colonies. Sir, that policy was, from the beginning, purely commercial, and the commercial system was wholly restrictive. It was the system of a monopoly. No trade was let loose from that constraint but merely to enable the colonists to dispose of what, in the course of your trade, you could not take, or to enable them to dispose of such articles as we forced upon them, and for which, without some degree of liberty, they could not pay. Hence all your specific and detailed enumerations, hence the innumerable checks and counterchecks, hence that infinite variety of paper chains by which you bind together this complicated system of the colonies. This principle of commercial monopoly runs through no less than twenty-nine Acts of Parliament, from the year 1660 to the unfortunate period of 1764.

In all those Acts the system of commerce is established as that from whence alone you proposed to make the colonies contribute (I mean directly and by the operation of your superintending legislative power) to the strength of the empire. I venture to say, that during that whole period, a parliamentary revenue from thence was never once in contemplation. Accordingly, in all the number of laws passed with regard to the plantations, the words which distinguish revenue laws specifically as such were, I think, premeditatedly avoided. I do not say, Sir, that a form of words alters the nature of the law or abridges the power of the lawgiver. It certainly does not. However, titles and formal preambles are not always idle words, and the lawyers frequently argue from them. I state these facts to show, not what was your right, but what has been your settled policy. Our revenue laws have usually a *title* purporting their being *grants*, and the words *give* and *grant* usually precede the enacting parts. Although duties were imposed on America in Acts of King Charles II, and in Acts of King William, no one title of giving "an aid to his Majesty," or any other of the usual titles to revenue Acts, was to be found in any of them till 1764, nor were the words "give and grant" in any preamble until the 6th of George II.[9] However, the title of this Act of George II, notwithstanding the words of donation, considers it merely as a regulation of trade, "an Act for the better securing of the trade of his Majesty's sugar colonies in America." This Act was made on a compromise of all, and at the express desire of a part, of the colonies themselves. It was therefore in some measure with their consent; and having a title directly purporting only a *commercial regulation*, and being in truth nothing more, the words were passed by, at a time when no jealousy was entertained and things were little scrutinised. Even Governor Bernard, in his second printed letter, dated in 1763, gives it as his opinion that it "was an Act of *prohibition* not of revenue." This is certainly true, that no act avowedly for the purpose of revenue, and with the ordinary title and recital taken together, is found in the statute book until the year 1764. All before this period stood on commercial regulation and restraint. The scheme of a colony revenue by British authority appeared therefore to the Americans in the light of a great innovation. The words of Governor Bernard's ninth letter, written in Nov. 1765, state this idea very strongly: "It must," says he, "have been supposed, *such an innovation as a parliamentary taxation* would cause a great *alarm*, and meet with much *opposition* in most parts of America; it was *quite new* to the people, and had no *visible bounds* set to it." After stating the weakness of government there, he says, "was this a time to introduce *so great a novelty* as a parliamentary inland taxation in America?" Whatever the right might have been, this mode of using it was absolutely new in policy and practice.

Sir, they who are friends to the schemes of American revenue say that the commercial restraint is full as hard a law for America to live under. I think so too. I think it, if uncompensated, to be a condition of as rigorous servitude as men can be subject to. But America bore it from the fundamental Act of Navigation until 1764.[10] Why? Because men do bear the inevitable constitution of their original nature with all its infirmities. The Act of Navigation attended the colonies from their infancy, grew with their growth, and strengthened with their strength. They were confirmed in obedience to it, even more by usage than by law. They scarcely had remembered a time when they were not subject to such restraint. Besides, they were indemnified for it by a pecu-

[9] The Molasses Act, 1733.
[10] Referring to the Navigation Act of 1660.

niary compensation. Their monopolist happened to be one of the richest men in the world. By his immense capital (primarily employed not for their benefit but his own) they were enabled to proceed with their fisheries, their agriculture, their shipbuilding (and their trade too within the limits), in such a manner as got far the start of the slow, languid operations of unassisted nature. This capital was a hotbed to them. Nothing in the history of mankind is like their progress. For my part, I never cast an eye on their flourishing commerce and their cultivated and commodious life, but they seem to me rather ancient nations grown to perfection through a long series of fortunate events and a train of successful industry, accumulating wealth in many centuries, than the colonies of yesterday, than a set of miserable outcasts, a few years ago, not so much sent as thrown out, on the bleak and barren shore of a desolate wilderness, three thousand miles from all civilised intercourse.

All this was done by England, whilst England pursued trade and forgot revenue. You not only acquired commerce, but you actually created the very objects of trade in America; and by that creation you raised the trade of this kingdom at least fourfold. America had the compensation of your capital, which made her bear her servitude. She had another compensation, which you are now going to take away from her. She had, except the commercial restraint, every characteristic mark of a free people in all her internal concerns. She had the image of the British constitution. She had the substance. She was taxed by her own representatives. She chose most of her own magistrates. She paid them all. She had in effect the sole disposal of her own internal government. This whole state of commercial servitude and civil liberty, taken together, is certainly not perfect freedom, but comparing it with the ordinary circumstances of human nature it was a happy and a liberal condition.

I know, Sir, that great and not unsuccessful pains have been taken to inflame our minds by an outcry, in this House and out of it, that in America the Act of Navigation neither is, nor ever was, obeyed. But if you take the colonies through, I affirm, that its authority never was disputed, that it was nowhere disputed for any length of time, and, on the whole, that it was well observed. Wherever the Act pressed hard many individuals indeed evaded it. This is nothing. These scattered individuals never denied the law and never obeyed it. Just as it happens whenever the laws of trade, whenever the laws of revenue, press hard upon the people in England, in that case all your shores are full of contraband. Your right to give a monopoly to the East India Company, your right to lay immense duties on French brandy, are not disputed in England. You do not make this charge on any man. But you know that there is not a creek from Pentland Frith to the Isle of Wight in which they do not smuggle immense quantities of teas, East India goods, and brandies. I take it for granted that the authority of Governor Bernard in this point is indisputable. Speaking of these laws as they regarded that part of America now in so unhappy a condition, he says, "I believe they are nowhere better supported than in this province; I do not pretend that it is entirely free from a breach of these laws, but that such a breach, if discovered, is justly punished." What more can you say of the obedience to any laws in any country? An obedience to these laws formed the acknowledgment, instituted by yourselves, for your superiority, and was the payment you originally imposed for your protection.

Whether you were right or wrong in establishing the colonies on the principles of commercial monopoly rather than on that of revenue, is at this day a problem of mere speculation. You cannot have both by the same authority. To join together the restraints of an universal internal and external monopoly with an universal internal and external taxation is an unnatural union—perfect, uncompensated slavery. You have long since decided for yourself and them, and you and they have prospered exceedingly under that decision.

This nation, Sir, never thought of departing from that choice until the period immediately on the close of the last war. Then a scheme of government new in many things seemed to have been adopted. I saw, or I thought I saw, several symptoms of a great change whilst I sat in your gallery, a good while before I had the honour of a seat in this House. At that period the necessity was established of keeping up no less than twenty new regiments, with twenty colonels capable of seats in this House. This scheme was adopted with very general applause from all sides, at the very time that, by your conquests in America, your danger from foreign attempts in that part of the world was much lessened or indeed rather quite over. When this huge increase of military establishment was resolved on, a revenue was to be found to support so great a burthen. Country gentlemen, the great patrons of economy and the great resisters of a standing armed force, would not have entered with much alacrity into the vote for so large and so expensive an army if they had been very sure that they were to continue to pay for it.[11] But hopes of another kind were held out to them; and, in particular, I well remember, that Mr. Townshend, in a brilliant harangue on this subject, did dazzle them by playing before their eyes the image of a revenue to be raised in America.

Here began to dawn the first glimmerings of this new colony system. It appeared more distinctly afterwards, when it was devolved upon a person to whom, on other accounts, this country owes very great obligations. I do believe, that he had a very serious desire to benefit the public. But with no small study of the detail, he did not seem to have his view, at least equally, carried to the total circuit of our affairs. He generally considered his objects in lights that were rather too detached. Whether the business of an American revenue was imposed upon him altogether, whether it was entirely the result of his own speculation, or, what is more probable, that his own ideas rather coincided with the instructions he had received—certain it is that, with the best intentions in the world, he first brought this fatal scheme into form and established it by Act of Parliament.[12]

. . . Mr. Grenville thought better of the wisdom and power of human legislation than in truth it deserves. He conceived, and many conceived along with him, that the flourishing trade of this country was greatly owing to law and institution, and not quite so much to liberty; for but too many are apt to believe regulation to be commerce and taxes to be revenue. Among regulations, that which stood first in reputation was his idol. I mean the Act of Navigation. He has often professed it to be so. The policy of that Act is, I readily admit, in many respects well understood. But I do say that, if the Act be suffered to run the full length of its principle and is not changed and modified according to the change of times and the fluctuation of circumstances, it must do great mischief and frequently even defeat its own purpose.

---

[11] It should be noted that an army was still necessary, for the French threat had not been entirely removed. Moreover, Pontiac's rebellion had broken out and few of the colonies would send a contingent to help out, making the need for English troops even greater.

[12] Burke here follows with a eulogy on George Grenville, the subject of this paragraph, extolling his statesmanship and dedication.

After the war, and in the last years of it, the trade of America had increased far beyond the speculations of the most sanguine imaginations. It swelled out on every side. It filled all its proper channels to the brim. It overflowed with a rich redundance, and breaking its banks on the right and on the left, it spread out upon some places where it was indeed improper, upon others where it was only irregular. It is the nature of all greatness not to be exact, and great trade will always be attended with considerable abuses. The contraband will always keep pace in some measure with the fair trade. It should stand as a fundamental maxim, that no vulgar precaution ought to be employed in the cure of evils which are closely connected with the cause of our prosperity. Perhaps this great person turned his eyes somewhat less than was just towards the incredible increase of the fair trade, and looked with something of too exquisite a jealousy towards the contraband. He certainly felt a singular degree of anxiety on the subject, and even began to act from that passion earlier than is commonly imagined. For whilst he was First Lord of the Admiralty, though not strictly called upon in his official line, he presented a very strong memorial to the Lords of the Treasury (my Lord Bute was then at the head of the board) heavily complaining of the growth of the illicit commerce in America. Some mischief happened even at that time from this over-earnest zeal. Much greater happened afterwards, when it operated with greater power in the highest department of the finances. The bonds of the Act of Navigation were straitened so much that America was on the point of having no trade, either contraband or legitimate. They found, under the construction and execution then used, the Act no longer tying, but actually strangling them. All this coming with new enumerations of commodities, with regulations which in a manner put a stop to the mutual coasting intercourse of the colonies, with the appointment of courts of admiralty under various improper circumstances, with a sudden extinction of the paper currencies, with a compulsory provision for the quartering of soldiers—the people of America thought themselves proceeded against as delinquents, or, at best, as people under suspicion of delinquency, and in such a manner as, they imagined, their recent services in the war did not at all merit. Any of these innumerable regulations, perhaps, would not have alarmed alone; some might be thought reasonable; the multitude struck them with terror.

But the grand manœuvre in that business of new regulating the colonies, was the 15th Act of the fourth of George III., which, besides containing several of the matters to which I have just alluded, opened a new principle; and here properly began the second period of the policy of this country with regard to the colonies, by which the scheme of a regular plantation parliamentary revenue was adopted in theory and settled in practice. A revenue not substituted in the place of, but superadded to, a monopoly, which monopoly was enforced at the same time with additional strictness, and the execution put into military hands.

This Act, Sir, had for the first time the title of "granting duties in the colonies and plantations of America;" and for the first time it was asserted in the preamble, "that it was *just* and *necessary* that a revenue should be raised there." Then came the technical words of "giving and granting," and thus a complete American Revenue Act was made in all the forms, and with a full avowal of the right, equity, policy, and even necessity of taxing the colonies, without any formal consent of theirs. There are contained also in the preamble to that Act these very remarkable words: the commons, etc.—"being desirous to make *some* provision in the *present* session of Parliament *towards* raising the said revenue." By these words it appeared to the colonies that this Act was but a beginning of sorrows; that every session was to produce something of the same kind, that we were to go on, from day to day, in charging them with such taxes as we pleased, for such a military force as we should think proper. Had this plan been pursued it was evident that the provincial assemblies, in which the Americans felt all their portion of importance and beheld their sole image of freedom, were *ipso facto* annihilated. This ill prospect before them seemed to be boundless in extent and endless in duration. Sir, they were not mistaken. The Ministry valued themselves when this Act passed, and when they gave notice of the Stamp Act, that both of the duties came very short of their ideas of American taxation. Great was the applause of this measure here. In England we cried out for new taxes on America, whilst they cried out that they were nearly crushed with those which the war and their own grants had brought upon them.

Sir, it has been said in the debate that when the first American Revenue Act (the Act in 1764 imposing the port duties) passed the Americans did not object to the principle. It is true they touched it but very tenderly. It was not a direct attack. They were, it is true, as yet novices, as yet unaccustomed to direct attacks upon any of the rights of Parliament. The duties were port duties, like those they had been accustomed to bear; with this difference, that the title was not the same, the preamble not the same, and the spirit altogether unlike. But of what service is this observation to the cause of those that make it? It is a full refutation of the pretence for their present cruelty to America, for it shows, out of their own mouths, that our colonies were backward to enter into the present vexatious and ruinous controversy.

There is also another circulation abroad (spread with a malignant intention, which I cannot attribute to those who say the same thing in this House) that Mr. Grenville gave the colony agents an option for their assemblies to tax themselves, which they had refused. I find that much stress is laid on this as a fact. However, it happens neither to be true nor possible. I will observe, first, that Mr. Grenville never thought fit to make this apology for himself in the innumerable debates that were had upon the subject. He might have proposed to the colony agents that they should agree in some mode of taxation as the ground of an Act of Parliament. But he never could have proposed that they should tax themselves on requisition, which is the assertion of the day. Indeed, Mr. Grenville well knew that the colony agents could have no general powers to consent to it, and they had no time to consult their assemblies for particular powers before he passed his first Revenue Act. If you compare dates you will find it impossible. Burthened as the agents knew the colonies were at that time, they could not give the least hope of such grants. His own favourite governor was of opinion that the Americans were not then taxable objects:

"Nor was the time less favourable to the equity *of such a taxation. I don't mean to dispute the reasonableness of America contributing to the charges of Great Britain* when she is able; *nor, I believe, would the Americans themselves have disputed it, at a* proper time and season. *But it should be considered that the American governments themselves have, in the prosecution of the late war, contracted very large debts, which it will take some years to pay off, and in the mean time occasion very* burdensome taxes for that purpose *only. . . . "*

These are the words of Governor Bernard's letter to a member of the old Ministry, and which he has since printed. Mr. Grenville could not have made this proposition to the agents for another reason. He was of opinion, which he has declared in this House an hundred times, that the colonies could not legally grant any revenue to the crown, and that infinite mischiefs would be the consequence of such a power. When Mr. Grenville had passed the first Revenue Act, and in the same session had made this House come to a resolution for laying a stamp duty on America, between that time and the passing the Stamp Act into a law he told a considerable and most respectable merchant, a member of this House, whom I am truly sorry I do not now see in his place, when he represented against this proceeding, that if the stamp duty was disliked, he was willing to exchange it for any other equally productive, but that, if he objected to the Americans being taxed by Parliament, he might save himself the trouble of the discussion as he was determined on the measure. This is the fact, and, if you please, I will mention a very unquestionable authority for it.

Thus, Sir, I have disposed of this falsehood. But falsehood has a perennial spring. It is said, that no conjecture could be made of the dislike of the colonies to the principle. This is as untrue as the other. After the resolution of the House, and before the passing of the Stamp Act, the colonies of Massachusetts Bay and New York did send remonstrances, objecting to this mode of parliamentary taxation. What was the consequence? They were suppressed, they were put under the table, notwithstanding an order of council to the contrary, by the Ministry which composed the very council that had made the order; and thus the House proceeded to its business of taxing without the least regular knowledge of the objections which were made to it. But to give that House its due, it was not over-desirous to receive information or to hear remonstrance. On the 15th February, 1765, whilst the Stamp Act was under deliberation, they refused with scorn even so much as to receive four petitions presented from so respectable colonies as Connecticut, Rhode Island, Virginia, and Carolina, besides one from the traders of Jamaica. As to the colonies, they had no alternative left to them, but to disobey, or to pay the taxes imposed by that Parliament which was not suffered, or did not suffer itself, even to hear them remonstrate upon the subject.

This was the state of the colonies before his Majesty thought fit to change his ministers. It stands upon no authority of mine. It is proved by uncontrovertible records. The honourable gentleman has desired some of us to lay our hands upon our hearts and answer to his queries upon the historical part of this consideration, and by his manner (as well as my eyes could discern it) he seemed to address himself to me.

Sir, I will answer him as clearly as I am able, and with great openness; I have nothing to conceal. In the year sixty-five, being in a very private station, far enough from any line of business, and not having the honour of a seat in this House, it was my fortune, unknowing and unknown to the then Ministry, by the intervention of a common friend, to become connected with a very noble person, and at the head of the Treasury department. It was indeed in a situation of little rank and no consequence, suitable to the mediocrity of my talents and pretensions. But a situation near enough to enable me to see, as well as others, what was going on, and I did see in that noble person such sound principles, such an enlargement of mind, such clear and sagacious sense, and such unshaken fortitude, as have bound me, as well as others much better than me, by an inviolable attachment to him from that time forward. Sir, Lord Rockingham very early in that summer received a strong representation from many weighty English merchants and manufacturers, from governors of provinces and commanders of men of war, against almost the whole of the American commercial regulations, and particularly with regard to the total ruin which was threatened to the Spanish trade. I believe, Sir, the noble lord soon saw his way in this business. But he did not rashly determine against Acts which it might be supposed were the result of much deliberation. However, Sir, he scarcely began to open the ground when the whole veteran body of office took the alarm. A violent outcry of all (except those who knew and felt the mischief) was raised against any alteration. On one hand, his attempt was a direct violation of treaties and public law; on the other, the Act of Navigation and all the corps of trade laws were drawn up in array against it.

The first step the noble lord took was to have the opinion of his excellent, learned, and ever-lamented friend, the late Mr. Yorke, then Attorney-General, on the point of law. When he knew that formally and officially, which in substance he had known before, he immediately despatched orders to redress the grievance. But I will say it for the then minister, he is of that constitution of mind that I know he would have issued, on the same critical occasion, the very same orders, if the Acts of trade had been, as they were not, directly against him, and would have cheerfully submitted to the equity of Parliament for his indemnity.

On the conclusion of this business of the Spanish trade, the news of the troubles on account of the Stamp Act arrived in England. It was not until the end of October that these accounts were received. No sooner had the sound of that mighty tempest reached us in England than the whole of the then opposition, instead of feeling humbled by the unhappy issue of their measures, seemed to be infinitely elated, and cried out that the Ministry, from envy to the glory of their predecessors, were prepared to repeal the Stamp Act. Near nine years after, the honourable gentleman takes quite opposite ground, and now challenges me to put my hand to my heart and say whether the Ministry had resolved on the repeal till a considerable time after the meeting of Parliament. Though I do not very well know what the honourable gentleman wishes to infer from the admission or from the denial of this fact, on which he so earnestly adjures me, I do put my hand on my heart and assure him that they did *not* come to a resolution directly to repeal. They weighed this matter as its difficulty and importance required. They considered maturely among themselves. They consulted with all who could give advice or information. It was not determined until a little before the meeting of Parliament; but it was determined, and the main lines of their own plan marked out, before that meeting. Two questions arose—(I hope I am not going into a narrative troublesome to the House)—

[A cry of, Go on, go on.]

The first of the two considerations was, whether the repeal should be total, or whether only partial; taking out everything burthensome and productive, and reserving only an empty acknowledgment, such as a stamp on cards or dice. The other question was, on what principle the Act should be repealed? On this head also two principles were stated. One that the legislative rights of this country, with regard to America, were not entire, but had certain restrictions and limitations. The other principle was, that taxes of this kind were contrary to the fundamental principles of commerce on which the colonies were founded, and contrary to every idea of political equity; by which equity we are bound, as much as possible, to extend the spirit and benefit of the British constitution to every part of the British dominions. The option, both of the measure and of the principle of repeal, was made before the session, and I wonder how any one can read the king's speech at the opening of that session without seeing in that speech both the Repeal and the Declaratory Act very sufficiently crayoned out. Those who cannot see this can see nothing.

Surely the honourable gentleman will not think that a great deal less time than was then employed ought to have been spent in deliberation when he considers that the news of the troubles did not arrive till towards the end of October. The Parliament sat to fill the vacancies on the 14th day of December, and on business the 14th of the following January.

Sir, a partial repeal, or, as the *bon ton* of the court then was, a *modification*, would have satisfied a timid, unsystematic, procrastinating Ministry, as such a measure has since done such a Ministry. A modification is the constant resource of weak, undeciding minds. To repeal by the denial of our right to tax in the preamble (and this, too, did not want advisers) would have cut, in the heroic style, the Gordian knot with a sword. Either measure would have cost no more than a day's debate. But when the total repeal was adopted, and adopted on principles of policy, of equity, and of commerce, this plan made it necessary to enter into many and difficult measures. It became necessary to open a very large field of evidence commensurate to these extensive views. But then this labour did knight's service. It opened the eyes of several to the true state of the American affairs; it enlarged their ideas, it removed prejudices, and it conciliated the opinions and affections of men. The noble lord, who then took the lead in administration, my honourable friend[13] under me, and a right honourable gentleman[14] (if he will not reject his share, and it was a large one, of this business) exerted the most laudable industry in bringing before you the fullest, most impartial, and least garbled body of evidence that ever was produced to this House. I think the inquiry lasted in the committee for six weeks, and, at its conclusion, this House, by an independent, noble, spirited, and unexpected majority, by a majority that will redeem all the acts ever done by majorities in Parliament, in the teeth of all the old mercenary Swiss of state, in despite of all the speculators and augurs of political events, in defiance of the whole embattled legion of veteran pensioners and practised instruments of a court, gave a total repeal to the Stamp Act, and (if it had been so permitted) a lasting peace to this whole empire.

I state, Sir, these particulars because this act of spirit and fortitude has lately been, in the circulation of the season and in some hazarded declamations in this House, attributed to timidity. If, Sir, the conduct of Ministry, in proposing the repeal, had arisen from timidity with regard to themselves, it would have been

[13] William Dowdeswell.
[14] General Conway.

greatly to be condemned. Interested timidity disgraces as much
in the cabinet, as personal timidity does in the field. But timidity,
with regard to the well-being of our country, is heroic virtue. The
noble lord who then conducted affairs, and his worthy colleagues,
whilst they trembled at the prospect of such distresses as you have
since brought upon yourselves, were not afraid steadily to look in
the face that glaring and dazzling influence at which the eyes of
eagles have blenched. He looked in the face one of the ablest, and,
let me say, not the most scrupulous, oppositions that perhaps ever
was in this House, and withstood it, unaided by even one of the
usual supports of administration. He did this when he repealed
the Stamp Act. He looked in the face of a person he had long
respected and regarded, and whose aid was then particularly wanting—I mean Lord Chatham. He did this when he passed the
Declaratory Act.

It is now given out, for the usual purposes by the usual emis-
saries, that Lord Rockingham did not consent to the repeal of this
Act until he was bullied into it by Lord Chatham; and the reporters have gone so far as publicly to assert, in a hundred companies, that the honourable gentleman under the gallery[15] who
proposed the repeal in the American committee, had another set
of resolutions in his pocket directly the reverse of those he moved.
These artifices of a desperate cause are at this time spread abroad
with incredible care, in every part of the town, from the highest
to the lowest companies, as if the industry of the circulation were
to make amends for the absurdity of the report. . . .[16]

Sir, this act of supreme magnanimity has been represented as
if it had been a measure of an administration that, having no
scheme of their own, took a middle line, pilfered a bit from one
side and a bit from the other. Sir, they took *no* middle lines. They
differed fundamentally from the schemes of both parties; but they
preserved the objects of both. They preserved the authority of
Great Britain. They preserved the equity of Great Britain. They
made the Declaratory Act; they repealed the Stamp Act. They did
both *fully*, because the Declaratory Act was *without qualification*,

[15] General Conway.

[16] At this point Burke stresses the difficulty of Rockingham's position in 1765–1766 and panegyrizes the latter's fixity of principle and
strength of character. He follows that with a short description of the
greeting that Gen. Conway received after moving the motion for repeal
in 1766. The people "clung about him as captives about their redeemer.
All England, all America joined to his applause."

and the repeal of the Stamp Act *total*. This they did in the situation I have described.

Now, Sir, what will the adversary say to both these Acts? If the principle of the Declaratory Act was not good, the principle we are contending for this day is monstrous. If the principle of the repeal was not good, why are we not at war for a real, substantial, effective revenue? If both were bad, why has this Ministry incurred all the inconveniences of both and of all schemes? Why have they enacted, repealed, enforced, yielded, and now attempt to enforce again?

Sir, I think I may as well now as at any other time speak to a certain matter of fact, not wholly unrelated to the question under your consideration. We, who would persuade you to revert to the ancient policy of this kingdom, labour under the effect of this short current phrase, which the court leaders have given out to all their corps in order to take away the credit of those who would prevent you from that frantic war you are going to wage upon your colonies. Their cant is this: "All the disturbances in America have been created by the repeal of the Stamp Act." I suppress for a moment my indignation at the falsehood, baseness, and absurdity of this most audacious assertion. Instead of remarking on the motives and character of those who have issued it for circulation, I will clearly lay before you the state of America antecedently to that repeal, after the repeal, and since the renewal of the schemes of American taxation.

It is said that the disturbances, if there were any, before the repeal were slight, and without difficulty or inconvenience might have been suppressed. For an answer to this assertion I will send you to the great author and patron of the Stamp Act, who certainly meaning well to the authority of this country and fully apprised of the state of that, made, before a repeal was so much as agitated in this House, the motion which is on your journals, and which, to save the clerk the trouble of turning to it, I will now read to you. It was for an amendment to the address of the 17th of December 1765:

"To express our just resentment and indignation at the outrages, tumults, and insurrections *which have been excited and carried on in North America; and at the resistance given, by* open *and* rebellious *force, to the execution of the laws in that part of his Majesty's dominions. And to assure his Majesty, that his faithful Commons, animated with the warmest duty and attachment to*

his royal person and government, will firmly and effectually sup-
port his Majesty in all such measures as shall be necessary for
preserving and supporting the legal dependence of the colonies on
the mother country," etc. etc.

Here was certainly a disturbance preceding the repeal, such a
disturbance as Mr. Grenville thought necessary to qualify by the
name of an *insurrection* and the epithet of a *rebellious* force:
terms much stronger than any by which those who then supported
his motion have ever since thought proper to distinguish the subsequent disturbances in America. They were disturbances which
seemed to him and his friends to justify as strong a promise of
support as hath been usual to give in the beginning of a war with
the most powerful and declared enemies. When the accounts of
the American governors came before the House, they appeared
stronger even than the warmth of public imagination had painted
them; so much stronger, that the papers on your table bear me
out in saying, that all the late disturbances, which have been at
one time the minister's motives for the repeal of five out of six
of the new court taxes, and are now his pretences for refusing to
repeal that sixth, did not amount—why do I compare them?—no,
not to a tenth part of the tumults and violence which prevailed
long before the repeal of that Act.

Ministry cannot refuse the authority of the commander-in-chief,
General Gage, who, in his letter of the 4th of November, from
New York, thus represents the state of things:

"It is difficult to say, from the highest to the lowest, *who has not
been* accessory *to this* insurrection, *either by writing or* mutual
agreements, *to oppose the Act, by what they are pleased to term
all legal opposition to it. Nothing effectual has been proposed,
either to prevent or quell the tumult.* The rest of the provinces are
in the same situation *as to a positive refusal to take the stamps;
and threatening those who shall take them* to plunder and murder
them; *and this affair stands* in all the provinces, *that unless the
Act, from its own nature, enforces itself, nothing but a* very
considerable military force can do it."

It is remarkable, Sir, that the persons who formerly trumpeted
forth the most loudly the violent resolutions of the assemblies, the
universal insurrections, the seizing and burning the stamped
papers, the forcing stamp officers to resign their commissions
under the gallows, the rifling and pulling down of the houses of
magistrates, and the expulsion from their country of all who

dared to write or speak a single word in defence of the powers of
Parliament—those very trumpeters are now the men that represent the whole as a mere trifle, and choose to date all the disturbances from the repeal of the Stamp Act, which put an end to them.
Hear your officers abroad, and let them refute this shameless falsehood, who, in all their correspondence, state the disturbances as
owing to their true causes, the discontent of the people from the
taxes. You have this evidence in your own archives—and it will
give you complete satisfaction, if you are not so far lost to all
parliamentary ideas of information as rather to credit the lie of
the day than the records of your own House.

Sir, this vermin of court reporters, when they are forced into
day upon one point, are sure to burrow in another; but they shall
have no refuge—I will make them bolt out of all their holes. Conscious that they must be baffled, when they attribute a precedent
disturbance to a subsequent measure, they take other ground,
almost as absurd, but very common in modern practice and very
wicked, which is, to attribute the ill effect of ill-judged conduct to
the arguments which had been used to dissuade us from it. They
say that the opposition made in Parliament to the Stamp Act at
the time of its passing encouraged the Americans to their resistance. This has even formally appeared in print in a regular volume, from an advocate of that faction, a Dr. Tucker. This Dr.
Tucker is already a dean, and his earnest labours in this vineyard
will, I suppose, raise him to a bishopric. But this assertion too,
just like the rest, is false. In all the papers which have loaded your
table, in all the vast crowd of verbal witnesses that appeared at
your bar, witnesses which were indiscriminately produced from
both sides of the House, not the least hint of such a cause of disturbance has ever appeared. As to the fact of a strenuous opposition to the Stamp Act, I sat as a stranger in your gallery when
the Act was under consideration. Far from anything inflammatory, I never heard a more languid debate in this House. No more
than two or three gentlemen, as I remember, spoke against the
Act, and that with great reserve and remarkable temper. There
was but one division in the whole progress of the bill; and the
minority did not reach to more than 39 or 40. In the House of
Lords I do not recollect that there was any debate or division at
all. I am sure there was no protest. In fact, the affair passed with
so very, very little noise, that in town they scarcely knew the nature of what you were doing. The opposition to the bill in England

never could have done this mischief, because there scarcely ever was less of opposition to a bill of consequence.

Sir, the agents and distributors of falsehoods have, with their usual industry, circulated another lie of the same nature with the former. It is this, that the disturbances arose from the account which had been received in America of the change in the Ministry. No longer awed, it seems, with the spirit of the former rulers, they thought themselves a match for what our calumniators chose to qualify by the name of so feeble a Ministry as succeeded. Feeble in one sense these men certainly may be called; for, with all their efforts, and they have made many, they have not been able to resist the distempered vigour and insane alacrity with which you are rushing to your ruin. But it does so happen, that the falsity of this circulation is (like the rest) demonstrated by indisputable dates and records.

So little was the change known in America, that the letters of your governors, giving an account of these disturbances long after they had arrived at their highest pitch, were all directed to the *old Ministry*, and particularly to the *Earl of Halifax*, the Secretary of State corresponding with the colonies, without once in the smallest degree intimating the slightest suspicion of any ministerial revolution whatsoever. . . .[17]

Thus are blown away the insect race of courtly falsehoods! thus perish the miserable inventions of the wretched runners for a wretched cause, which they have fly-blown into every weak and rotten part of the country, in vain hopes that when their maggots had taken wing their importunate buzzing might sound something like the public voice!

Sir, I have troubled you sufficiently with the state of America before the repeal. Now I turn to the honourable gentleman who so stoutly challenges us to tell, whether, after the repeal, the provinces were quiet? This is coming home to the point. Here I meet him directly, and answer most readily, *They were quiet.* And I, in my turn, challenge him to prove when, and where, and by whom, and in what numbers, and with what violence, the other laws of trade, as gentlemen assert, were violated in consequence of your concession? or that even your other revenue laws were attacked? But I quit the vantage-ground on which I stand, and where I

[17] He then cited the letters of Governors Bernard (Mass.) and Fauquier (Va.) as late as September 7, having first reminded his listeners that the ministry changed on July 10.

might leave the burthen of the proof upon him: I walk down upon the open plain, and undertake to show that they were not only quiet, but showed many unequivocal marks of acknowledgment and gratitude. And to give him every advantage, I select the obnoxious colony of Massachusetts Bay, which at this time (but without hearing her) is so heavily a culprit before parliament— I will select their proceedings even under circumstances of no small irritation. For, a little imprudently I must say, Governor Bernard mixed in the administration of the lenitive of the repeal no small acrimony arising from matters of a separate nature. Yet see, Sir, the effect of that lenitive, though mixed with these bitter ingredients, and how this rugged people can express themselves on a measure of concession.

"If it is not in our power" (say they in their address to Governor Bernard), *"in so full a manner as will be expected, to show our respectful gratitude to the mother country, or to make a dutiful and affectionate return to the indulgence of the king and Parliament, it shall be no fault of ours; for this we intend, and hope we shall be able fully to effect."*

Would to God that this temper had been cultivated, managed, and set in action! other effects than those which we have since felt would have resulted from it. On the requisition for compensation to those who had suffered from the violence of the populace, in the same address they say, *"The recommendation enjoined by Mr. Secretary Conway's letter, and in consequence thereof made to us, we will embrace the first convenient opportunity to consider and act upon."* They did consider; they did act upon it. They obeyed the requisition. I know the mode has been chicaned upon, but it was substantially obeyed; and much better obeyed than I fear the parliamentary requisition of this session will be, though enforced by all your rigour and backed with all your power. In a word, the damages of popular fury were compensated by legislative gravity. Almost every other part of America in various ways demonstrated their gratitude. I am bold to say that so sudden a calm recovered after so violent a storm is without parallel in history. To say that no other disturbance should happen from any other cause is folly. But as far as appearances went, by the judicious sacrifice of one law you procured an acquiescence in all that remained. After this experience nobody shall persuade me, when a whole people are concerned, that acts of lenity are not means of conciliation.

I hope the honourable gentleman has received a fair and full answer to his question.

I have done with the third period of your policy, that of your repeal, and the return of your ancient system, and your ancient tranquillity and concord. Sir, this period was not as long as it was happy. Another scene was opened, and other actors appeared on the stage. The state, in the condition I have described it, was delivered into the hands of Lord Chatham—a great and celebrated name—a name that keeps the name of this country respectable in every other on the globe. It may be truly called—

> "Clarum etvenerabile nomen
> Gentibus, et multum nostræ quod proderat urbi."[18]

Sir, the venerable age of this great man, his merited rank, his superior eloquence, his splendid qualities, his eminent services, the vast space he fills in the eye of mankind, and, more than all the rest, his fall from power, which, like death, canonises and sanctifies a great character, will not suffer me to censure any part of his conduct. I am afraid to flatter him; I am sure I am not disposed to blame him. Let those who have betrayed him by their adulation insult him with their malevolence. But what I do not presume to censure I may have leave to lament. For a wise man, he seemed to me at that time to be governed too much by general maxims. I speak with the freedom of history, and I hope without offence. One or two of these maxims, flowing from an opinion not the most indulgent to our unhappy species, and surely a little too general, led him into measures that were greatly mischievous to himself, and for that reason among others fatal to his country; measures, the effects of which, I am afraid, are for ever incurable. He made an administration, so chequered and speckled; he put together a piece of joinery, so crossly indented and whimsically dovetailed: a cabinet so variously inlaid; such a piece of diversified mosaic; such a tessellated pavement without cement; here a bit of black stone, and there a bit of white; patriots and courtiers, king's friends and republicans; whigs and tories; treacherous friends and open enemies—that it was indeed a very curious show, but utterly unsafe to touch, and unsure to stand on. The colleagues whom he had assorted at the same boards stared at each other, and

[18] "An illustrious name, venerable to the world, and one which has much helped our city," Lucan, IX, V, 202.

were obliged to ask, "Sir, your name?—Sir, you have the advantage of me—Mr. Such-a-one—I beg a thousand pardons—" I venture to say, it did so happen that persons had a single office divided between them, who had never spoke to each other in their lives until they found themselves, they knew not how, pigging together, heads and points, in the same truckle-bed.

Sir, in consequence of this arrangement, having put so much the larger part of his enemies and opposers into power, the confusion was such that his own principles could not possibly have any effect or influence in the conduct of affairs. If ever he fell into a fit of the gout, or if any other cause withdrew him from public cares, principles directly the contrary were sure to predominate. When he had executed his plan he had not an inch of ground to stand upon. When he had accomplished his scheme of administration he was no longer a minister.

When his face was hid but for a moment his whole system was on a wide sea, without chart or compass. The gentlemen, his particular friends, who, with the names of various departments of Ministry, were admitted to seem as if they acted a part under him, with a modesty that becomes all men, and with a confidence in him which was justified even in its extravagance by his superior abilities, had never, in any instance, presumed upon any opinion of their own. Deprived of his guiding influence, they were whirled about, the sport of every gust, and easily driven into any port; and as those who joined with them in manning the vessel were the most directly opposite to his opinions, measures, and character, and far the most artful and most powerful of the set, they easily prevailed, so as to seize upon the vacant, unoccupied, and derelict minds of his friends; and instantly they turned the vessel wholly out of the course of his policy. As if it were to insult as well as to betray him, even long before the close of the first session of his administration, when everything was publicly transacted, and with great parade, in his name, they made an Act declaring it highly just and expedient to raise a revenue in America. For even then, Sir, even before this splendid orb was entirely set, and while the western horizon was in a blaze with his descending glory, on the opposite quarter of the heavens arose another luminary, and for his hour became lord of the ascendant.

This light too is passed and set for ever. You understand, to be sure, that I speak of Charles Townshend, officially the reproducer of this fatal scheme, whom I cannot even now remember without some degree of sensibility. In truth, Sir, he was the delight and ornament of this House, and the charm of every private society which he honoured with his presence. Perhaps there never arose in this country, nor in any country, a man of a more pointed and finished wit; and (where his passions were not concerned) of a more refined, exquisite, and penetrating judgment. If he had not so great a stock, as some have had who flourished formerly, of knowledge long treasured up, he knew better by far than any man I ever was acquainted with how to bring together within a short time all that was necessary to establish, to illustrate, and to decorate that side of the question he supported. He stated his matter skilfully and powerfully. He particularly excelled in a most luminous explanation and display of his subject. His style of argument was neither trite and vulgar nor subtle and abstruse. He hit the House just between wind and water. And not being troubled with too anxious a zeal for any matter in question, he was never more tedious, or more earnest, than the pre-conceived opinions and present temper of his hearers required, to whom he was always in perfect unison. He conformed exactly to the temper of the House, and he seemed to guide, because he was also sure to follow it.

I beg pardon, Sir, if, when I speak of this and of other great men, I appear to digress in saying something of their characters. In this eventful history of the revolutions of America, the characters of such men are of much importance. Great men are the guide-posts and landmarks in the state. The credit of such men at court, or in the nation, is the sole cause of all the public measures. . . . There are many young members in the House (such of late has been the rapid succession of public men) who never saw that prodigy, Charles Townshend, nor of course know what a ferment he was able to excite in everything by the violent ebullition of his mixed virtues and failings. For failings he had undoubtedly—many of us remember them; we are this day considering the effect of them. But he had no failings which were not owing to a noble cause, to an ardent, generous, perhaps an immoderate, passion for fame—a passion which is the instinct of all great souls. He worshipped that goddess wheresoever she appeared; but he paid his particular devotions to her in her favourite habitation, in her chosen temple, the House of Commons. Besides the characters of the individuals that compose our body, it is impossible, Mr. Speaker, not to observe that this House has a collective character of its own. That character too, however imperfect, is not unamiable. Like all great public collections of men, you possess a marked love of virtue and an abhorrence of vice. But among vices, there is none which the House abhors in the same degree with *obstinacy*. Obstinacy, Sir, is certainly a great vice; and in the changeful state of political affairs it is frequently the cause of great mischief. It happens, however, very unfortunately, that almost the whole line of the great and masculine virtues, constancy, gravity, magnanimity, fortitude, fidelity, and firmness, are closely allied to this disagreeable quality, of which you have so just an abhorrence, and, in their excess, all these virtues very easily fall into it. He who paid such a punctilious attention to all your feelings certainly took care not to shock them by that vice which is the most disgustful to you.

That fear of displeasing those who ought most to be pleased betrayed him sometimes into the other extreme. He had voted, and, in the year 1765, had been an advocate, for the Stamp Act. Things and the disposition of men's minds were changed. In short, the Stamp Act began to be no favourite in this House. He therefore attended at the private meeting, in which the resolutions moved by a right honourable gentleman were settled, resolutions leading to the repeal. The next day he voted for that repeal, and he would have spoken for it too if an illness (not, as was then given out, a political, but to my knowledge a very real illness) had not prevented it.

The very next session, as the fashion of this world passeth away, the repeal began to be in as bad an odour in this House as the Stamp Act had been in the session before. To conform to the temper which began to prevail, and to prevail mostly amongst those most in power, he declared very early in the winter that a revenue must be had out of America. Instantly he was tied down to his engagements by some who had no objection to such experiments when made at the cost of persons for whom they had no particular regard. The whole body of courtiers drove him onward. They always talked as if the king stood in a sort of humiliated state until something of the kind should be done.

Here this extraordinary man, then Chancellor of the Exchequer, found himself in great straits. To please universally was the object of his life, but to tax and to please, no more than to love and to be wise, is not given to men. However, he attempted it. To render the tax palatable to the partisans of American revenue, he had a preamble stating the necessity of such a revenue. To close with the American distinction, this revenue was *external* or port duty; but again, to soften it to the other party, it was a duty of *supply*. To gratify the *colonists*, it was laid on British manufactures; to satisfy the *merchants of Britain*, the duty was trivial, and (except that on tea, which touched only the devoted East India Company) on none of the grand objects of commerce. To counterwork the American contraband, the duty on tea was reduced from a shilling to threepence. But to secure the favour of those who would tax America, the scene of collection was changed, and, with the rest, it was levied in the colonies. What need I say more? This fine-spun scheme had the usual fate of all exquisite policy. But the original plan of the duties and the mode of executing that plan both arose singly and solely from a love of our applause. He was truly the child of the House. He never thought, did, or said anything, but with a view to you. He every day adapted himself to your disposition, and adjusted himself before it as at a looking-glass. . . .[19]

Hence arose this unfortunate Act, the subject of this day's debate; from a disposition which, after making an American revenue to please one, repealed it to please others, and again revived it in hopes of pleasing a third, and of catching something in the ideas of all.

This Revenue Act of 1767 formed the fourth period of American policy. How we have fared since then—what woeful variety of schemes have been adopted; what enforcing and what repealing; what bullying and what submitting; what doing and undoing; what straining and what relaxing; what assemblies dissolved for not obeying and called again without obedience; what troops sent out to quell resistance and, on meeting that resistance, recalled; what shiftings and changes and jumblings of all kinds of men at home, which left no possibility of order, consistency, vigour, or even so much as a decent unity of colour in any one public measure—it is a tedious, irksome task. My duty may call me to open it out some other time; on a former occasion[20] I tried your temper on a part of it, for the present I shall forbear.

After all these changes and agitations, your immediate situation upon the question on your paper is at length brought to this.

[19] He goes off on a short tangent here, needling those of the "country party" who tended too often to sit on the fence during important debates such as that on the Townshend Act.
[20] See above, pp. 7-21.

You have an Act of Parliament, stating that "it is *expedient* to raise a revenue in America." By a partial repeal you annihilated the greatest part of that revenue which this preamble declares to be so expedient. You have substituted no other in the place of it. A Secretary of State has disclaimed, in the king's name, all thoughts of such a substitution in future. The principle of this disclaimer goes to what has been left as well as what has been repealed. The tax which lingers after its companions (under a preamble declaring an American revenue expedient, and for the sole purpose of supporting the theory of that preamble) militates with the assurance authentically conveyed to the colonies, and is an exhaustless source of jealousy and animosity. On this state, which I take to be a fair one, not being able to discern any grounds of honour, advantage, peace, or power, for adhering either to the Act or to the preamble, I shall vote for the question which leads to the repeal of both.

If you do not fall in with this motion, then secure something to fight for consistent in theory and valuable in practice. If you must employ your strength, employ it to uphold you in some honourable right or some profitable wrong. If you are apprehensive that the concession recommended to you, though proper, should be a means of drawing on you further but unreasonable claims, why then employ your force in supporting that reasonable concession against those unreasonable demands. You will employ it with more grace, with better effect, and with great probable concurrence of all the quiet and rational people in the provinces, who are now united with, and hurried away by, the violent— having indeed different dispositions, but a common interest. If you apprehend that on a concession you shall be pushed by meta- physical process to the extreme lines and argued out of your whole authority, my advice is this: when you have recovered your old, your strong, your tenable position, then face about—stop short—do nothing more—reason not at all—oppose the ancient policy and practice of the empire as a rampart against the specu- lations of innovators on both sides of the question, and you will stand on great, manly, and sure ground. On this solid basis fix your machines, and they will draw worlds towards you.

Your ministers, in their own and his Majesty's name, have already adopted the American distinction of internal and external duties. It is a distinction, whatever merit it may have, that was originally moved by the Americans themselves, and I think they will acquiesce in it, if they are not pushed with too much logic and too little sense, in all the consequences. That is, if external taxation be understood, as they and you understand it, when you please, to be not a distinction of geography, but of policy; that it is a power for regulating trade, and not for supporting establishments. The distinction, which is as nothing with regard to right, is of most weighty consideration in practice. Recover your old ground and your old tranquillity—try it—I am persuaded the Americans will compromise with you. When confidence is once restored, the odious and suspicious *summum jus* will perish of course. The spirit of practicability, of moderation, and mutual convenience will never call in geometrical exactness as the arbitrator of amicable settlement. Consult and follow your experience. Let not the long story with which I have exercised your patience prove fruitless to your interests.

For my part, I should choose (if I could have my wish) that the proposition of the honourable gentleman for the repeal could go to America without the attendance of the penal bills. Alone I could almost answer for its success. I cannot be certain of its reception in the bad company it may keep. In such heterogeneous assortments, the most innocent person will lose the effect of his innocency. Though you should send out this angel of peace, yet you are sending out a destroying angel too; and what would be the effect of the conflict of these two adverse spirits, or which would predominate in the end, is what I dare not say: whether the lenient measures would cause American passion to subside, or the severe would increase its fury—all this in the hand of Providence. Yet now, even now, I should confide in the prevailing virtue and efficacious operation of lenity, though working in darkness and in chaos, in the midst of all this unnatural and turbid combination, I should hope it might produce order and beauty in the end.

Let us, Sir, embrace some system or other before we end this session. Do you mean to tax America and to draw a productive revenue from thence? If you do, speak out; name, fix, ascertain this revenue; settle its quantity; define its objects; provide for its collection; and then fight when you have something to fight for. If you murder, rob; if you kill, take possession: and do not appear in the character of madmen as well as assassins, violent, vindictive, bloody, and tyrannical, without an object. But may better counsels guide you!

Again and again revert to your own principles—seek peace and ensue it—leave America, if she has taxable matter in her, to tax herself. I am not here going into the distinctions of rights, not attempting to mark their boundaries. I do not enter into these metaphysical distinctions; I hate the very sound of them. Leave the Americans as they anciently stood, and these distinctions, born of our unhappy contest, will die along with it. They and we, and their and our ancestors, have been happy under that system. Let the memory of all actions in contradiction to that good old mode, on both sides, be extinguished for ever. Be content to bind America by laws of trade; you have always done it. Let this be your reason for binding their trade. Do not burthen them by taxes; you were not used to do so from the beginning. Let this be your reason for not taxing. These are the arguments of states and kingdoms. Leave the rest to the schools, for there only they may be discussed with safety. But if, intemperately, unwisely, fatally, you sophisticate and poison the very source of government, by urging subtle deductions and consequences odious to those you govern, from the unlimited and illimitable nature of supreme sovereignty, you will teach them by these means to call that sovereignty itself in question. When you drive him hard, the boar will surely turn upon the hunters. If that sovereignty and their freedom cannot be reconciled, which will they take? They will cast your sovereignty in your face. Nobody will be argued into slavery. Sir, let the gentlemen on the other side call forth all their ability, let the best of them get up and tell me, what one character of liberty the Americans have, and what one brand of slavery they are free from, if they are bound in their property and industry by all the restraints you can imagine on commerce, and at the same time are made pack-horses of every tax you choose to impose, without the least share in granting them. When they bear the burthens of unlimited monopoly, will you bring them to bear the burthens of unlimited revenue too? The Englishman in America will feel that this is slavery—that it is *legal* slavery will be no compensation either to his feelings or his understanding.

A noble lord,[21] who spoke some time ago, is full of the fire of ingenuous youth; and when he has modelled the ideas of a lively imagination by further experience he will be an ornament to his country in either House. He has said that the Americans are our children, and how can they revolt against their parent? He says

---

[21] Lord Carmarthen.

that if they are not free in their present state, England is not free, because Manchester and other considerable places are not represented. So then, because some towns in England are not represented, America is to have no representative at all. They are "our children"; but when children ask for bread we are not to give a stone. Is it because the natural resistance of things and the various mutations of time hinder our Government, or any scheme of government, from being any more than a sort of approximation to the right, is it therefore that the colonies are to recede from it infinitely? When this child of ours wishes to assimilate to its parent and to reflect with a true filial resemblance the beauteous countenance of British liberty, are we to turn to them the shameful parts of our constitution? are we to give them our weakness for their strength? our opprobrium for their glory? and the slough of slavery, which we are not able to work off, to serve them for their freedom?

If this be the case, ask yourselves this question, Will they be content in such a state of slavery? If not, look to the consequences. Reflect how you are to govern a people who think they ought to be free and think they are not. Your scheme yields no revenue, it yields nothing but discontent, disorder, disobedience; and such is the state of America, that after wading up to your eyes in blood, you could only end just where you begun; that is, to tax where no revenue is to be found, to—my voice fails me; my inclination indeed carries me no farther—all is confusion beyond it.

Well, Sir, I have recovered a little, and before I sit down I must say something to another point with which gentlemen urge us. What is to become of the Declaratory Act asserting the entireness of British legislative authority if we abandon the practice of taxation?

For my part I look upon the rights stated in that Act exactly in the manner in which I viewed them on its very first proposition, and which I have often taken the liberty, with great humility, to lay before you. I look, I say, on the imperial rights of Great Britain and the privileges which the colonists ought to enjoy under these rights to be just the most reconcilable things in the world. The Parliament of Great Britain sits at the head of her extensive empire in two capacities: one as the local legislature of this island, providing for all things at home, immediately, and by no other instrument than the executive power; the other, and I think her nobler capacity, is what I call her *imperial character*,

in which, as from the throne of heaven, she superintends all the
several inferior legislatures, and guides and controls them all,
without annihilating any. As all these provincial legislatures are
only co-ordinate to each other, they ought all to be subordinate
to her; else they can neither preserve mutual peace, nor hope for
mutual justice, nor effectually afford mutual assistance. It is
necessary to coerce the negligent, to restrain the violent, and to
aid the weak and deficient by the overruling plentitude of her
power. She is never to intrude into the place of the others, whilst
they are equal to the common ends of their institution. But in
order to enable Parliament to answer all these ends of provident
and beneficent superintendence, her powers must be boundless.
The gentlemen who think the powers of Parliament limited, may
please themselves to talk of requisitions. But suppose the requisitions are not obeyed? What! Shall there be no reserved power in
the empire, to supply a deficiency which may weaken, divide, and
dissipate the whole? We are engaged in war—the Secretary of
State calls upon the colonies to contribute—some would do it, I
think most would cheerfully furnish whatever is demanded—one
or two, suppose, hang back, and, easing themselves, let the stress
of the draft lie on the others—surely it is proper, that some authority might legally say—"Tax yourselves for the common supply, or Parliament will do it for you." This backwardness was, as
I am told, actually the case of Pennsylvania for some short time
towards the beginning of the last war, owing to some internal
dissensions in the colony. But whether the fact were so, or otherwise, the case is equally to be provided for by a competent sovereign power. But then this ought to be no ordinary power, nor ever
used in the first instance. This is what I meant, when I have said
at various times that I consider the power of taxing in Parliament
as an instrument of empire and not as a means of supply.

Such, Sir, is my idea of the constitution of the British empire,
as distinguished from the constitution of Britain; and on these
grounds I think subordination and liberty may be sufficiently reconciled through the whole, whether to serve a refining speculatist
or a factious demagogue, I know not, but enough surely for the
ease and happiness of man.

Sir, whilst we held this happy course, we drew more from the
colonies than all the impotent violence of despotism ever could
extort from them. We did this abundantly in the last war. It has
never been once denied—and what reason have we to imagine that

the colonies would not have proceeded in supplying government as liberally, if you had not stepped in and hindered them from contributing, by interrupting the channel in which their liberality flowed with so strong a course, by attempting to take, instead of being satisfied to receive? Sir William Temple says that Holland has loaded itself with ten times the impositions which it revolted from Spain rather than submit to. He says true. Tyranny is a poor provider. It knows neither how to accumulate nor how to extract.

I charge therefore to this new and unfortunate system the loss not only of peace, of union, and of commerce, but even of revenue, which its friends are contending for. It is morally certain that we have lost at least a million of free grants since the peace. I think we have lost a great deal more, and that those who look for a revenue from the provinces never could have pursued, even in that light, a course more directly repugnant to their purposes.

Now, Sir, I trust I have shown, first on that narrow ground which the honourable gentleman measured, that you are likely to lose nothing by complying with the motion, except what you have lost already. I have shown afterwards, that in time of peace you flourished in commerce, and, when war required it, had sufficient aid from the colonies while you pursued your ancient policy; that you threw everything into confusion when you made the Stamp Act; and that you restored everything to peace and order when you repealed it. I have shown that the revival of the system of taxation has produced the very worst effects, and that the partial repeal has produced, not partial good, but universal evil. Let these considerations, founded on facts not one of which can be denied, bring us back to our reason by the road of our experience.

I cannot, as I have said, answer for mixed measures; but surely this mixture of lenity would give the whole a better chance of success. When you once regain confidence, the way will be clear before you. Then you may enforce the Act of Navigation when it ought to be enforced. You will yourselves open it where it ought still further to be opened. Proceed in what you do, whatever you do, from policy and not from rancour. Let us act like men, let us act like statesmen. Let us hold some sort of consistent conduct.— It is agreed that a revenue is not to be had in America. If we lose the profit, let us get rid of the odium.

On this business of America I confess I am serious even to

sadness. I have had but one opinion concerning it since I sat, and before I sat, in Parliament. The noble lord[22] will, as usual, probably attribute the part taken by me and my friends in this business to a desire of getting his places. Let him enjoy this happy and original idea. If I deprived him of it, I should take away most of his wit and all his argument. But I had rather bear the brunt of all his wit, and indeed blows much heavier, than stand answerable to God for embracing a system that tends to the destruction of some of the very best and fairest of his works. But I know the map of England as well as the noble lord, or as any other person, and I know that the way I take is not the road to preferment. My excellent and honourable friend under me on the floor[23] has trod that road with great toil for upwards of twenty years together. He is not yet arrived at the noble lord's destination. However, the tracks of my worthy friend are those I have ever wished to follow, because I know they lead to honour. Long may we tread the same road together, whoever may accompany us, or whoever may laugh at us on our journey! I honestly and solemnly declare, I have in all seasons adhered to the system of 1766, for no other reason than that I think it laid deep in your truest interest—and that, by limiting the exercise, it fixes on the firmest foundations a real, consistent, well-grounded authority in Parliament. Until you come back to that system there will be no peace for England.

[22] Lord North.
[23] William Dowdeswell.

6

SPEECH IN SUPPORT OF
RESOLUTIONS FOR CONCILIATION
WITH THE AMERICAN COLONIES

MARCH 22, 1775[1]

*Throughout 1774 relations between England and the colonies had fur-
ther deteriorated. The King and Parliament rebuffed the "olive branch
petition" of the First Continental Congress (October, 1774) and now
in the early part of 1775 Parliament debated motions designed to
punish the colonies by prohibiting trade between them and England,
Ireland, and the British West Indies. Burke prepared his own scheme
for the reconciliation of America and England which he presented in
the following famous speech.*

I HOPE, Sir, that, notwithstanding the austerity of the
Chair, your good-nature will incline you to some degree of indulgence towards human frailty. You will not think it unnatural that
those who have an object depending, which strongly engages their
hopes and fears, should be somewhat inclined to superstition. As
I came into the House full of anxiety about the event of my motion, I found, to my infinite surprise, that the grand penal bill[2]
by which we had passed sentence on the trade and sustenance of
America, is to be returned to us from the other House. I do con-

[1] *Works*, II, 99-186.
[2] The Act to restrain the trade and commerce of the provinces of
Massachusetts Bay and New Hampshire, and colonies of Connecticut
and Rhode Island, and Providence Plantation, in North America, to
Great Britain, Ireland, and the British Islands in the West Indies; and
to prohibit such provinces and colonies from carrying on any fishery
on the banks of Newfoundland, and other places therein mentioned,
under certain conditions and limitations.

fess, I could not help looking on this event as a fortunate omen. I look upon it as a sort of providential favour, by which we are put once more in possession of our deliberative capacity upon a business so very questionable in its nature, so very uncertain in its issue. By the return of this bill, which seemed to have taken its flight for ever, we are at this very instant nearly as free to choose a plan for our American government as we were on the first day of the session. If, Sir, we incline to the side of conciliation, we are not at all embarrassed (unless we please to make ourselves so) by any incongruous mixture of coercion and restraint. We are therefore called upon, as it were by a superior warning voice, again to attend to America; to attend to the whole of it together, and to review the subject with an unusual degree of care and calmness.

Surely it is an awful subject, or there is none so on this side of the grave. When I first had the honour of a seat in this House, the affairs of that continent pressed themselves upon us as the most important and most delicate object of parliamentary attention. My little share in this great deliberation oppressed me. I found myself a partaker in a very high trust, and having no sort of reason to rely on the strength of my natural abilities for the proper execution of that trust, I was obliged to take more than common pains to instruct myself in everything which relates to our colonies. I was not less under the necessity of forming some fixed ideas concerning the general policy of the British empire. Something of this sort seemed to be indispensable, in order, amidst so vast a fluctuation of passions and opinions, to concentre my thoughts, to ballast my conduct, to preserve me from being blown about by every wind of fashionable doctrine. I really did not think it safe, or manly, to have fresh principles to seek upon every fresh mail which should arrive from America.

At that period I had the fortune to find myself in perfect concurrence with a large majority in this House. Bowing under that high authority, and penetrated with the sharpness and strength of that early impression, I have continued ever since, without the least deviation, in my original sentiments. Whether this be owing to an obstinate perseverance in error or to a religious adherence to what appears to me truth and reason, it is in your equity to judge.

Sir, Parliament having an enlarged view of objects, made during this interval more frequent changes in their sentiments and their conduct than could be justified in a particular person upon the contracted scale of private information. But though I do not hazard anything approaching to censure on the motives of former Parliaments to all those alterations, one fact is undoubted—that under them the state of America has been kept in continual agitation. Everything administered as remedy to the public complaint, if it did not produce, was at least followed by an heightening of the distemper; until, by a variety of experiments, that important country has been brought into her present situation—a situation which I will not miscall, which I dare not name, which I scarcely know how to comprehend in the terms of any description.

In this posture, Sir, things stood at the beginning of the session. About that time, a worthy member[3] of great parliamentary experience, who in the year 1766 filled the chair of the American committee with much ability, took me aside, and, lamenting the present aspect of our politics, told me things were come to such a pass that our former methods of proceeding in the House would be no longer tolerated. That the public tribunal (never too indulgent to a long and unsuccessful opposition) would now scrutinise our conduct with unusual severity. That the very vicissitudes and shiftings of ministerial measures, instead of convicting their authors of inconstancy and want of system, would be taken as an occasion of charging us with a predetermined discontent which nothing could satisfy; whilst we accused every measure of vigour as cruel and every proposal of lenity as weak and irresolute. The public, he said, would not have patience to see us play the game out with our adversaries: we must produce our hand. It would be expected that those who for many years had been active in such affairs should show that they had formed some clear and decided idea of the principles of colony government, and were capable of drawing out something like a platform of the ground which might be laid for future and permanent tranquillity.

I felt the truth of what my hon. friend represented, but I felt my situation too. His application might have been made with far greater propriety to many other gentlemen. No man was indeed ever better disposed, or worse qualified, for such an undertaking than myself. Though I gave so far in to his opinion that I immediately threw my thoughts into a sort of parliamentary form, I was by no means equally ready to produce them. It generally argues

[3] Rose Fuller.

some degree of natural impotence of mind, or some want of knowledge of the world, to hazard plans of government except from a seat of authority. Propositions are made, not only ineffectually, but somewhat disreputably, when the minds of men are not properly disposed for their reception; and for my part I am not ambitious of ridicule, not absolutely a candidate for disgrace.

Besides, Sir, to speak the plain truth, I have in general no very exalted opinion of the virtue of paper government, nor of any politics in which the plan is to be wholly separated from the execution. But when I saw that anger and violence prevailed every day more and more, and that things were hastening towards an incurable alienation of our colonies, I confess my caution gave way. I felt this as one of those few moments in which decorum yields to a higher duty. Public calamity is a mighty leveller; and there are occasions when any, even the slightest, chance of doing good, must be laid hold on even by the most inconsiderable person. . . .[4]

The proposition is peace. Not peace through the medium of war; not peace to be hunted through the labyrinth of intricate and endless negotiations; not peace to arise out of universal discord fomented from principle in all parts of the empire; not peace to depend on the juridical determination of perplexing questions or the precise marking the shadowy boundaries of a complex government. It is simple peace, sought in its natural course, and in its ordinary haunts—it is peace sought in the spirit of peace, and laid in principles purely pacific. I propose, by removing the ground of the difference, and by restoring the *former unsuspecting confidence of the colonies in the mother country*, to give permanent satisfaction to your people; and (far from a scheme of ruling by discord) to reconcile them to each other in the same act, and by the bond of the very same interest which reconciles them to British government.

My idea is nothing more. Refined policy ever has been the parent of confusion, and ever will be so as long as the world endures. Plain good intention, which is as easily discovered at the first view as fraud is surely detected at last, is, let me say, of no mean force in the government of mankind. Genuine simplicity of heart is an healing and cementing principle. My plan, therefore, being formed upon the most simple grounds imaginable, may disappoint some people when they hear it. It has nothing to recommend to it the

[4] Burke continues to humble himself and justifies the presentation of his plan on the grounds of its reasonableness.

pruriency of curious ears. There is nothing at all new and capti-
vating in it. It has nothing of the splendour of the project which
has been lately laid upon your table by the noble lord in the blue
riband. It does not propose to fill your lobby with squabbling
colony agents, who will require the interposition of your mace at
every instant to keep the peace amongst them. It does not institute
a magnificent auction of finance, where captivated provinces come
to general ransom by bidding against each other, until you knock
down the hammer and determine a proportion of payments beyond
all the powers of algebra to equalise and settle.

The plan which I shall presume to suggest derives, however,
one great advantage from the proposition and registry of that
noble lord's project. The idea of conciliation is admissible. First,
the House, in accepting the resolution moved by the noble lord,
has admitted, notwithstanding the menacing front of our address,
notwithstanding our heavy bill of pains and penalties—that we do
not think ourselves precluded from all ideas of free grace and
bounty.

The House has gone further, it has declared conciliation admissible, *previous* to any submission on the part of America. It has
even shot a good deal beyond that mark, and has admitted that the
complaints of our former mode of exerting the right of taxation
were not wholly unfounded. That right thus exerted is allowed
to have had something reprehensible in it, something unwise or
something grievous, since in the midst of our heat and resentment we, of ourselves, have proposed a capital alteration; and, in
order to get rid of what seemed so very exceptionable, have instituted a mode that is altogether new, one that is, indeed, wholly
alien from all the ancient methods and forms of Parliament.

The *principle* of this proceeding is large enough for my purpose.
The means proposed by the noble lord for carrying his ideas into
execution, I think, indeed, are very indifferently suited to the end;
and this I shall endeavour to show you before I sit down. But, for
the present, I take my ground on the admitted principle. I mean
to give peace. Peace implies reconciliation, and, where there has
been a material dispute, reconciliation does in a manner always
imply concession on the one part or on the other. In this state of
things I make no difficulty in affirming that the proposal ought to
originate from us. Great and acknowledged force is not impaired,
either in effect or in opinion, by an unwillingness to exert itself.
The superior power may offer peace with honour and with safety.
Such an offer from such a power will be attributed to magnanim-

ity. But the concessions of the weak are the concessions of fear. When such a one is disarmed he is wholly at the mercy of his superior, and he loses for ever that time and those chances which, as they happen to all men, are the strength and resources of all inferior power.

The capital leading questions on which you must this day decide are these two: First, whether you ought to concede; and secondly, what your concession ought to be. On the first of these questions we have gained (as I have just taken the liberty of observing to you) some ground. But I am sensible that a good deal more is still to be done. Indeed, Sir, to enable us to determine both on the one and the other of these great questions with a firm and precise judgment, I think it may be necessary to consider distinctly the true nature and the peculiar circumstances of the object which we have before us. Because after all our struggle, whether we will or not, we must govern America according to that nature and to those circumstances, and not according to our own imaginations, nor according to abstract ideas of right—by no means according to mere general theories of government, the resort to which appears to me, in our present situation, no better than arrant trifling. I shall therefore endeavour, with your leave, to lay before you some of the most material of these circumstances in as full and as clear a manner as I am able to state them.

The first thing that we have to consider with regard to the nature of the object is—the number of people in the colonies. I have taken for some years a good deal of pains on that point. I can by no calculation justify myself in placing the number below two millions of inhabitants of our own European blood and colour, besides at least 500,000 others, who form no inconsiderable part of the strength and opulence of the whole. This, Sir, is, I believe, about the true number. There is no occasion to exaggerate where plain truth is of so much weight and importance. But whether I put the present numbers too high or too low is a matter of little moment. Such is the strength with which population shoots in that part of the world that, state the numbers as high as we will, whilst the dispute continues, the exaggeration ends. Whilst we are discussing any given magnitude, they are grown to it. Whilst we spend our time in deliberating on the mode of governing two millions, we shall find we have millions more to manage. Your children do not grow faster from infancy to manhood than they spread from families to communities, and from villages to nations.

I put this consideration of the present and the growing num-

bers in the front of our deliberation, because, Sir, this consideration will make it evident to a blunter discernment than yours that
no partial, narrow, contracted, pinched, occasional system will be
at all suitable to such an object. It will show you, that it is not to
be considered as one of those *minima* which are out of the eye
and consideration of the law; not a paltry excrescence of the state,
not a mean dependent, who may be neglected with little damage
and provoked with little danger. It will prove that some degree of
care and caution is required in the handling such an object; it will
show that you ought not, in reason, to trifle with so large a mass
of the interests and feelings of the human race. You could at no
time do so without guilt, and be assured you will not be able to
do it long with impunity.

But the population of this country, the great and growing population, though a very important consideration, will lose much of
its weight if not combined with other circumstances. The commerce of your colonies is out of all proportion beyond the numbers
of the people. This ground of their commerce indeed has been
trod some days ago, and with great ability, by a distinguished
person, at your bar.[5] This gentleman, after thirty-five years—it is
so long since he first appeared at the same place to plead for the
commerce of Great Britain—has come again before you to plead
the same cause, without any other effect of time than that to the
fire of imagination and extent of erudition which even then
marked him as one of the first literary characters of his age, he
has added a consummate knowledge in the commercial interest of
his country, formed by a long course of enlightened and discrimi-
nating experience.

Sir, I should be inexcusable in coming after such a person with
any detail, if a great part of the members who now fill the House
had not the misfortune to be absent when he appeared at your bar.
Besides, Sir, I propose to take the matter at periods of time somewhat different from his. There is, if I mistake not, a point of view
from whence if you will look at this subject it is impossible that
it should not make an impression upon you.

I have in my hand two accounts: one a comparative state of the
export trade of England to its colonies, as it stood in the year
1704 and as it stood in the year 1772; the other a state of the
export trade of this country to its colonies alone, as it stood in

[5] Mr. Glover.

1772, compared with the whole trade of England to all parts of the world (the colonies included) in the year 1704. They are from good vouchers, the latter period from the accounts on your table, the earlier from an original manuscript of Davenant, who first established the inspector-general's office, which has been ever since his time so abundant a source of parliamentary information.

The export trade to the colonies consists of three great branches. The African, which, terminating almost wholly in the colonies, must be put to the account of their commerce; the West Indian, and the North American. All these are so interwoven that the attempt to separate them would tear to pieces the contexture of the whole, and, if not entirely destroy, would very much depreciate the value of all the parts. I therefore consider these three denominations to be, what in effect they are, one trade.

The trade to the colonies, taken on the export side, at the beginning of this century, that is in the year 1704, stood thus:

Exports to North America and the West Indies	£ 483,265
To Africa	86,665
	£ 569,930

In the year 1772, which I take as a middle year between the highest and lowest of those lately laid on your table, the account was as follows:

To North America and the West Indies	£ 4,791,734
To Africa	866,398
To which if you add the export trade from Scotland, which had in 1704 no existence	364,000
	£ 6,022,132

From five hundred and odd thousand it has grown to six millions. It has increased no less than twelve-fold. This is the state of the colony trade as compared with itself at these two periods within this century—and this is matter for meditation. But this is not all. Examine my second account. See how the export trade to the colonies alone in 1772 stood in the other point of view, that is, as compared to the whole trade of England in 1704.

The whole export trade of England, including that to the colonies, in 1704	£ 6,509,000
Export to the colonies alone, in 1772	6,024,000
Difference	£ 485,000

The trade with America alone is now within less than £500,000 of being equal to what this great commercial nation, England, carried on at the beginning of this century with the whole world! If I had taken the largest year of those on your table it would rather have exceeded. But it will be said, is not this American trade an unnatural protuberance that has drawn the juices from the rest of the body? The reverse. It is the very food that has nourished every other part into its present magnitude. Our general trade has been greatly augmented, and augmented more or less in almost every part to which it ever extended; but with this material difference, that of the six millions which in the beginning of the century constituted the whole mass of our export commerce, the colony trade was but one-twelfth part; it is now (as a part of sixteen millions) considerably more than a third of the whole. This is the relative proportion of the importance of the colonies at these two periods; and all reasoning concerning our mode of treating them must have this proportion as its basis, or it is a reasoning weak, rotten, and sophistical.

Mr. Speaker, I cannot prevail on myself to hurry over this great consideration. It is good for us to be here. We stand where we have an immense view of what is, and what is past. Clouds, indeed, and darkness rest upon the future. Let us, however, before we descend from this noble eminence, reflect that this growth of our national prosperity has happened within the short period of the life of man. It has happened within sixty-eight years. There are those alive whose memory might touch the two extremities. For instance, my Lord Bathurst might remember all the stages of the progress. He was in 1704 of an age at least to be made to comprehend such things. He was then old enough *acta parentum jam legere, et quæ sit poterit cognoscere virtus.*[6] Suppose, Sir, that the angel of this auspicious youth, foreseeing the many virtues which made him one of the most amiable as he is one of the most fortunate men of his age, had opened to him in vision that when, in the fourth generation, the third prince of the House of Brunswick had sat twelve years on the throne of that nation which (by the happy issue of moderate and healing councils) was to be made Great Britain, he should see his son, Lord Chancellor of England, turn back the current of hereditary dignity to its fountain and raise him to a higher rank of peerage, whilst he enriched the family

[6] "To study the doings of his forebears, and to learn what virtue is."

with a new one—if amidst these bright and happy scenes of domestic honour and prosperity, that angel should have drawn up
the curtain and unfolded the rising glories of his country, and
whilst he was gazing with admiration on the then commercial
grandeur of England, the genius should point out to him a little
speck, scarce visible in the mass of the national interest, a small
seminal principle rather than a formed body, and should tell him—
"Young man, there is America, which at this day serves for little
more than to amuse you with stories of savage men and uncouth
manners, yet shall, before you taste of death, show itself equal to
the whole of that commerce which now attracts the envy of the
world. Whatever England has been growing to by a progressive
increase of improvement, brought in by varieties of people, by
succession of civilising conquests and civilising settlements in a
series of seventeen hundred years, you shall see as much added
to her by America in the course of a single life!" If this state of
his country had been foretold to him, would it not require all the
sanguine credulity of youth, and all the fervid glow of enthusi-
asm, to make him believe it? Fortunate man, he has lived to see
it! Fortunate indeed if he lives to see nothing that shall vary the
prospect and cloud the setting of his day!

Excuse me, Sir, if turning from such thoughts I resume this
comparative view once more. You have seen it on a large scale,
look at it on a small one. I will point out to your attention a particular instance of it in the single province of Pennsylvania. In
the years 1704, that province called for £11,459 in value of your
commodities, native and foreign. This was the whole. What did it
demand in 1772? Why nearly fifty times as much; for in that year
the export to Pennsylvania was £507,909, nearly equal to the
export to all the colonies together in the first period.

I choose, Sir, to enter into these minute and particular details,
because generalities, which in all other cases are apt to heighten
and raise the subject, have here a tendency to sink it. When we
speak of the commerce with our colonies fiction lags after truth,
invention is unfruitful, and imagination cold and barren.

So far, Sir, as to the importance of the object in view of its
commerce, as concerned in the exports from England. If I were to
detail the imports, I could show how many enjoyments they procure which deceive the burthen of life, how many materials which
invigorate the springs of national industry, and extend and ani-
mate every part of our foreign and domestic commerce. This

would be a curious subject indeed—but I must prescribe bounds to myself in a matter so vast and various.

I pass therefore to the colonies in another point of view, their agriculture. This they have prosecuted with such a spirit that, besides feeding plentifully their own growing multitude, their annual export of grain, comprehending rice, has some years ago exceeded a million in value. Of their last harvest, I am persuaded they will export much more. At the beginning of the century some of these colonies imported corn from the mother country. For some time past, the Old World has been fed from the New. The scarcity which you have felt would have been a desolating famine if this child of your old age, with a true filial piety, with a Roman charity, had not put the full breast of its youthful exuberance to the mouth of its exhausted parent.

As to the wealth which the colonies have drawn from the sea by their fisheries, you had all that matter fully opened at your bar. You surely thought these acquisitions of value, for they seemed even to excite your envy; and yet the spirit by which that enterprising employment has been exercised ought rather, in my opinion, to have raised your esteem and admiration. And pray, Sir, what in the world is equal to it? Pass by the other parts, and look at the manner in which the people of New England have of late carried on the whale fishery. Whilst we follow them among the tumbling mountains of ice, and behold them penetrating into the deepest frozen recesses of Hudson's Bay and Davis's Straits, whilst we are looking for them beneath the arctic circle, we hear that they have pierced into the opposite region of polar cold, that they are at the antipodes, and engaged under the frozen serpent of the south. Falkland Island, which seemed too remote and romantic an object for the grasp of national ambition, is but a stage and resting-place in the progress of their victorious industry. Nor is the equinoctial heat more discouraging to them than the accumulated winter of both the poles. We know that whilst some of them draw the line and strike the harpoon on the coast of Africa, others run the longitude and pursue their gigantic game along the coast of Brazil. No sea but what is vexed by their fisheries. No climate that is not witness to their toils. Neither the perseverance of Holland, nor the captivity of France, nor the dexterous and firm sagacity of English enterprise ever carried this most perilous mode of hard industry to the extent to which it has been pushed by this recent people—a people who are still, as it were, but in the gristle, and not yet hardened into the bone of manhood. When I contemplate these things, when I know that the colonies in general owe little or nothing to any care of ours, and that they are not squeezed into this happy form by the constraints of watchful and suspicious government, but that, through a wise and salutary neglect, a generous nature has been suffered to take her own way to perfection; when I reflect upon these effects, when I see how profitable they have been to us, I feel all the pride of power sink, and all presumption in the wisdom of human contrivances melt and die away within me. My rigour relents. I pardon something to the spirit of liberty.

I am sensible, Sir, that all which I have asserted in my detail, is admitted in the gross, but that quite a different conclusion is drawn from it. America, gentlemen say, is a noble object. It is an object well worth fighting for. Certainly it is, if fighting a people be the best way of gaining them. Gentlemen in this respect will be led to their choice of means by their complexions and their habits. Those who understand the military art will of course have some predilection for it. Those who wield the thunder of the state may have more confidence in the efficacy of arms. But I confess, possibly for want of this knowledge, my opinion is much more in favour of prudent management than of force, considering force not as an odious, but a feeble instrument for preserving a people so numerous, so active, so growing, so spirited as this in a profitable and subordinate connection with us.

First, Sir, permit me to observe that the use of force alone is but *temporary*. It may subdue for a moment, but it does not remove the necessity of subduing again; and a nation is not governed which is perpetually to be conquered.

My next objection is its *uncertainty*. Terror is not always the effect of force, and an armament is not a victory. If you do not succeed, you are without resource; for, conciliation failing, force remains, but, force failing, no further hope of reconciliation is left. Power and authority are sometimes bought by kindness, but they can never be begged as alms by an impoverished and defeated violence.

A further objection to force is, that you *impair the object* by your very endeavours to preserve it. The thing you fought for is not the thing which you recover, but depreciated, sunk, wasted, and consumed in the contest. Nothing less will content me than *whole America*. I do not choose to consume its strength along with

our own, because in all parts it is the British strength that I consume. I do not choose to be caught by a foreign enemy at the end
of this exhausting conflict; and still less in the midst of it. I may
escape, but I can make no assurance against such an event. Let me
add, that I do not choose wholly to break the American spirit,
because it is the spirit that has made the country.

Lastly, we have no sort of *experience* in favour of force as an
instrument in the rule of our colonies. Their growth and their
utility has been owing to methods altogether different. Our ancient indulgence has been said to be pursued to a fault. It may be
so. But we know, if feeling is evidence, that our fault was more
tolerable than our attempt to mend it, and our sin far more salutary than our penitence.

These, Sir, are my reasons for not entertaining that high opinion of untried force by which many gentlemen, for whose sentiments in other particulars I have great respect, seem to be so
greatly captivated. But there is still behind a third consideration
concerning this object, which serves to determine my opinion on
the sort of policy which ought to be pursued in the management
of America, even more than its population and its commerce—I
mean its *temper and character.*

In this character of the Americans, a love of freedom is the
predominating feature which marks and distinguishes the whole;
and as an ardent is always a jealous affection, your colonies become suspicious, restive, and untractable whenever they see the
least attempt to wrest from them by force or shuffle from them
by chicane what they think the only advantage worth living for.
The fierce spirit of liberty is stronger in the English colonies
probably than in any other people of the earth; and this from a
great variety of powerful causes, which, to understand the true
temper of their minds and the direction which this spirit takes, it
will not be amiss to lay open somewhat more largely.

First, the people of the colonies are descendants of Englishmen.
England, Sir, is a nation which still I hope respects, and formerly
adored, her freedom. The colonists emigrated from you when this
part of your character was most predominant, and they took this
bias and direction the moment they parted from your hands. They
are therefore not only devoted to liberty, but to liberty according
to English ideas and on English principles. Abstract liberty, like
other mere abstractions, is not to be found. Liberty inheres in
some sensible object; and every nation has formed to itself some

favourite point, which by way of eminence becomes the criterion of their happiness. It happened you know, Sir, that the great contests for freedom in this country were from the earliest times chiefly upon the question of taxing. Most of the contests in the ancient commonwealths turned primarily on the right of election of magistrates, or on the balance among the several orders of the state. The question of money was not with them so immediate. But in England it was otherwise. On this point of taxes the ablest pens and most eloquent tongues have been exercised; the greatest spirits have acted and suffered. In order to give the fullest satisfaction concerning the importance of this point, it was not only necessary for those who in argument defended the excellence of the English constitution to insist on this privilege of granting money as a dry point of fact, and to prove that the right had been acknowledged in ancient parchments and blind usages to reside in a certain body called a House of Commons. They went much further; they attempted to prove, and they succeeded, that in theory it ought to be so, from the particular nature of a House of Commons, as an immediate representative of the people, whether the old records had delivered this oracle or not. They took infinite pains to inculcate, as a fundamental principle, that in all monarchies the people must in effect themselves, mediately or immediately, possess the power of granting their own money, or no shadow of liberty could subsist. The colonies draw from you, as with their life-blood, these ideas and principles. Their love of liberty, as with you, fixed and attached on this specific point of taxing. Liberty might be safe or might be endangered in twenty other particulars, without their being much pleased or alarmed. Here they felt its pulse, and as they found that beat they thought themselves sick or sound. I do not say whether they were right or wrong in applying your general arguments to their own case. It is not easy indeed to make a monopoly of theorems and corollaries. The fact is, that they did thus apply those general arguments; and your mode of governing them, whether through lenity or indolence, through wisdom or mistake, confirmed them in the imagination that they, as well as you, had an interest in these common principles.

They were further confirmed in this pleasing error by the form of their provincial legislative assemblies. Their governments are popular in a high degree, some are merely popular, in all the popular representative is the most weighty, and this share of the people in their ordinary government never fails to inspire them with lofty sentiments and with a strong aversion from whatever tends to deprive them of their chief importance.

If anything were wanting to this necessary operation of the form of government, religion would have given it a complete effect. Religion, always a principle of energy, in this new people is no way worn out or impaired, and their mode of professing it is also one main cause of this free spirit. The people are Protestants, and of that kind which is the most adverse to all implicit submission of mind and opinion. This is a persuasion not only favourable to liberty, but built upon it. I do not think, Sir, that the reason of this averseness in the dissenting churches, from all that looks like absolute government, is so much to be sought in their religious tenets as in their history. Every one knows that the Roman Catholic religion is at least coeval with most of the governments where it prevails, that it has generally gone hand in hand with them, and received great favour and every kind of support from authority. The Church of England, too, was formed from her cradle under the nursing care of regular government. But the dissenting interests have sprung up in direct opposition to all the ordinary powers of the world, and could justify that opposition only on a strong claim to natural liberty. Their very existence depended on the powerful and unremitted assertion of that claim. All Protestantism, even the most cold and passive, is a sort of dissent. But the religion most prevalent in our northern colonies is a refinement on the principle of resistance; it is the dissidence of dissent and the Protestantism of the Protestant religion. This religion, under a variety of denominations agreeing in nothing but in the communion of the spirit of liberty, is predominant in most of the northern provinces, where the Church of England, notwithstanding its legal rights, is in reality no more than a sort of private sect, not composing most probably the tenth of the people. The colonists left England when this spirit was high, and in the emigrants was the highest of all; and even that stream of foreigners, which has been constantly flowing into these colonies, has, for the greatest part, been composed of dissenters from the establishments of their several countries, and have brought with them a temper and character far from alien to that of the people with whom they mixed.

Sir, I can perceive by their manner that some gentlemen object to the latitude of this description; because in the southern colonies the Church of England forms a large body and has a regular establishment. It is certainly true. There is, however, a circumstance attending these colonies which, in my opinion, fully counterbalances this difference, and makes the spirit of liberty still more high and haughty than in those to the northward. It is, that in Virginia and the Carolinas they have a vast multitude of slaves. Where this is the case in any part of the world, those who are free are by far the most proud and jealous of their freedom. Freedom is to them not only an enjoyment, but a kind of rank and privilege. Not seeing there that freedom, as in countries where it is a common blessing and as broad and general as the air, may be united with much abject toil, with great misery, with all the exterior of servitude liberty looks amongst them like something that is more noble and liberal. I do not mean, Sir, to commend the superior morality of this sentiment, which has at least as much pride as virtue in it; but I cannot alter the nature of man. The fact is so; and these people of the southern colonies are much more strongly, and with a higher and more stubborn spirit, attached to liberty than those to the northward. Such were all the ancient commonwealths, such were our Gothic ancestors, such in our days were the Poles, and such will be all masters of slaves who are not slaves themselves. In such a people, the haughtiness of domination combines with the spirit of freedom, fortifies it, and renders it invincible.

Permit me, Sir, to add another circumstance in our colonies, which contributes no mean part towards the growth and effect of this untractable spirit. I mean their education. In no country perhaps in the world is the law so general a study. The profession itself is numerous and powerful, and in most provinces it takes the lead. The greater number of the deputies sent to the congress were lawyers. But all who read, and most do read, endeavour to obtain some smattering in that science. I have been told by an eminent bookseller that in no branch of his business, after tracts of popular devotion, were so many books as those on the law exported to the plantations. The colonists have now fallen into the way of printing them for their own use. I hear that they have sold nearly as many of Blackstone's Commentaries in America as in England. General Gage marks out this disposition very particularly in a letter on your table. He states that all the people in his government are lawyers, or smatterers in law, and that in Boston they have been enabled, by successful chicane, wholly to evade many parts of one of your capital penal constitutions. The smartness of debate will say, that this knowledge ought to teach them more clearly the rights of legislature, their obligations to obedience, and the penalties of rebellion. All this is mighty well. But my honourable and learned friend[7] on the floor, who condescends to mark what I say for animadversion, will disdain that ground. He has heard, as well as I, that when great honours and great emoluments do not win over this knowledge to the service of the state, it is a formidable adversary to government. If the spirit be not tamed and broken by these happy methods, it is stubborn and litigious. *Abeunt studia in mores.*[8] This study renders men acute, inquisitive, dexterous, prompt in attack, ready in defence, full of resources. In other countries, the people, more simple and of a less mercurial cast, judge of an ill principle in government only by an actual grievance; here they anticipate the evil and judge of the pressure of the grievance by the badness of the principle. They augur misgovernment at a distance, and snuff the approach of tyranny in every tainted breeze.

The last cause of this disobedient spirit in the colonies is hardly less powerful than the rest, as it is not merely moral, but laid deep in the natural constitution of things. Three thousand miles of ocean lie between you and them. No contrivance can prevent the effect of this distance in weakening government. Seas roll, and months pass, between the order and the execution, and the want of a speedy explanation of a single point is enough to defeat a whole system. . . . The Sultan gets such obedience as he can. He governs with a loose rein that he may govern at all; and the whole of the force and vigour of his authority in his centre is derived from a prudent relaxation in all his borders. Spain, in her provinces, is, perhaps, not so well obeyed as you are in yours. She complies too, she submits, she watches time. This is the immutable condition, the eternal law, of extensive and detached empire.

Then, Sir, from these six capital sources: of descent, of form of government, of religion in the northern provinces, of manners in the southern, of education, of the remoteness of situation from the first mover of government—from all these causes a fierce spirit of liberty has grown up. It has grown with the growth of the people in your colonies, and increased with the increase of their wealth; a spirit that unhappily meeting with an exercise

[7] Attorney General, Edward Thurlow.
[8] "Pursuits influence character."

of power in England which, however lawful, is not reconcilable to any ideas of liberty, much less with theirs, has kindled this flame that is ready to consume us.

I do not mean to commend either the spirit in this excess or the moral causes which produce it. Perhaps a more smooth and accommodating spirit of freedom in them would be more acceptable to us. Perhaps ideas of liberty might be desired more reconcilable with an arbitrary and boundless authority. Perhaps we might wish the colonists to be persuaded that their liberty is more secure when held in trust for them by us (as their guardians during a perpetual minority) than with any part of it in their own hands. The question is, not whether their spirit deserves praise or blame, but—what, in the name of God, shall we do with it? You have before you the object, such as it is, with all its glories, with all its imperfections on its head. You see the magnitude, the importance, the temper, the habits, the disorders. By all these considerations we are strongly urged to determine something concerning it. We are called upon to fix some rule and line for our future conduct which may give a little stability to our politics and prevent the return of such unhappy deliberations as the present. Every such return will bring the matter before us in a still more untractable form. For, what astonishing and incredible things have we not seen already! What monsters have not been generated from this unnatural contention! Whilst every principle of authority and resistance has been pushed, upon both sides, as far as it would go, there is nothing so solid and certain, either in reasoning or in practice, that has not been shaken. Until very lately, all authority in America seemed to be nothing but an emanation from yours. Even the popular part of the colony constitution derived all its activity, and its first vital movement, from the pleasure of the crown. We thought, Sir, that the utmost which the discontented colonists could do was to disturb authority; we never dreamt they could of themselves supply it, knowing in general what an operose business it is to establish a government absolutely new. But having, for our purposes in this contention, resolved that none but an obedient assembly should sit, the humours of the people there, finding all passage through the legal channel stopped, with great violence broke out another way. Some provinces have tried their experiment, as we have tried ours— and theirs has succeeded. They have formed a government, sufficient for its purposes, without the bustle of a revolution or the troublesome formality of an election. Evident necessity and tacit consent have done the business in an instant. So well they have done it, that Lord Dunmore (the account is among the fragments on your table) tells you that the new institution is infinitely better obeyed than the ancient government ever was in its most fortunate periods. Obedience is what makes government and not the names by which it is called; not the name of governor, as formerly, or committee, as at present. This new government has originated directly from the people, and was not transmitted through any of the ordinary artificial media of a positive constitution. It was not a manufacture ready formed and transmitted to them in that condition from England. The evil arising from hence is this: that the colonists, having once found the possibility of enjoying the advantages of order in the midst of a struggle for liberty, such struggles will not henceforward seem so terrible to the settled and sober part of mankind as they had appeared before the trial.

Pursuing the same plan of punishing by the denial of the exercise of government to still greater lengths, we wholly abrogated the ancient government of Massachusetts. We were confident that the first feeling, if not the very prospect of anarchy, would instantly enforce a complete submission. The experiment was tried. A new, strange, unexpected face of things appeared. Anarchy is found tolerable. A vast province has now subsisted, and subsisted in a considerable degree of health and vigour, for near a twelve-month, without governor, without public council, without judges, without executive magistrates. How long it will continue in this state, or what may arise out of this unheard-of situation, how can the wisest of us conjecture? Our late experience has taught us that many of those fundamental principles, formerly believed infallible, are either not of that importance they were imagined to be, or that we have not at all adverted to some other far more important and far more powerful principles which entirely overrule those we had considered as omnipotent. I am much against any further experiments, which tend to put to the proof any more of these allowed opinions, which contribute so much to the public tranquillity. In effect, we suffer as much at home by this loosening of all ties, and this concussion of all established opinions, as we do abroad. For, in order to prove that the Americans have no right to their liberties, we are every day endeavouring to subvert the maxims which preserve the whole spirit of our own. To prove that the Americans ought not to be free, we are obliged to depreciate the value of freedom itself; and we never seem to gain a paltry advantage over them in debate without attacking some of those principles, or deriding some of those feelings, for which our ancestors have shed their blood.

But, Sir, in wishing to put an end to pernicious experiments, I do not mean to preclude the fullest inquiry. Far from it. Far from deciding on a sudden or partial view, I would patiently go round and round the subject and survey it minutely in every possible aspect. Sir, if I were capable of engaging you to an equal attention, I would state that, as far as I am capable of discerning, there are but three ways of proceeding relative to this stubborn spirit which prevails in your colonies and disturbs your government. These are: to change that spirit, as inconvenient, by removing the causes; to prosecute it as criminal; or, to comply with it as necessary. I would not be guilty of an imperfect enumeration; I can think of but these three. Another has indeed been started, that of giving up the colonies; but it met so slight a reception that I do not think myself obliged to dwell a great while upon it. It is nothing but a little sally of anger, like the frowardness of peevish children, who, when they cannot get all they would have, are resolved to take nothing.

The first of these plans, to change the spirit as inconvenient by removing the causes, I think is the most like a systematic proceeding. It is radical in its principle; but it is attended with great difficulties, some of them little short, as I conceive, of impossibilities. This will appear by examining into the plans which have been proposed.

As the growing population in the colonies is evidently one cause of their resistance, it was last session mentioned in both Houses, by men of weight, and received not without applause, that in order to check this evil it would be proper for the crown to make no further grants of land. But to this scheme there are two objections. The first, that there is already so much unsettled land in private hands as to afford room for an immense future population, although the crown not only withheld its grants, but annihilated its soil. If this be the case, then the only effect of this avarice of desolation, this hoarding of a royal wilderness, would be to raise the value of the possessions in the hands of the great private monopolists, without any adequate check to the growing and alarming mischief of population.

But if you stopped your grants, what would be the consequence? The people would occupy without grants. They have already so occupied in many places. You cannot station garrisons in every part of these deserts. If you drive the people from one place, they will carry on their annual tillage, and remove with their flocks and herds to another. Many of the people in the back settlements are already little attached to particular situations. Already they have topped the Appalachian mountains. From thence they behold before them an immense plain, one vast, rich, level meadow—a square of five hundred miles. Over this they would wander without a possibility of restraint; they would change their manners with the habits of their life, would soon forget a government by which they were disowned, would become hordes of English Tartars, and, pouring down upon your unfortified frontiers a fierce and irresistible cavalry, become masters of your governors and your counsellors, your collectors and comptrollers, and of all the slaves that adhered to them. Such would, and in no long time must be, the effect of attempting to forbid as a crime, and to suppress as an evil, the command and blessing of Providence, "Increase and multiply." Such would be the happy result of an endeavour to keep as a lair of wild beasts that earth which God, by an express charter, has given to the children of men. Far different and surely much wiser has been our policy hitherto. Hitherto we have invited our people, by every kind of bounty, to fixed establishments. We have invited the husbandman to look to authority for his title. We have taught him piously to believe in the mysterious virtue of wax and parchment. We have thrown each tract of land, as it was peopled, into districts, that the ruling power should never be wholly out of sight. We have settled all we could, and we have carefully attended every settlement with government.

Adhering, Sir, as I do, to this policy, as well as for the reasons I have just given, I think this new project of hedging-in population to be neither prudent nor practicable.

To impoverish the colonies in general, and in particular to arrest the noble course of their marine enterprises, would be a more easy task. I freely confess it. We have shown a disposition to a system of this kind—a disposition even to continue the restraint after the offence; looking on ourselves as rivals to our colonies, and persuaded that of course we must gain all that they shall lose. Much mischief we may certainly do. The power inadequate to all other things is often more than sufficient for this. I do not look on the direct and immediate power of the colonies to resist our violence as very formidable. In this, however, I may be mistaken. But when I consider that we have colonies for no purpose but to be servicable to us, it seems to my poor understanding a little preposterous to make them unserviceable in order to keep them obedient. It is, in truth, nothing more than the old and, as I thought, exploded problem of tyranny, which proposes to beggar its subjects into submission. But remember, when you have completed your system of impoverishment, that nature still proceeds in her ordinary course; that discontent will increase with misery; and that there are critical moments in the fortune of all states, when they who are too weak to contribute to your prosperity may be strong enough to complete your ruin. *Spoliatis arma supersunt.*[9]

The temper and character which prevail in our colonies are, I am afraid, unalterable by any human art. We cannot, I fear, falsify the pedigree of this fierce people, and persuade them that they are not sprung from a nation in whose veins the blood of freedom circulates. The language in which they would hear you tell them this tale would detect the imposition—your speech would betray you. An Englishman is the unfittest person on earth to argue another Englishman into slavery.

I think it is nearly as little in our power to change their republican religion as their free descent, or to substitute the Roman Catholic as a penalty, or the Church of England as an improvement. The mode of inquisition and dragooning is going out of fashion in the Old World, and I should not confide much to their efficacy in the New. The education of the Americans is also on the same unalterable bottom with their religion. You cannot persuade them to burn their books of curious science, to banish their lawyers from their courts of laws, or to quench the lights of their assemblies by refusing to choose those persons who are best read in their privileges. It would be no less impracticable to think of wholly annihilating the popular assemblies in which these lawyers sit. The army, by which we must govern in their place, would be far more chargeable to us, not quite so effectual, and, perhaps, in the end full as difficult to be kept in obedience.

With regard to the high aristocratic spirit of Virginia and the southern colonies, it has been proposed, I know, to reduce it by

[9] "Arms remain to those despoiled," Juvenal, Satires, VIII, 124.

declaring a general enfranchisement of their slaves. This project has had its advocates and panegyrists; yet I never could argue myself into any opinion of it. Slaves are often much attached to their masters. A general wild offer of liberty would not always be accepted. History furnishes few instances of it. It is sometimes as hard to persuade slaves to be free as it is to compel freemen to be slaves; and in this auspicious scheme we should have both these pleasing tasks on our hands at once. But when we talk of enfranchisement, do we not perceive that the American master may enfranchise too, and arm servile hands in defence of freedom? A measure to which other people have had recourse more than once, and not without success, in a desperate situation of their affairs.

Slaves as these unfortunate black people are, and dull as all men are from slavery, must they not a little suspect the offer of freedom from that very nation which has sold them to their present masters?—from that nation, one of whose causes of quarrel with those masters is their refusal to deal any more in that inhuman traffic? An offer of freedom from England would come rather oddly, shipped to them in an African vessel, which is refused an entry into the ports of Virginia or Carolina, with a cargo of three hundred Angola negroes. It would be curious to see the Guinea captain attempting at the same instant to publish his proclamation of liberty, and to advertise his sale of slaves.

But let us suppose all these moral difficulties got over. The ocean remains. You cannot pump this dry; and as long as it continues in its present bed, so long all the causes which weaken authority by distance will continue. "Ye gods, annihilate but space and time and make two lovers happy!" was a pious and passionate prayer; but just as reasonable as many of the serious wishes of very grave and solemn politicians.

If then, Sir, it seems almost desperate to think of any alternative course for changing the moral causes (and not quite easy to remove the natural) which produce prejudices irreconcilable to the late exercise of our authority, but that the spirit infallibly will continue, and, continuing, will produce such effects as now embarrass us, the second mode under consideration is, to prosecute that spirit in its overt acts as *criminal*.

At this proposition I must pause a moment. The thing seems a great deal too big for my ideas of jurisprudence. It should seem to my way of conceiving such matters that there is a very wide difference in reason and policy between the mode of proceeding on their regular conduct of scattered individuals, or even of bands of men, who disturb order within the state and the civil dissensions which may, from time to time, on great questions, agitate the several communities which compose a great empire. It looks to me to be narrow and pedantic to apply the ordinary ideas of criminal justice to this great public contest. I do not know the method of drawing up an indictment against a whole people. I cannot insult and ridicule the feelings of millions of my fellow-creatures as Sir Edward Coke insulted one excellent individual (Sir Walter Raleigh) at the bar. I hope I am not ripe to pass sentence on the gravest public bodies, entrusted with magistracies of great authority and dignity and charged with the safety of their fellow-citizens, upon the very same title that I am. I really think that for wise men this is not judicious; for sober men, not decent; for minds tinctured with humanity, not mild and merciful.

Perhaps, Sir, I am mistaken in my idea of an empire as distinguished from a single state or kingdom. But my idea of it is this: that an empire is the aggregate of many states under one common head, whether this head be a monarch or a presiding republic. It does, in such constitutions, frequently happen (and nothing but this dismal, cold, dead uniformity of servitude can prevent its happening) that the subordinate parts have many local privileges and immunities. Between these privileges and the supreme common authority the line may be extremely nice. Of course disputes, often, too, very bitter disputes, and much ill blood, will arise. But though every privilege is an exemption (in the case) from the ordinary exercise of the supreme authority, it is no denial of it. The claim of a privilege seems rather, *ex vi termini*,[10] to imply a superior power. For to talk of the privileges of a state, or of a person, who has no superior, is hardly any better than speaking nonsense. Now, in such unfortunate quarrels among the component parts of a great political union of communities, I can scarcely conceive anything more completely imprudent than for the head of the empire to insist that, if any privilege is pleaded against his will or his acts, his whole authority is denied—instantly to proclaim rebellion, to beat to arms, and to put the offending provinces under the ban. Will not this, Sir, very soon teach the provinces to make no distinctions on their part? Will it not teach them that

[10] "From the force of the term."

the government, against which a claim of liberty is tantamount to high treason, is a government to which submission is equivalent to slavery? It may not always be quite convenient to impress dependent communities with such an idea.

We are, indeed, in all disputes with the colonies, by the necessity of things, the judge. It is true, Sir. But I confess that the character of judge in my own cause is a thing that frightens me. Instead of filling me with pride, I am exceedingly humbled by it. I cannot proceed with a stern, assured, judicial confidence, until I find myself in something more like a judicial character. I must have these hesitations as long as I am compelled to recollect that, in my little reading upon such contests as these, the sense of mankind has, at least, as often decided against the superior as the subordinate power. Sir, let me add too, that the opinion of my having some abstract right in my favour would not put me much at my ease in passing sentence, unless I could be sure that there were no rights which, in their exercise under certain circumstances, were not the most odious of all wrongs and the most vexatious of all injustice. Sir, these considerations have great weight with me, when I find things so circumstanced that I see the same party at once a civil litigant against me in point of right and a culprit before me. . . .

There is Sir, also a circumstance which convinces me that this mode of criminal proceeding is not (at least in the present stage of our contest) altogether expedient; which is nothing less than the conduct of those very persons who have seemed to adopt that mode by lately declaring a rebellion in Massachusetts Bay, as they had formerly addressed to have traitors brought hither, under an Act of Henry the Eighth, for trial. For though rebellion is declared, it is not proceeded against as such, nor have any steps been taken towards the apprehension or conviction of any individual offender, either on our later or our former address; but modes of public coercion have been adopted, and such as have much more resemblance to a sort of qualified hostility towards an independent power than the punishment of rebellious subjects. All this seems rather inconsistent, but it shows how difficult it is to apply the juridical ideas to our present case.

In this situation, let us seriously and coolly ponder. What is it we have got by all our menaces, which have been many and ferocious? What advantage have we derived from the penal laws we have passed, and which for the time have been severe and numerous? What advances have we made towards our object by the sending of a force which, by land and sea, is no contemptible strength? Has the disorder abated? Nothing less. When I see things in this situation, after such confident hopes, bold promises, and active exertions, I cannot, for my life, avoid a suspicion that the plan itself is not correctly right.

If then the removal of the causes of this spirit of American liberty be, for the greater part, or rather entirely, impracticable; if the ideas of criminal process be inapplicable, or, if applicable, are in the highest degree inexpedient—what way yet remains? No way is open, but the third and last—to comply with the American spirit as necessary, or, if you please, to submit to it as a necessary evil.

If we adopt this mode, if we mean to conciliate and concede, let us see of what nature the concession ought to be: to ascertain the nature of our concession, we must look at their complaint. The colonies complain that they have not the characteristic mark and seal of British freedom. They complain that they are taxed in a Parliament in which they are not represented. If you mean to satisfy them at all, you must satisfy them with regard to this complaint. If you mean to please any people, you must give them the boon which they ask; not what you may think better for them, but of a kind totally different. Such an act may be a wise regulation, but it is no concession: whereas our present theme is the mode of giving satisfaction.

Sir, I think you must perceive that I am resolved this day to have nothing at all to do with the question of the right of taxation. Some gentlemen startle—but it is true; I put it totally out of the question. It is less than nothing in my consideration. I do not indeed wonder, nor will you, Sir, that gentlemen of profound learning are fond of displaying it on this profound subject. But my consideration is narrow, confined, and wholly limited to the policy of the question. I do not examine whether the giving away a man's money be a power excepted and reserved out of the general trust of government; and how far all mankind, in all forms of polity, are entitled to an exercise of that right by the charter of nature. Or whether, on the contrary, a right of taxation is necessarily involved in the general principle of legislation and inseparable from the ordinary supreme power. These are deep questions, where great names militate against each other, where reason is perplexed, and an appeal to authorities only thickens the confusion. For high and reverend authorities lift up their heads on both sides, and there is no sure footing in the middle. This point is the *great Serbonian bog betwixt Damiata and Mount Casius old, where armies whole have sunk.* I do not intend to be overwhelmed in that bog, though in such respectable company. The question with me is, not whether you have a right to render your people miserable, but whether it is not your interest to make them happy. It is not what a lawyer tells me I *may* do, but what humanity, reason, and justice tell me I ought to do. Is a politic act the worse for being a generous one? Is no concession proper but that which is made from your want of right to keep what you grant? Or does it lessen the grace or dignity of relaxing in the exercise of an odious claim because you have your evidence-room full of titles, and your magazines stuffed with arms to enforce them? What signify all those titles and all those arms? Of what avail are they, when the reason of the thing tells me that the assertion of my title is the loss of my suit, and that I could do nothing but wound myself by the use of my own weapons?

Such is stedfastly my opinion of the absolute necessity of keeping up the concord of this empire by a unity of spirit, though in a diversity of operations, that, if I were sure the colonists had at their leaving this country sealed a regular compact of servitude, that they had solemnly abjured all the rights of citizens, that they had made a vow to renounce all ideas of liberty for them and their posterity to all generations, yet I should hold myself obliged to conform to the temper I found universally prevalent in my own day, and to govern two millions of men, impatient of servitude, on the principles of freedom. I am not determining a point of law; I am restoring tranquillity—and the general character and situation of a people must determine what sort of government is fitted for them. That point nothing else can or ought to determine.

My idea, therefore, without considering whether we yield as matter of right, or grant as matter of favour, is *to admit the people of our colonies into an interest in the constitution*; and, by recording that admission in the journals of Parliament, to give them as strong an assurance as the nature of the thing will admit that we mean for ever to adhere to that solemn declaration of systematic indulgence.

Some years ago the repeal of a revenue Act, upon its understood principle, might have served to show that we intended an unconditional abatement of the exercise of taxing power. Such a measure was then sufficient to remove all suspicion and to give perfect content. But unfortunate events since that time may make something further necessary; and not more necessary for the satisfaction of the colonies than for the dignity and consistency of our own future proceedings.

I have taken a very incorrect measure of the disposition of the House if this proposal in itself would be received with dislike. I think, Sir, we have few American financiers. But our misfortune is we are too acute, we are too exquisite in our conjectures of the future, for men oppressed with such great and present evils. The more moderate among the opposers of parliamentary concession freely confess that they hope no good from taxation; but they apprehend the colonists have further views, and if this point were conceded, they would instantly attack the trade laws. These gentlemen are convinced that this was the intention from the beginning, and the quarrel of the Americans with taxation was no more than a cloak and cover to this design. Such has been the language of a gentleman of real moderation, and of a natural temper well adjusted to fair and equal government.[11] I am, however, Sir, not a little surprised at this kind of discourse whenever I hear it; and I am the more surprised on account of the arguments which I constantly find in company with it, and which are often urged from the same mouths and on the same day.

For instance, when we allege that it is against reason to tax a people under so many restraints in trade as the Americans, the noble lord[12] in the blue riband shall tell you that the restraints on trade are futile and useless; of no advantage to us and of no burthen to those on whom they are imposed; that the trade to America is not secured by the Acts of Navigation, but by the natural and irresistible advantage of a commercial preference.

Such is the merit of the trade laws in this posture of the debate. But when strong internal circumstances are urged against the taxes, when the scheme is dissected, when experience and the nature of things are brought to prove, and do prove, the utter impossibility of obtaining an effective revenue from the colonies—when these things are pressed, or rather press themselves, so as to drive the advocates of colony taxes to a clear admission of the futility of the scheme, then, Sir, the sleeping trade laws revive from their trance, and this useless taxation is to be kept sacred, not for its

[11] George Rice.
[12] Lord North.

own sake, but as a counter-guard and security of the laws of trade.

Then, Sir, you keep up revenue laws which are mischievous, in order to preserve trade laws that are useless. Such is the wisdom of our plan in both its members. They are separately given up as of no value; and yet one is always to be defended for the sake of the other. But I cannot agree with the noble lord, nor with the pamphlet from whence he seems to have borrowed these ideas, concerning the inutility of the trade laws. For, without idolising them, I am sure they are still, in many ways, of great use to us; and in former times they have been of the greatest. They do confine, and they do greatly narrow, the market for the Americans. But my perfect conviction of this does not help me in the least to discern how the revenue laws form any security whatsoever to the commercial regulations, or that these commercial regulations are the true ground of the quarrel, or that the giving way, in any one instance of authority, is to lose all that may remain unconceded.

One fact is clear and indisputable. The public and avowed origin of this quarrel was on taxation. This quarrel has indeed brought on new disputes on new questions, but certainly the least bitter, and the fewest of all, on the trade laws. To judge which of the two be the real, radical cause of quarrel we have to see whether the commercial dispute did, in order of time, precede the dispute on taxation? There is not a shadow of evidence for it. Next, to enable us to judge whether at this moment a dislike to the trade laws be the real cause of quarrel, it is absolutely necessary to put the taxes out of the question by a repeal. See how the Americans act in this position, and then you will be able to discern correctly what is the true object of the controversy, or whether any controversy at all will remain. Unless you consent to remove this cause of difference it is impossible, with decency, to assert that the dispute is not upon what it is avowed to be. And I would, Sir, recommend to your serious consideration whether it be prudent to form a rule for punishing people, not on their own acts, but on your conjectures? Surely it is preposterous at the very best. It is not justifying your anger by their misconduct, but it is converting your ill-will into their delinquency.

But the colonies will go further. Alas! alas! when will this speculating against fact and reason end? What will quiet these panic fears which we entertain of the hostile effect of a conciliatory conduct? Is it true that no case can exist in which it is proper for the sovereign to accede to the desires of his discontented subjects? Is there anything peculiar in this case to make a rule for itself? Is all authority of course lost when it is not pushed to the extreme? Is it a certain maxim that the fewer causes of dissatisfaction are left by Government the more the subject will be inclined to resist and rebel?

All these objections being in fact no more than suspicions, conjectures, divinations, formed in defiance of fact and experience, they did not, Sir, discourage me from entertaining the idea of a conciliatory concession, founded on the principles which I have just stated.

. . . I am sure that I shall not be misled when, in a case of constitutional difficulty, I consult the genius of the English constitution. Consulting at that oracle (it was with all due humility and piety) I found four capital examples in a similar case before me, those of Ireland, Wales, Chester, and Durham.

Ireland, before the English conquest, though never governed by a despotic power, had no Parliament. How far the English Parliament itself was at that time modelled according to the present form is disputed among antiquarians. But we have all the reason in the world to be assured that a form of parliament, such as England then enjoyed, she instantly communicated to Ireland, and we are equally sure that almost every successive improvement in constitutional liberty as fast as it was made here was transmitted thither. . . . It was not English arms but the English constitution that conquered Ireland. From that time Ireland has ever had a general Parliament, as she had before a partial Parliament. You changed the people, you altered the religion, but you never touched the form or the vital substance of free government in that kingdom. You deposed kings, you restored them, you altered the succession to theirs as well as to your own crown, but you never altered their constitution, the principle of which was respected by usurpation, restored with the restoration of monarchy, and established, I trust, for ever by the glorious Revolution. This has made Ireland the great and flourishing kingdom that it is; and from a disgrace and a burthen intolerable to this nation has rendered her a principal part of our strength and ornament. This country cannot be said to have ever formally taxed her. The irregular things done in the confusion of mighty troubles and on the hinge of great revolutions, even if all were done that is said to have been done, form no example. If they have any effect in argument they make an exception to prove the rule. None of your own liberties could stand a moment if the casual deviations from them at such times were suffered to be used as proofs of their nullity. By the lucrative amount of such casual breaches in the constitution judge what the stated and fixed rule of supply has been in that kingdom. Your Irish pensioners would starve if they had no other fund to live on than taxes granted by English authority. Turn your eyes to those popular grants from whence all your great supplies are come, and learn to respect that only source of public wealth in the British empire.

My next example is Wales. This country was said to be reduced by Henry the Third. It was said more truly to be so by Edward the First. But though then conquered it was not looked upon as any part of the realm of England. Its old constitution, whatever that might have been, was destroyed, and no good one was substituted in its place. The care of that tract was put into the hands of lords marchers—a form of government of a very singular kind, a strange heterogeneous monster, something between hostility and government; perhaps it has a sort of resemblance, according to the modes of those times, to that of commander-in-chief at present, to whom all civil power is granted as secondary. The manners of the Welsh nation followed the genius of the government; the people were ferocious, restive, savage, and uncultivated, sometimes composed, never pacified. Wales within itself was in perpetual disorder, and it kept the frontier of England in perpetual alarm. Benefits from it to the state there were none. Wales was only known to England by incursion and invasion.

Sir, during that state of things, Parliament was not idle. They attempted to subdue the fierce spirit of the Welsh by all sorts of rigorous laws. They prohibited by statute the sending of all sorts of arms into Wales, as you prohibit by proclamation (with something more of doubt on the legality) the sending arms to America. They disarmed the Welsh by statute, as you attempted (but still with more questions on the legality) to disarm New England by an instruction. They made an Act to drag offenders from Wales into England for trial, as you have done (but with more hardship) with regard to America. By another Act, where one of the parties was an Englishman, they ordained that his trial should be always by English. They made Acts to restrain trade, as you do; and they prevented the Welsh from the use of fairs and markets, as you do the Americans from fisheries and foreign ports. In short, when the statute book was not quite so much swelled as it is now, you find no less than fifteen Acts of penal regulation on the subject of Wales.

Here we rub our hands—A fine body of precedents for the authority of Parliament and the use of it! I admit it fully; and pray add likewise to these precedents that all the while Wales rid this kingdom like an incubus; that it was an unprofitable and oppressive burthen; and that an Englishman travelling in that country could not go six yards from the high-road without being murdered.

The march of the human mind is slow. Sir, it was not until after two hundred years discovered that, by an eternal law, Providence had decreed vexation to violence and poverty to rapine. Your ancestors did, however, at length open their eyes to the ill husbandry of injustice. They found that the tyranny of a free people could of all tyrannies the least be endured, and that laws made against a whole nation were not the most effectual methods for securing its obedience. Accordingly, in the twenty-seventh year of Henry VIII, the course was entirely altered. With a preamble stating the entire and perfect rights of the crown of England, it gave to the Welsh all the rights and privileges of English subjects. A political order was established; the military power gave way to the civil; the marches were turned into counties. But that a nation should have a right to English liberties and yet no share at all in the fundamental security of these liberties—the grant of their own property—seemed a thing so incongruous that, eight years after, that is, in the thirty-fifth of that reign, a complete and not ill-proportioned representation by counties and boroughs was bestowed upon Wales by Act of Parliament. From that moment, as by a charm, the tumults subsided, obedience was restored, peace, order, and civilisation followed in the train of liberty. . . .

The very same year the county palatine of Chester received the same relief from its oppressions and the same remedy to its disorders. Before this time Chester was little less distempered than Wales. The inhabitants, without rights themselves, were the fittest to destroy the rights of others; and from thence Richard II drew the standing army of archers with which for a time he oppressed England. The people of Chester applied to Parliament in a petition penned as I shall read to you:

"To the king our sovereign lord, in most humble wise shown unto your excellent Majesty, the inhabitants of your Grace's county palatine of Chester: That where the said county palatine of Chester is and has been always hitherto exempt, excluded, and separated out and from your high court of Parliament, to have any knights and burgesses within the said court; by reason whereof the said inhabitants have hitherto sustained manifold disherisons, losses, and damages, as well in their lands, goods, and bodies, as in the good, civil, and politic governance and maintenance of the commonwealth of their said country: (2.) And forasmuch as the said inhabitants have always hitherto been bound by the acts and statutes made and ordained by your said Highness and your most noble progenitors, by authority of the said court, as far forth as other counties, cities, and boroughs have been, that have had their knights and burgesses within your said court of Parliament, and yet have had neither knight ne burgess there for the said county palatine; the said inhabitants, for lack thereof, have been oftentimes touched and grieved with acts and statutes made within the said court, as well derogatory unto the most ancient jurisdictions, liberties, and privileges of your said county palatine, as prejudicial unto the commonwealth, quietness, rest, and peace of your Grace's most bounden subjects inhabiting within the same."

What did Parliament with this audacious address?—Reject it as a libel? Treat it as an affront to Government? Spurn it as a derogation from the rights of legislature? Did they toss it over the table? Did they burn it by the hands of the common hangman? They took the petition of grievance, all rugged as it was, without softening or temperament, unpurged of the original bitterness and indignation of complaint; they made it the very preamble to their Act of address, and consecrated its principle to all ages in the sanctuary of legislation.

Here is my third example. It was attended with the success of the two former. Chester, civilised as well as Wales, has demonstrated that freedom, and not servitude, is the cure of anarchy; as religion, and not atheism, is the true remedy for superstition. Sir, this pattern of Chester was followed in the reign of Charles II with regard to the county palatine of Durham, which is my fourth example. This county had long lain out of the pale of free legislation. So scrupulously was the example of Chester followed that the style of the preamble is nearly the same with that of the

Chester Act; and, without affecting the abstract extent of the authority of Parliament, it recognizes the equity of not suffering any considerable district, in which the British subjects may act as a body, to be taxed without their own voice in the grant.

Now if the doctrines of policy contained in these preambles, and the force of these examples in the Acts of Parliament, avail anything, what can be said against applying them with regard to America? Are not the people of America as much Englishmen as the Welsh? The preamble of the Act of Henry VIII says the Welsh speak a language no way resembling that of his Majesty's English subjects. Are the Americans not as numerous? If we may trust the learned and accurate Judge Barrington's account of North Wales, and take that as a standard to measure the rest, there is no comparison. The people cannot account to above 200,000; not a tenth part of the number in the colonies. Is America in rebellion? Wales was hardly ever free from it. Have you attempted to govern America by penal statutes? You made fifteen for Wales. But your legislative authority is perfect with regard to America; was it less perfect in Wales, Chester, and Durham? But America is virtually represented. What! does the electric force of virtual representation more easily pass over the Atlantic than pervade Wales, which lies in your neighbourhood; or than Chester and Durham, surrounded by abundance of representation that is actual and palpable? But, Sir, your ancestors thought this sort of virtual representation, however ample, to be totally insufficient for the freedom of the inhabitants of territories that are so near, and comparatively so inconsiderable. How then can I think it sufficient for those which are infinitely greater, and infinitely more remote?

You will now, Sir, perhaps imagine, that I am on the point of proposing to you a scheme for a representation of the colonies in Parliament. Perhaps I might be inclined to entertain some such thought; but a great flood stops me in my course. *Opposuit natura* —I cannot remove the eternal barriers of the creation. The thing, in that mode, I do not know to be possible. . . .

Fortunately I am not obliged for the ways and means of [a] substitute to tax my own unproductive invention. I am not even obliged to go to the rich treasury of the fertile framers of imaginary commonwealths; not to the Republic of Plato; not to the Utopia of More; not to the Oceana of Harrington. It is before me—it is at my feet, *and the rude swain treads daily on it with his clouted shoon.* I only wish you to recognise, for the theory, the ancient constitutional policy of this kingdom with regard to representation, as that policy has been declared in Acts of Parliament; and, as to the practice, to return to that mode which an uniform experience has marked out to you as best, and in which you walked with security, advantage, and honour until the year 1763.

My resolutions therefore mean to establish the equity and justice of a taxation of America by *grant*, and not by *imposition*. To mark the *legal competency* of the colony assemblies for the support of their government in peace, and for public aids in time of war. To acknowledge that this legal competency has had *a dutiful and beneficial exercise*; and that experience has shown the *benefit of their grants*, and the *futility of parliamentary taxation as a method of supply*.

These solid truths compose six fundamental propositions. There are three more resolutions corrollary to these. If you admit the first set, you can hardly reject the others. But if you admit the first, I shall be far from solicitous whether you accept or refuse the last. I think these six massive pillars will be of strength sufficient to support the temple of British concord. I have no more doubt than I entertain of my existence that, if you admitted these, you would command an immediate peace, and, with but tolerable future management, a lasting obedience in America. I am not arrogant in this confident assurance. The propositions are all mere matters of fact; and if they are such facts as draw irresistible conclusions even in the stating, this is the power of truth and not any management of mine.

Sir, I shall open the whole plan to you, together with such observations on the motions as may tend to illustrate them where they may want explanation. The first is a resolution: "That the colonies and plantations of Great Britain in North America, consisting of fourteen separate governments, and containing two millions and upwards of free inhabitants, have not had the liberty and privilege of electing and sending any knights and burgesses, or others, to represent them in the high court of Parliament." This is a plain matter of fact, necessary to be laid down, and (excepting the description) it is laid down in the language of the constitution; it is taken nearly *verbatim* from Acts of Parliament.

The second is like unto the first: "That the said colonies and plantations have been liable to, and bounden by, several subsidies, payments, rates, and taxes, given and granted by Parliament, though the said colonies and plantations have not their knights and burgesses in the said high court of Parliament, of their own election, to represent the condition of their country; by lack whereof they have been oftentimes touched and grieved by subsidies given, granted, and assented to, in the said court, in a manner prejudicial to the commonwealth, quietness, rest, and peace of the subjects inhabiting within the same."

Is this description too hot, or too cold, too strong, or too weak? Does it arrogate too much to the supreme legislature? Does it lean too much to the claims of the people? If it runs into any of these errors, the fault is not mine. It is the language of your own ancient Acts of Parliament.

> "Non meus hic sermo, sed quæ præcepit Ofellus,
> Rusticus, abnormis sapiens."[13]

It is the genuine produce of the ancient, rustic, manly, home-bred sense of this country. I did not dare to rub off a particle of the venerable rust that rather adorns and preserves than destroys the metal. It would be a profanation to touch with a tool the stones which construct the sacred altar of peace. I would not violate with modern polish the ingenuous and noble roughness of these truly constitutional materials. Above all things, I was resolved not to be guilty of tampering—the odious vice of restless and unstable minds. I put my foot in the tracks of our forefathers, where I can neither wander nor stumble. . . .

There are indeed words expressive of grievance in this second resolution, which those who are resolved always to be in the right will deny to contain matter of fact, as applied to the present case, although Parliament thought them true with regard to the counties of Chester and Durham. They will deny that the Americans were ever "touched and grieved" with the taxes. If they consider nothing in taxes but their weight as pecuniary impositions, there might be some pretence for this denial. But men may be sorely touched and deeply grieved in their privileges as well as in their purses. Men may lose little in property by the act which takes away all their freedom. When a man is robbed of a trifle on the

[13]   *"Ofellus shall set forth,*
'Twas he that taught me it, a shrewd clear wit,
Though country bred, and for the schools unfit."
                              —HORACE, *Serm.* ii. 2, 3.

highway, it is not the twopence lost that constitutes the capital outrage. This is not confined to privileges. Even ancient indulgences withdrawn without offence on the part of those who enjoyed such favours operate as grievances. But were the Americans then not touched and grieved by the taxes, in some measure, merely as taxes? If so, why were they almost all either wholly repealed or exceedingly reduced? Were they not touched and grieved even by the regulating duties of the sixth of George II? Else why were the duties first reduced to one third in 1764, and afterwards to a third of that third in the year 1766? Were they not touched and grieved by the Stamp Act? I shall say they were until that tax is revived. Were they not touched and grieved by the duties of 1767, which were likewise repealed, and which Lord Hillsborough tells you (for the Ministry) were laid contrary to the true principle of commerce? Is not the assurance given by that noble person to the colonies of a resolution to lay no more taxes on them an admission that taxes would touch and grieve them? Is not the resolution of the noble lord in the blue riband, now standing on your journals, the strongest of all proofs that parliamentary subsidies really touched and grieved them? Else why all these changes, modifications, repeals, assurances, and resolutions?

The next proposition is: "That, from the distance of the said colonies, and from other circumstances, no method hath hitherto been devised for procuring a representation in Parliament for the said colonies." This is an assertion of a fact. I go no further on the paper, though, in my private judgment, an useful representation is impossible; I am sure it is not desired by them, nor ought it perhaps by us—but I abstain from opinions.

The fourth resolution is: "That each of the said colonies hath within itself a body, chosen in part or in the whole by the freemen, freeholders, or other free inhabitants thereof, commonly called the general assembly, or general court, with powers legally to raise, levy, and assess, according to the several usage of such colonies, duties and taxes towards defraying all sorts of public services."

This competence in the colony assemblies is certain. It is proved by the whole tenor of their Acts of supply in all the assemblies, in which the constant style of granting is an "aid to his Majesty"; and Acts granting to the crown have regularly for near a century passed the public offices without dispute. Those who have been pleased paradoxically to deny this right, holding that none but the British Parliament can grant to the crown, are wished to look to what is done, not only in the colonies, but in Ireland, in one uniform unbroken tenor every session. Sir, I am surprised that this doctrine should come from some of the law servants of the crown. I say, that if the crown could be responsible, his Majesty— but certainly the ministers, and even these law officers themselves through whose hands the Acts pass biennially in Ireland, or annually in the colonies, are in an habitual course of committing impeachable offences. What habitual offenders have been all presidents of the council, all secretaries of state, all first lords of trade, all attorneys, and all solicitors-general! However, they are safe, as no one impeaches them; and there is no ground of charge against them except in their own unfounded theories.

The fifth resolution is also a resolution of fact: "That the said general assemblies, general courts, or other bodies legally qualified as aforesaid, have at sundry times freely granted several large subsidies and public aids for his Majesty's service, according to their abilities, when required thereto by letter from one of his Majesty's principal secretaries of state; and that their right to grant the same, and their cheerfulness and sufficiency in the said grants, have been at sundry times acknowledged by Parliament." To say nothing of their great expenses in the Indian wars; and not to take their exertion in foreign ones, so high as the supplies in the year 1695; not to go back to their public contributions in the year 1710, I shall begin to travel only where the journals give me light, resolving to deal in nothing but fact, authenticated by parliamentary record, and to build, myself wholly on that solid basis. . . .[14]

Sir, here is the repeated acknowledgment of Parliament that the colonies not only gave but gave to satiety. This nation has formally acknowledged two things: first, that the colonies had gone beyond their abilities, Parliament having thought it necessary to reimburse them; secondly, that they had acted legally and laudably in their grants of money and their maintenance of troops, since the compensation is expressly given as reward and encouragement. Reward is not bestowed for acts that are unlawful, and

[14] He then mentioned a number of resolutions granting compensation. They are: April 4, 1748; January 28, February 3, 1756; May 16 and 19, 1757; June 1, 1758; April 26 and 30, 1759; March 26 and 31, April 28, 1760; January 9 and 20, 1761; January 22 and 26, 1762; and March 14 and 17, 1763.

encouragement is not held out to things that deserve reprehension. My resolution therefore does nothing more than collect into one proposition what is scattered through your journals. I give you nothing but your own, and you cannot refuse in the gross what you have so often acknowledged in detail. The admission of this, which will be so honourable to them and to you, will indeed be mortal to all the miserable stories by which the passions of the misguided people have been engaged in an unhappy system. The people heard, indeed, from the beginning of these disputes one thing continually dinned in their ears, that reason and justice demanded that the Americans, who paid no taxes, should be compelled to contribute. How did that fact of their paying nothing stand when the taxing system began? When Mr. Grenville began to form his system of American revenue, he stated in this House that the colonies were then in debt two million six hundred thousand pounds sterling money, and was of opinion they would discharge that debt in four years. On this state those untaxed people were actually subject to the payment of taxes to the amount of six hundred and fifty thousand a year. In fact, however, Mr. Grenville was mistaken. The funds given for sinking the debt did not prove quite so ample as both the colonies and he expected. The calculation was too sanguine; the reduction was not completed till some years after, and at different times in different colonies. However, the taxes after the war continued too great to bear any addition with prudence or propriety; and when the burthens imposed in consequence of former requisitions were discharged our tone became too high to resort again to requisition. No colony since that time ever has had any requisition whatsoever made to it.

We see the sense of the crown and the sense of Parliament on the productive nature of a *revenue by grant*. Now search the same journals for the produce of the *revenue by imposition*. Where is it?—let us know the volume and the page; what is the gross, what is the net produce? to what service is it applied? how have you appropriated its surplus? What, can none of the many skilful index-makers that we are now employing find any trace of it? Well, let them and that rest together. But are the journals which say nothing of the revenue as silent on the discontent? Oh no! a child may find it. It is the melancholy burthen and blot of every page.

I think then I am, from those journals, justified in the sixth and last resolution, which is: "That it hath been found by experience that the manner of granting the said supplies and aids, by the said general assemblies, hath been more agreeable to the said colonies and more beneficial and conducive to the public service than the mode of giving and granting aids in Parliament, to be raised and paid in the said colonies." This makes the whole of the fundamental part of the plan. The conclusion is irresistible. You cannot say that you were driven by any necessity to an exercise of the utmost rights of legislature. You cannot assert that you took on yourselves the task of imposing colony taxes from the want of another legal body that is competent to the purpose of supplying the exigencies of the state without wounding the prejudices of the people. Neither is it true that the body so qualified, and having that competence, had neglected the duty.

The question now, on all this accumulated matter, is, whether you will choose to abide by a profitable experience, or a mischievous theory; whether you choose to build on imagination or fact; whether you prefer enjoyment or hope; satisfaction in your subjects or discontent?

If these propositions are accepted, everything which has been made to enforce a contrary system must, I take it for granted, fall along with it. On that ground I have drawn the following resolution, which, when it comes to be moved, will naturally be divided in a proper manner: "That it may be proper to repeal an Act, made in the seventh year of the reign of his present Majesty, intituled, An Act for granting certain duties in the British colonies and plantations in America; for allowing a drawback of the duties of customs upon the exportation from this kingdom of coffee and cocoanuts of the produce of the said colonies or plantations; for discontinuing the drawbacks payable on China earthenware exported to America; and for more effectually preventing the clandestine running of goods in the said colonies and plantations. And that it may be proper to repeal an Act, made in the fourteenth year of the reign of his present Majesty, intituled, An Act to discontinue, in such manner and for such time as are therein mentioned, the landing and discharging, lading or shipping, of goods, wares, and merchandise at the town and within the harbour of Boston, in the province of Massachusetts Bay, in North America. And that it may be proper to repeal an Act, made in the fourteenth year of the reign of his present Majesty, intituled, An Act for the impartial administration of justice in the cases of persons questioned for any acts done by them in the execution of the law, or for the suppression of riots and tumults, in the province of Massachusetts Bay, in New England. And that it may be proper to repeal an Act, made in the fourteenth year of the reign of his present Majesty, intituled, An Act for the better regulating the government of the province of Massachusetts Bay, in New England. And, also, that it may be proper to explain and amend an Act, made in the thirty-fifth year of the reign of King Henry the Eighth, intituled, An Act for the trial of treasons committed out of the king's dominions."

I wish, Sir, to repeal the Boston Port Bill, because (independently of the dangerous precedent of suspending the rights of the subject during the king's pleasure) it was passed, as I apprehend, with less regularity and on more partial principles than it ought. The corporation of Boston was not heard before it was condemned. Other towns, full as guilty as she was, have not had their ports blocked up. Even the restraining bill of the present session does not go to the length of the Boston Port Act. The same ideas of prudence, which induced you not to extend equal punishment to equal guilt, even when you were punishing, induced me, who mean not to chastise but to reconcile, to be satisfied with the punishment already partially inflicted.

Ideas of prudence and accommodation to circumstances prevent you from taking away the charters of Connecticut and Rhode Island, as you have taken away that of Massachusetts colony, though the crown has far less power in the two former provinces than it enjoyed in the latter, and though the abuses have been full as great and as flagrant in the exempted as in the punished. The same reasons of prudence and accommodation have weight with me in restoring the charter of Massachusetts Bay. Besides, Sir, the Act which changes the charter of Massachusetts is in many particulars so exceptionable, that if I did not wish absolutely to repeal I would by all means desire to alter it, as several of its provisions tend to the subversion of all public and private justice. Such, among others, is the power in the governor to change the sheriff at his pleasure, and to make a new returning officer for every special cause. It is shameful to behold such a regulation standing among English laws.

The Act for bringing persons accused of committing murder under the orders of Government to England for trial is but temporary. That Act has calculated the probable duration of our quarrel with the colonies, and is accommodated to that supposed duration. I would hasten the happy moment of reconciliation, and therefore must, on my principle, get rid of that most justly obnoxious Act.

The Act of Henry the Eighth for the trial of treasons I do not mean to take away, but to confine it to its proper bounds and original intention; to make it expressly for trial of treasons (and the greatest treasons may be committed) in places where the jurisdiction of the crown does not extend.

Having guarded the privileges of local legislature, I would next secure to the colonies a fair and unbiassed judicature; for which purpose, Sir, I propose the following resolution: "That, from the time when the general assembly or general court of any colony or plantation in North America shall have appointed by Act of Assembly, duly confirmed, a settled salary to the offices of the chief justice and other judges of the superior court, it may be proper that the said chief justice and other judges of the superior courts of such colony shall hold his and their office and offices during their good behaviour; and shall not be removed therefrom, but when the said removal shall be adjudged by his Majesty in council, upon a hearing on complaint from the general assembly, or on a complaint from the governor or council, or the House of Representatives severally, or of the colony in which the said chief justice and other judges have exercised the said offices."

The next resolution relates to the courts of Admiralty.

It is this: "That it may be proper to regulate the courts of Admiralty or Vice-Admiralty, authorised by the fifteenth chapter of the fourth of George the Third, in such a manner as to make the same more commodious to those who sue, or are sued, in the said courts, and to provide for the more decent maintenance of the judges in the same."

These courts I do not wish to take away; they are in themselves proper establishments. This court is one of the capital securities of the Act of Navigation. The extent of its jurisdiction, indeed, has been increased; but this is altogether as proper, and is indeed on many accounts more eligible where new powers were wanted, than a court absolutely new. But courts incommodiously situated in effect deny justice; and a court partaking in the fruits of its own condemnation is a robber. The Congress complain, and complain justly, of this grievance.

These are the three consequential propositions. I have thought of two or three more, but they come rather too near detail, and to the province of executive government, which I wish Parliament always to superintend, never to assume. If the first six are granted, congruity will carry the latter three. If not, the things that remain unrepealed will be, I hope, rather unseemly encumbrances on the building than very materially detrimental to its strength and stability.

Here, Sir, I should close, but I plainly perceive some objections remain, which I ought, if possible, to remove. The first will be that, in resorting to the doctrine of our ancestors, as contained in the preamble to the Chester Act, I prove too much; that the grievance from a want of representation, stated in that preamble, goes to the whole of legislation as well as to taxation. And that the colonies, grounding themselves upon that doctrine, will apply it to all parts of legislative authority.

To this objection, with all possible deference and humility, and wishing as little as any man living to impair the smallest particle of our supreme authority, I answer, that *the words are the words of Parliament and not mine*; and that all false and inconclusive inferences drawn from them are not mine, for I heartily disclaim any such inference. I have chosen the words of an Act of Parliament, which Mr. Grenville, surely a tolerably zealous and very judicious advocate for the sovereignty of Parliament, formerly moved to have read at your table in confirmation of his tenets. It is true that Lord Chatham considered these preambles as declaring strongly in favor of his opinions. He was a no less powerful advocate for the privileges of the Americans. Ought I not from hence to presume that these preambles are as favourable as possible to both, when properly understood; favourable both to the rights of Parliament and to the privilege of the dependencies of this crown? But, Sir, the object of grievance in my resolution I have not taken from the Chester, but from the Durham Act, which confines the hardship of want of representation to the case of subsidies, and which, therefore, falls in exactly with the case of the colonies. But whether the unrepresented counties were *de jure*, or *de facto*, bound, the preambles do not accurately distinguish; nor indeed was it necessary, for whether *de jure* or *de facto* the legislature thought the exercise of the power of taxing as of right, or as of fact without right, equally a grievance and equally oppressive.

I do not know that the colonies have, in any general way, or in any cool hour, gone much beyond the demand of immunity in relation to taxes. It is not fair to judge of the temper or dispositions of any man or any set of men, when they are composed and at rest from their conduct, or their expressions in a state of disturbance and irritation. It is besides a very great mistake to imagine that mankind follow up practically any speculative principle, either of government or of freedom, as far as it will go in argument and logical illation. We Englishmen stop very short of the principles upon which we support any given part of our constitution, or even the whole of it together. I could easily, if I had not already tired you, give you very striking and convincing instances of it. This is nothing but what is natural and proper. All government, indeed every human benefit and enjoyment, every virtue, and every prudent act, is founded on compromise and barter. We balance inconveniences, we give and take, we remit some rights that we may enjoy others, and we choose rather to be happy citizens than subtle disputants. As we must give away some natural liberty to enjoy civil advantages, so we must sacrifice some civil liberties for the advantages to be derived from the communion and fellowship of a great empire. But in all fair dealings the thing bought must bear some proportion to the purchase paid. . . . In every arduous enterprise we consider what we are to lose as well as what we are to gain, and the more and better stake of liberty every people possess the less they will hazard in a vain attempt to make it more. These are *the cords of man.* Man acts from adequate motives relative to his interest, and not on metaphysical speculations. Aristotle, the great master of reasoning, cautions us, and with great weight and propriety, against this species of delusive geometrical accuracy in moral arguments as the most fallacious of all sophistry.

The Americans will have no interest contrary to the grandeur and glory of England, when they are not oppressed by the weight of it; and they will rather be inclined to respect the acts of a superintending legislature, when they see them the acts of that power which is itself he security, not the rival, of their secondary importance. In this assurance my mind most perfectly acquiesces; and I confess I feel not the least alarm from the discontents which are to arise from putting people at their ease, nor do I apprehend the destruction of this empire from giving, by an act of free grace and indulgence, to two millions of my fellow citizens some share of those rights upon which I have always been taught to value myself.

It is said, indeed, that this power of granting, vested in American assemblies, would dissolve the unity of the empire, which was preserved entire, although Wales, and Chester, and Durham were added to it. Truly, Mr. Speaker, I do not know what this unity means, nor has it ever been heard of, that I know, in the constitutional policy of this country. The very idea of subordination of parts excludes this notion of simple and undivided unity. England is the head; but she is not the head and the members too. Ireland has ever had from the beginning a separate, but not an independent, legislature, which, far from distracting, promoted the union of the whole. Everything was sweetly and harmoniously disposed through both islands for the conservation of English dominion and the communication of English liberties. I do not see that the same principles might not be carried into twenty islands, and with the same good effect. This is my model with regard to America, as far as the internal circumstances of the two countries are the same. I know no other unity of this empire than I can draw from its example during these periods, when it seemed to my poor understanding more united than it is now, or than it is likely to be by the present methods.

But since I speak of these methods I recollect, Mr. Speaker, almost too late, that I promised before I finished to say something of the proposition of the noble lord on the floor, which has been so lately received, and stands on your journals.[15] I must be deeply concerned whenever it is my misfortune to continue a difference with the majority of this House. But as the reasons for that difference are my apology for thus troubling you, suffer me to state them in a very few words. I shall compress them into as small a body as I possibly can, having already debated that matter at large when the question was before the committee. First, then, I cannot admit that proposition of a ransom by auction—because it is a mere project. It is a thing new, unheard of, supported by no experience, justified by no analogy, without example of our ancestors or root in the constitution.

It is neither regular parliamentary taxation, nor colony grant. *Experimentum in corpore vili*,[16] is a good rule, which will ever make me adverse to any trial of experiments on what is certainly the most valuable of all subjects, the peace of this empire.

---

[15] This refers to Lord North's plan of reconciliation, presented to the Commons in February, 1775, which reaffirmed Parliament's supremacy but offered to refrain from taxing those colonies that granted requisitions requested by England.

[16] "Experiment on an inferior body or object."

Secondly, it is an experiment which must be fatal in the end to our constitution. For what is it but a scheme for taxing the colonies in the antechamber of the noble lord and his successors? To settle the quotas and proportions in this House is clearly impossible. You, Sir, may flatter yourself you shall sit a state auctioneer, with your hammer in your hand, and knock down to each colony as it bids. But to settle (on the plan laid down by the noble lord) the true proportional payment for four or five and twenty governments, according to the absolute and the relative wealth of each, and according to the British proportion of wealth and burthen, is a wild and chimerical notion. This new taxation must therefore come in by the backdoor of the constitution. Each quota must be brought to this House ready formed; you can neither add nor alter. You must register it. You can do nothing further. For on what grounds can you deliberate either before or after the proposition? You cannot hear the counsel for all these provinces, quarrelling each on its own quantity of payment and its proportion to others. If you should attempt it, the committee of provincial ways and means, or by whatever other name it will delight to be called, must swallow up all the time of Parliament.

Thirdly, it does not give satisfaction to the complaint of the colonies. They complain that they are taxed without their consent; you answer that you will fix the sum at which they shall be taxed. That is you give them the very grievance for the remedy. You tell them indeed that you will leave the mode to themselves. I really beg pardon—it gives me pain to mention it—but you must be sensible that you will not perform this part of the compact. For suppose the colonies were to lay the duties which furnished their contingent upon the importation of your manufactures, you know you would never suffer such a tax to be laid. You know, too, that you would not suffer many other modes of taxation. So that when you come to explain yourself it will be found that you will neither leave to themselves the quantum nor the mode, nor indeed anything. The whole is delusion from one end to the other.

Fourthly, this method of ransom by auction, unless it be *universally* accepted, will plunge you into great and inextricable difficulties. In what year of our Lord are the proportions of payments to be settled? To say nothing of the impossibility that colony agents should have general powers of taxing the colonies at their discretion, consider, I implore you, that the communication by special messages, and orders between these agents and their constituents on each variation of the case, when the parties come to contend together, and to dispute on their relative proportions, will be a matter of delay, perplexity, and confusion that never can have an end.

If all the colonies do not appear at the outcry, what is the condition of those assemblies who offer by themselves or their agents to tax themselves up to your ideas of their proportion? The refractory colonies, who refuse all composition, will remain taxed only to your old impositions, which, however grievous in principle, are trifling as to production. The obedient colonies in this scheme are heavily taxed; the refractory remain unburthened. What will you do? Will you lay new and heavier taxes by Parliament on the disobedient? Pray consider in what way you can do it. You are perfectly convinced that, in the way of taxing, you can do nothing but at the ports. Now suppose it is Virginia that refuses to appear at your auction, while Maryland and North Carolina bid handsomely for their ransom, and are taxed to your quota, how will you put these colonies on a par? Will you tax the tobacco of Virginia? If you do you give its death wound to your English revenue at home and to one of the very greatest articles of your own foreign trade. If you tax the import of that rebellious colony, what do you tax but your own manufactures, or the goods of some other obedient and already well-taxed colony? Who has said one word on this labyrinth of detail, which bewilders you more and more as you enter into it? Who has presented, who can present you with a clue to lead you out of it? I think, Sir, it is impossible that you should not recollect that the colony bounds are so implicated in one another (you know it by your other experiments in the bill for prohibiting the New England fishery), that you can lay no possible restraints on almost any of them which may not be presently eluded, if you do not confound the innocent with the guilty, and burthen those whom, upon every principle, you ought to exonerate. He must be grossly ignorant of America who thinks that, without falling into this confusion of all rules of equity and policy, you can restrain any single colony, especially Virginia and Maryland, the central and most important of them all.[17]

Let it also be considered that, either in the present confusion you settle a permanent contingent, which will and must be trifling,

[17] Referring to Governor Thomas Pownall, an authority on American affairs who supported North's plan of reconciliation (see immediately above, footnote 15). North, it should be noted, never planned or plotted any such "ransom" as Burke maintains.

and then you have no effectual revenue; or you change the quota at every exigency, and then on every new repartition you will have a new quarrel.

Reflect, besides, that when you have fixed a quota for every colony, you have not provided for prompt and punctual payment. Suppose one, two, five, ten years' arrears. You cannot issue a treasury extent against the failing colony. You must make new Boston Port Bills, new restraining laws, new Acts for dragging men to England for trial. You must send out new fleets, new armies. All is to begin again. From this day forward the empire is never to know an hour's tranquillity. An intestine fire will be kept alive in the bowels of the colonies which one time or other must consume this whole empire. I allow indeed that the empire of Germany raises her revenue and her troops by quotas and contingents; but the revenue of the empire, and the army of the empire, is the worst revenue and the worst army in the world.

Instead of a standing revenue, you will therefore have a perpetual quarrel. Indeed the noble lord who proposed this project of a ransom by auction seemed himself to be of that opinion. His project was rather designed for breaking the union of the colonies than for establishing a revenue. He confessed he apprehended that his proposal would not be to *their taste*. I say this scheme of disunion seems to be at the bottom of the project; for I will not suspect that the noble lord meant nothing but merely to delude the nation by an airy phantom which he never intended to realise. But whatever his views may be, as I propose the peace and union of the colonies as the very foundation of my plan, it cannot accord with one whose foundation is perpetual discord.

Compare the two. This I offer to give you is plain and simple. The other full of perplexed and intricate mazes. This is mild; that harsh. This is found by experience effectual for its purposes; the other is a new project. This is universal; the other calculated for certain colonies only. This is immediate in its conciliatory operation; the other remote, contingent, full of hazard. Mine is what becomes the dignity of a ruling people; gratuitous, unconditional, and not held out as matter of bargain and sale. I have done my duty in proposing it to you. I have indeed tired you by a long discourse, but this is the misfortune of those to whose influence nothing will be conceded, and who must win every inch of their ground by argument. You have heard me with goodness. May you decide with wisdom! For my part I feel my mind greatly disburthened by what I have done to-day. I have been the less fearful of trying your patience because on this subject I mean to spare it altogether in future. I have this comfort that in every stage of the American affairs I have steadily opposed the measures that have produced the confusion and may bring on the destruction of this empire. I now go so far as to risk a proposal of my own. If I cannot give peace to my country I give it to my conscience.

But what (says the financier) is peace to us without money? Your plan gives us no revenue. No! But it does—For it secures to the subject the power of REFUSAL; the first of all revenues. Experience is a cheat, and fact a liar, if this power in the subject of proportioning his grant, or of not granting at all, has not been found the richest mine of revenue ever discovered by the skill or by the fortune of man. It does not indeed vote you £152,750 : 11 : 2¾ths, nor any other paltry limited sum. But it gives the strong box itself, the fund, the bank, from whence only revenues can arise amongst a people sensible of freedom: *Posita luditur arca*.[18] Cannot you in England; cannot you at this time of day; cannot you, a House of Commons, trust to the principle which has raised so mighty a revenue, and accumulated a debt of near 140 millions in this country? Is this principle to be true in England and false everywhere else? Is it not true in Ireland? Has it not hitherto been true in the colonies? Why should you presume that in any country a body duly constituted for any function will neglect to perform its duty and abdicate its trust? Such a presumption would go against all governments in all modes. But in truth this dread of penury of supply from a free assembly has no foundation in nature. For first observe that besides the desire which all men have naturally of supporting the honour of their own Government, that sense of dignity and that security to property which ever attends freedom has a tendency to increase the stock of the free community. Most may be taken where most is accumulated. And what is the soil or climate where experience has not uniformly proved that the voluntary flow of heaped-up plenty, bursting from the weight of its own rich luxuriance, has ever run with a more copious stream of revenue than could be squeezed from the dry husks of oppressed indigence, by the straining of all the politic machinery in the world.

. . . And so may I speed in the great object I propose to you, as I think it would not only be an act of injustice, but would be

---

[18] "Even the strong boxes were staked." Juvenal, I, 90.

the worst economy in the world to compel the colonies to a sum certain either in the way of ransom or in the way of compulsory compact.

But to clear up my ideas on this subject—a revenue from America transmitted hither—do not delude yourselves—you never can receive it—No, not a shilling. We have experience that from remote countries it is not to be expected. If, when you attempted to extract revenue from Bengal, you were obliged to return in loan what you had taken in imposition, what can you expect from North America? For certainly, if ever there was a country qualified to produce wealth, it is India; or an institution fit for the transmission, it is the East India Company. America has none of these aptitudes. If America gives you taxable objects on which you lay your duties here, and gives you at the same time a surplus by a foreign sale of her commodities to pay the duties on these objects which you tax at home, she has performed her part to the British revenue. But with regard to her own internal establishments, she may, I doubt not she will, contribute in moderation. I say in moderation, for she ought not to be permitted to exhaust herself. She ought to be reserved to a war, the weight of which, with the enemies that we are most likely to have, must be considerable in her quarter of the globe. There she may serve you, and serve you essentially.

For that service, for all service, whether of revenue, trade, or empire, my trust is in her interest in the British constitution. My hold of the colonies is in the close affection which grows from common names, from kindred blood, from similar privileges, and equal protection. These are ties which, though light as air, are as strong as links of iron. Let the colonies always keep the idea of their civil rights associated with your government; they will cling and grapple to you, and no force under heaven will be of power to tear them from their allegiance. But let it be once understood that your government may be one thing and their privileges another, that these two things may exist without any mutual relation; the cement is gone, the cohesion is loosened, and everything hastens to decay and dissolution. As long as you have the wisdom to keep the sovereign authority of this country as the sanctuary of liberty, the sacred temple consecrated to our common faith, wherever the chosen race and sons of England worship freedom, they will turn their faces towards you. The more they multiply, the more friends you will have; the more ardently they love liberty, the more perfect will be their obedience. Slavery they can

have anywhere. It is a weed that grows in every soil. They may
have it from Spain, they may have it from Prussia. But until you
become lost to all feeling of your true interest and your natural
dignity, freedom they can have from none but you. This is the
commodity of price of which you have the monopoly. This is
the true act of navigation which binds to you the commerce of the
colonies, and through them secures to you the wealth of the world.
Deny them this participation of freedom and you break that sole
bond which originally made and must still preserve the unity of
the empire. Do not entertain so weak an imagination as that your
registers and your bonds, your affidavits and your sufferances,
your cockets and your clearances are what form the great securities of your commerce. Do not dream that your letters of office,
and your instructions, and your suspending clauses are the things
that hold together the great contexture of the mysterious whole.
These things do not make your government. Dead instruments,
passive tools as they are, it is the spirit of the English communion
that gives all their life and efficacy to them. It is the spirit of the
English constitution which, infused through the mighty mass,
pervades, feeds, unites, invigorates, vivifies every part of the empire, even down to the minutest member. . . .

All this, I know well enough, will sound wild and chimerical to
the profane herd of those vulgar and mechanical politicians, who
have no place among us; a sort of people who think that nothing
exists but what is gross and material; and who, therefore, far
from being qualified to be directors of the great movement of
empire, are not fit to turn a wheel in the machine. But to men
truly initiated and rightly taught, these ruling and master principles which, in the opinion of such men as I have mentioned, have
no substantial existence, are in truth everything and all in all.
Magnanimity in politics is not seldom the truest wisdom; and a
great empire and little minds go ill together. If we are conscious
of our situation, and glow with zeal to fill our place as becomes
our station and ourselves, we ought to auspicate all our public
proceedings on America with the old warning of the Church,
Sursum corda! We ought to elevate our minds to the greatness of
that trust to which the order of Providence has called us. By ad-
verting to the dignity of this high calling, our ancestors have
turned a savage wilderness into a glorious empire, and have made
the most extensive, and the only honourable conquests, not by destroying, but by promoting the wealth, the number, the happiness

of the human race. Let us get an American revenue as we have got an American empire. English privileges have made it all that it is; English privileges alone will make it all it can be.

In full confidence of this unalterable truth, I now (*quod felix faustumque sit*) lay the first stone of the temple of peace; and I move you—

"That the colonies and plantations of Great Britain in North America, consisting of fourteen separate governments, and containing two millions and upwards of free inhabitants, have not had the liberty and privilege of electing and sending any knights and burgesses, or others, to represent them in the High Court of Parliament."

7

SPEECH UPON PRESENTATION OF A BILL FOR COMPOSING THE PRESENT TROUBLES . . . IN AMERICA

NOVEMBER 16, 1775[1]

Burke's first scheme for Conciliation had been defeated. Since then news of the battles at Lexington and Concord had arrived and the King had declared the colonies to be in a state of rebellion (August, 1775). Burke had suggested several schemes to Rockingham and other friends for bringing everyone to their senses, but these had all been rejected. Burke was determined to make one last plea for conciliation and gave this less well known but very important speech on conciliation shortly after Parliament reconvened. He then began by presenting a petition from "The gentlemen, clergy, clothiers, manufacturers, and others, inhabitants of . . . Westbury, Warminster, and Trowbridge," etc., emphasizing the adverse effects of the restrictions on American trade on their own businesses and appealing for leniency. It was tabled but Burke continued.

M R. BURKE then rose. He said, that the signers were all men who manufactured for themselves; and he was authorized to say that they possessed more than 500,000 £. of English property. He wished the prayer of that petition to be considered as the exordium of what he had to say to the House. He complained of the difficulties which in civil wars lay upon moderate men who advised lenient measures; that their moderation was attributed to a want of zeal and their fears for the public safety to a want

[1] John Almon, *The Parliamentary Register*, III, 170-82, reprinted *PH*, XVIII, 963-82; *Gentleman's Magazine*, XLVI, 51-53.

of spirit; that on this particular occasion whatever they said to incline the House to lenity was construed into a countenance of rebellion; and so many arts and so many menaces had been used that if they had not been opposed with a good share of firmness by the friends to the peace of their country, all freedom of debate, and indeed all public deliberation, would have been put an end to.

He said that for his part he was no way intimidated by all these machinations from doing his duty; and that nothing that could be threatened by those whose measures had brought this country into so deplorable a situation, should hinder him from using his best endeavours to deliver it from its distresses.

The first step for this purpose was to get out of general discourse and vague sentiments, which had been one of the main causes of our present troubles, and to appreciate the value of the several plans that were, or might be proposed, by an exact detail of particulars.

He stated that there were three plans afloat. First, simple war, in order to a perfect conquest. Second, a mixture of war and treaty. And thirdly, peace grounded on concession.

As to the first plan, that of mere war, it was proposed in two ways: the one direct by conquest, the other indirect by distress. In either of these ways he thought it his duty before he voted for a war, to know distinctly that the means of carrying it on were adequate to the end. It did not satisfy his conscience to say that the resources of this nation were great; he must see them. Before he could trust to those resources, on the credit of what had been formerly done, he must find the situation of the country to be what it formerly was.

He then examined what the ministers had laid before the House as the means of carrying on the ensuing campaign. . . . On the whole, he saw reason to apprehend that we should not be very materially stronger at the beginning of the next year than we were at the beginning of the last. He said the probable number of troops, whether national or foreign, weighed very little in his judgment, as he thought the circumstances of the country were such as would disable them from effecting anything like a conquest of it.

As to the *predatory*, or war by distress (on the nature of which he greatly enlarged), he observed that it might irritate a people in the highest degree, but such a war had never yet induced any one people to receive the government of another. It was a kind of war adapted to distress an independent people and not to coerce disobedient subjects.

But his great objection to it was that it did not lead to a speedy decision. The longer our distractions continued, the greater chance there was for the interference of the Bourbon powers, which in a long protracted war, he considered not only as probable but in a manner certain. He was very sure this country was utterly incapable of carrying on a war with America and these powers acting in conjunction. He entered into a long and particular enumeration of all the dangers and difficulties which must attend such a war.

He stated the condition of France at the beginning of this century, and even within a few years, and compared it with her present situation. He observed that from being the *first*, she was, with regard to effective military power, only the *fifth* state in Europe; that she was fallen below her former rank solely from the advantages we had obtained over her; and that if *she* could humble *us*, she would certainly recover her situation. There was now an opportunity for her making herself, with very little hazard or difficulty, the first maritime power in the world and to invest herself with every branch of trade necessary to secure her in that preeminence. He admitted that at present there were circumstances (which he mentioned) that *might* prevent her from availing herself of this opportunity. But we must be made to trust such an interest as ours to such a chance; and that they who presumptuously trust to the *extraordinary* providence of God, by acting without prudence or foresight, deserve to be abandoned by his *ordinary* protection.

As he saw no probability of success in the *detail* of any of the arrangements that were proposed, neither did he see anything of *authority* to induce him to believe that they would succeed, not one military or naval officer having given an opinion in its favour and many of the greatest in both services having given their opinion directly against it.

As no man of *military experience* had vouched for the *sufficiency* of the force, so no man in the *commissariat* would answer for its *subsistence* from the moment it left the seacoast in America; therefore, its subsistence and its operation were become incompatible.

To the objection that at this rate the Americans might always bring us to unreasonable terms, by the supposed impossibility of reducing them by force, he said that he could not help the difficulties which arose from nature and the constitution of things; that he could not make America nearer to us than it is, or a country of another nature than what God has made it; that people who cannot contrive to reconcile their quarrels, must suffer the evils that happen to a divided nation; that he was of opinion that there was no dishonour at all in any kind of amicable adjustment of domestic quarrels; that he would rather yield an hundred points, when it was Englishmen who gave and received, than a single point to a foreign nation; and [that] we were in such circumstances that we must yield to either one or the other.

After an examination of the merits of the first plan, that of reducing the colonies to obedience by *simple war, in order to a perfect conquest* [*sic*], he entered into a discussion of the second, namely, *that of the mixture of war and treaty.*

Among the great and manifest diversity of sentiments which prevailed on the Treasury-bench, he thought he could discern that this plan had been the most generally adopted by ministers, or by those who acted as such. No light, however, had been let in upon the *particulars* of the scheme, except in the speech from the throne. It was, indeed, very little, and that little very fallacious. One would be inclined to think from that speech that nothing had retarded the restoration of peace but a doubt, whether those in arms might, upon laying them down, obtain a speedy pardon. However, the fact was no pardon had been ever applied for. If nothing had been wanting to conclude the peace but such a power, the commander-in-chief might be authorized to hold out mercy to all those who should submit; and then there would be no need of the laborious, expensive, uncertain, and dilatory process of a commission.

It was impossible to pass by the very exceptionable manner in which this power of pardoning was to be delegated: "they shall have authority," says the Speech from the throne, "to grant general or *particular* pardons or indemnities, in *such manner, and to such persons* as they shall think fit." A shocking, arbitrary power, not to be trusted to any persons, giving encouragement to *dangerous partialities* and tending rather to distract than to quiet the country. The rule of pardon—*singly* or *collectively,* men or bodies of men, whom they should judge friendly or adverse to the common cause—when delegated to subjects, ought not to be their *pleasure* or *displeasure,* but the compliance or non-compliance of the guilty with certain *fixed conditions*. Some such discretionary power as that mentioned in the speech seemed to be given already and to have produced the mischiefs which might be expected from it. For General Gage had already, whether by himself, or by order from minister, made a very indiscreet use of it, by offering mercy to those who were openly in arms and actually besieging him in his station and excluding from mercy those who were 500 miles from him[2] and then sitting in an assembly never declared by authority to be illegal, an assembly from which the minister in the House of Commons had at one time declared they were not without hopes of proposals, which might lead to accommodation. On this part of the speech from the throne he animadverted with great severity.

He said he understood that instead of the Americans waiting for pardons, they were to be persuaded by negotiation to accept them. Therefore it would be necessary to examine what *body* of men it was that administration proposed to negotiate with and what the *objects* of the negotiation were to be.

If he did not mistake the discourses of ministers, they did not now propose to negotiate with the present, or with any other *General Congress* or meeting, but with the *several assemblies* distinctly. In this scheme, he said, they know that they could not succeed because there was one principal province, that of Massachusett's Bay, whose assembly, under their charter, was destroyed by act of parliament. No assembly would sit in that province under the new constitution because if it should, the inhabitants must, as a preliminary, yield the principal object for which they had taken up arms and thus turn the negotiation against themselves, even before it should be opened. This province was the actual seat of war, as its suffering had been the cause of the war itself. Treaty must therefore stumble upon the threshold.

Besides this objection, (which was fundamental) a negotiation with so many provinces, of such different constitutions, tempers, and opinions, never could come to an end. In the meantime our hostile operations, with their whole train of disasters, accidents, and ruinous expences, would be continued, to the destruction of this country and of that. The hope of *dividing* the colonies, on which this part of the plan was founded, and which was even

---

[2] Hancock and Adams were excepted in the general pardon offered by General Gage, while Ward, Putnam, and others, besieging him, were *not* excepted.

avowed as a reason for adopting it, would be the most unfortunate thing that could happen, as it would protract the war and complicate its horrors and miseries, without a possibility of ending it. It was, he said, a vain imagination that any of the colonies would take up arms in favour of ministry for the execution of any of their plans; and a part of the colonies was sufficient, at least, to keep this war alive until the interference of foreign powers should render it utterly destructive.

With regard to the *objects* of the treaty, there must be concessions on the side of the colonies, or upon ours, or upon both. Upon their side they must be either *speculative* recognitions of rights upon *as large a scale as we had claimed them*—and this it was absolutely certain they never would submit to—or upon *a lesser, excluding taxation*, and its *consequences*, and this they had submitted to already; so that there seemed to be no object of the speculative kind, which made it necessary to postpone peace by a protracted negotiation.

The other object of treaty might be a *practical* recognition of our right of taxing for a revenue; this revenue was to be either *nominal* or beneficial. If only nominal, it amounted to nothing more than that speculative acknowledgement of right, which we knew they would forever refuse to make. If *beneficial* and productive, it was to be either by submitting to Lord North's proposition, namely, that of forcing them to furnish a *contingent* by authority of parliament, or, according to their ancient mode, by a *voluntary* grant of their own assemblies.

If the former, we know they have already rejected that proposition and never can submit to it without abandoning that point for the maintenance of which they have risked their all. If it only requires that they should resort to their ancient mode of granting by their assemblies, they have declared again and again, from the beginning of this contest to the end, that they were willing to contribute according to their ability, as *estimated by themselves*, who were the best judges of what their ability was. That ability would be lessened, if not totally destroyed, by the continuance of those troubles. This armed negotiation for taxes would therefore inevitably defeat its own purposes and prevent for ever the possibility of raising any revenue, either by our authority, or by that of their own assemblies.

If the ministers treated for a revenue, or for any other purpose, they had but two securities for the performance of the terms: either the same force which compelled these terms, or the honour, sincerity, and good inclination of the people. If they could trust the people *to keep* the terms without force, they might trust them *to make* them without force. If nothing but force could hold them, and they meant nothing but *independency*, as the Speech from the throne asserted, then the House was to consider how a standing army of 26,000 men and 70 ships of war, could be constantly kept up in America. A people meaning independency will not mean it the less because they have to avoid a present inconvenience, submitted to treaty. After all our struggles, our hold on America is, and must be, her good inclination. If this fails, all fails; and we had better trust to the honesty of the colonies before we had ruined ourselves than after, before we had irritated them than after we had alienated their affections for ever.

The troops sent for the purpose of *forwarding* would certainly impede the negotiation. It was impossible the provincials could be made enough to lay down their arms, while a great adverse military power remained in their country, without any assurance whatsoever of their obtaining any one of the points for which they had contended. This would not be to negotiate but to surrender at discretion. All the grievances they had complained of were contained in acts of parliament. Lord North had declared very truly that nobody could have power to negotiate for the repeal of an act of parliament.

But if the colonies should incline to put any confidence in the *certain* influence of ministry over parliament, even that grand confidence must fail them, as they cannot tell whether the same ministers will continue in power; and even at this very time no two persons upon the Treasury bench were of the same opinion on the conduct to be held towards America. Which of those opinions would finally prevail, no man living could divine. This uncertainty might continue the armed negotiation for several years, to the utter ruin of both countries.

He gave many other equally strong reasons against the scheme and concluded this part of his speech by observing that although the mixed plan of war and negotiation could answer no good end *in future*, it might have a *retrospective* operation—to justify the ministers in the use of their forcible proceedings. For *force* and *concession* going out together, if peace should be the result, ministers would attribute the success, not to the *concession*, but to the *force*. So that all this delay, blood-shed, and expence was incurred merely to furnish ministers with an excuse in debate.

After going through the two first plans, he spoke to the third (his own)—that of a *concession previous to treaty.*

He observed that as he put no great trust in any negotiation, and none at all in an *armed* negotiation, his idea was to have very little treaty, and that little as short as possible. The House was therefore at that time to judge whether it was necessary to make any concession to the colonies; if it should appear to them that such concession was necessary, he was clearly of opinion that they ought to make it immediately and of their own free grace. This he thought of more dignity with regard to themselves, and of much more efficacy with regard to the quiet of the colonies, than the *concession upon treaty* which had been proposed.

The first ground of treaty must be *confidence* and the colonies never could confide for the effect of any concession (as he had shewn in examining the foregoing plan) in a less assurance than that of parliament itself.

He then shewed, by a variety of instances, collected from the public proceedings during the last ten years, how necessary it was that government should be aided by parliament in re-establishing that confidence which had been shaken by those proceedings and that some firm ground should be laid as a foundation for future peace.

This foundation of confidence was become the more necessary from the constitution of the present ministry; that in no time or country, or under any form of government, was the power of ministers suffered to survive the success of their counsels, or the same men permitted to inflame a dependent people to arms and then to appease them by concessions. . . . In concession, the credit of a state is saved by the disgrace of a minister, because it is his *counsel* alone that is discredited. But when the same ministers do and undo, in consequence of the resistance they meet, it is the *nation* itself that submits. Besides, he alleged that all treaty is more easy and fewer concessions are required by all men when they have a confidence in those they treat with.

The mere removal of the offensive acts would have given satisfaction in former times and from amicable hands. But now things are on another footing; and if more concession is required, it is because injudicious coercion has made it necessary. He had always wished to preserve the legislative power of this kingdom entire in everything, and it was with great grief he saw that even an odious and scarcely ever to be exercised part of it was to be abandoned. But when the maxims of public councils are not steady, it is necessary that laws should supply the want of prudence. It was thus, and for this reason, that limits had been set to absolute power in all countries; and that power (though not absolute) had been preserved, not destroyed, by such limitations.

We are now in a *quarrel*, and in putting an end to any quarrel, it is necessary to look to its origin. The origin of this present difference had evidently been upon the subject of taxation. An arrangement of this question, either by enforcement or concession, was a preliminary essential to peace. The House ought to estimate the full value of the object to be conceded before they agree to give it up. If they were of opinion that the taxation of America could repay them their expences, or compensate their risks, they ought to pursue it. If, on the contrary, it was evident beyond all contradiction, and so evident as to enforce reiterated acknowledgments, that they never could enjoy a moment's quiet as long as that matter of contention continued—it was then altogether as essential to the preservation of their own authority in all other points, as to the liberty of America and quiet of the whole empire, to give it up, with such limitations in the concessions as the rights of sovereignty required.

The parliament of Great Britain were not the *representative*, but (as Lord John Cavendish had said, some days before, with great truth and propriety) the *sovereign* of America. The sovereignty was not in its nature an abstract idea of unity but was capable of great complexity and infinite modifications, according to the temper of those who are to be governed and to the circumstances of things, which—being infinitely diversified—government ought to be adapted to them and to conform itself to the nature of things and not to endeavour to force them. Although taxation was inherent in the *supreme power* of society, taken as an *aggregate*, it did not follow that it must reside in any *particular* power in that society. In the society of England, for instance, the king is the sovereign; but the power of the purse is not in his hands, and this does not derogate from his power in those things in which our constitution has attributed power to him. If parliament be the sovereign power of America, parliament may, by its own act, for wise purposes, put the local power of the purse into other hands than its own without disclaiming its just prerogative in other particulars.

Formerly, whatever this right might be to it, the kings of England were in the practice of levying taxes by their own authority upon the people of England. They contended that the crown, being charged with the public defence, must be furnished also with the means of providing for it; that it would be absurd to commit a trust into the hands of one person, and to leave the power of executing it to depend upon the will of another. They therefore held that this power was inseparable from the crown, and in general they made use of the very arguments in favour of the king's indefeasible right to tax the people of England that are now used by the parliament of England to tax the people of America. Notwithstanding all these arguments, one of the greatest of our kings, by an express and positive Act, cut off from the sovereign power this right of taxing.

This Act, which has been the foundation of the unity and happiness of England since that time, is the stat. *34* Edward I, called *Statutum de tallagio non concedendo*, [which] Mr. Burke made his pattern;[3] and from thence (if his plan should be adopted) he hoped the same good effects in future. This pattern statute was absolutely *silent about the right*, but confined itself to giving satisfaction in future, and it laid down no *general principles* which might tend to affect the royal prerogative in *other* particulars. In all human probability the preservation of the other branches of the prerogative was owing to the clear and absolute surrender of this.

He then moved that the first, fourth, and fifth chapter of the Statute *de tallegio non concedendo* might be read; which being done, he observed that this statute consisted of three capital parts: a renunciation of taxing, a repeal of all statutes which had been made upon a contrary principle, and a general pardon. He then read his own Bill and showed its conformity to the spirit of that Act, supposing Great Britain to stand in the place of the

[3] The notion that *de tallagio* was a statute arose in the seventeenth century when Englishmen differed with the Stuarts over the powers of parliament. Recently, however, it has been shown that *de tallagio* NEVER was enacted but was probably no more that a program or outline used by the barons in September 1297, in their efforts to obtain concessions from Edward I, which concessions were formally embodied in the *Confirmation Cartarum* of October 1297. It in turn was repudiated by Edward after he had appealed to the Pope, in 1305, on the grounds that it violated his coronation oath not to alienate any part of the crown. See Rothwell, "Confirmation of the Charter, 1297," *English Historical Review*, LX (1945), 16, 177, 300. For a slightly different view, see Edwards, "Confirmation Cartarum and the Baronial Grievances," *E.H.R.*, LVIII (1943), 147, 273.

sovereign and America in that of the subject. The circumstances are not indeed in every respect *exactly* parallel, but they are sufficiently so to justify his following an example that gave satisfaction and security on the subject of *taxes* and left all *other* rights and powers whatsoever exactly upon the bottom on which they stood before that arrangement had been made.

He then gave his reasons for not adopting the methods which (though not proposed in the House) had been frequently suggested in conversation by several friends and well-wishers to America.

And first he mentioned the proposal for repealing the Declaratory Act of 1766. On this occasion he entered into the history of that Act, the reasons for making colonies under it until, by the renewal of the scheme of actual taxation, their apprehensions were roused and they were taught to look with suspicion and terror upon the unlimited powers of the British legislature. The repeal of a Declaratory Act was a thing impossible, for it was nothing less than to make the legislature accuse itself of uttering propositions that were false and making claims that were groundless; that the disgrace of an English parliament could add nothing to the security of American liberty; that on the contrary our inconstancy would become a bad ground of trust; that the Declaratory Act had been misrepresented, as if it had been the cause of the taxation, whereas the grand scheme of taxation had *preceded* the Declaratory Act and not been the *consequence of it*; that the Act has said nothing in *particular* of taxation but is an affirmation of the *universality* of the legislative power of Great Britain over the colonies; that if this Act were repealed, it would be a *denial* of legislative power, as extensive as the affirmation of it in the Act so repealed; that he was averse to doing anything upon speculations of right because when parliament made a *positive* concession, the bounds of it were clear and precise, but when they made a concession founded in *theory and abstract principles*, the consequences of those principles were things out of the power of any legislature to limit; that this bill gave as effectual a security against future taxation as any declaration of right could possibly do; and that it put American liberty, in that point, upon just as good a footing as English liberty itself.

He next considered the proposition for repealing all the Acts since 1763. This he showed to be impossible without ruining the whole system of the trade laws and some of those laws which are extremely beneficial to America. All the laws which leaned upon the colonies, and were the cause or consequence of the quarrel, were to be repealed in this Bill, which made provision likewise for authorising such a negotiation as might tend to the settlement of all those lesser matter to the mutual advantage of the parties. The Congress did not require this sweeping repeal as a preliminary to peace; but even if it had, he was for treating the colonies and not receiving laws from them. He did not conceive that when men come to treat of peace they must of course persevere in demanding everything which they claimed in the height of the quarrel. The cause of quarrel was taxation; that being removed, the rest would not be difficult. For he denied that the desire of absolute independency was or could be general in the colonies. It was so contrary to their clearest interests, provided their liberties were preserved, that so far from disbelieving them when they denied such a design, he could scarcely credit them if they should assert it. He then stated five or six capital facts to prove that independency neither was or could be their object.

He said he was confident, both from the nature of the thing, and from information which did not use to fail him, that this Bill would restore immediate peace and as much obedience as could be expected after so rude a shock had been given to government and after so long a continuance of public disturbances; that in this Bill, a basis was laid for such satisfaction in the minds of all sober people in America as would enable government to fix and settle, if common prudence were employed in its future construction and management. That in the first operation it would be the true means of dividing America. Not the dangerous and fallacious method of dividing which had been proposed, and from which nothing but confusion could grow; not the division of province from province, or the rich from the poor; or the landed from the trading interest; but the division of the peaceable from the factious, the quiet from the ambitious, the friends to the unity of the empire from the projectors of independence. That this would put the standard of American liberty into the hands of the friends to British government. And when this was done, there was no doubt but that a sense of interest, natural affection, the dread of the horrors of war, and even the love of freedom itself, better secured by such an Act than by any schemes of hazardous speculation, would leave the really factious very few followers or companions.

He then strongly urged the necessity of granting peace to our colonies on terms of freedom, dilated largely on the uncertainty (to say no worse) of obtaining it upon any other, and the utter impossibility of preserving it in future without setting the minds of the people at rest. He dwelt largely on the mischiefs which we must suffer by the continuance of this quarrel. He rested little on the consideration of trade and revenue; he put that out of the question as a matter that would require a large discussion by itself and chiefly aimed at shewing that in the progress of this business new powers must be daily added to the crown, so that in seeking to destroy the freedom of others we may fail to obtain what we pursue and in the pursuit may lose our own liberty. On this head he dwelt very largely and concluded the whole with a warm and earnest address to the consciences of the members and an exhortation not to trust to general good intention and to an opinion that what they were doing was for the *support of government*, when it was far from evident that, under the name of government, it was not the ambition, the interest, the ignorance and obstinacy of particular men that they were supporting; that they were bound not to give confidence, where rational grounds of confidence did not appear; and that anarchy instead of government, and civil confusion instead of peace and obedience, would be the consequence of an encouragement given by that House to a blind perseverance in measures, which were not conceived with wisdom, or conducted with ability.

He moved "That leave be given to bring in a Bill for composing the present Troubles, and for quieting the minds of his Majesty's subjects in America."

The following is a Copy of the Bill.[4]

"Whereas, by the blessing of Almighty God, and the industry, enterprise and courage of several of the people of this realm, extensive and valuable territories have been acquired in America to the crown of Great Britain, which are now inhabited by great

[4] The text of Burke's bill is over 1800 words and space does not permit reprinting more than the preamble and the first three provisions dealing with taxation. The remainder simply provides for the recognition of a Continental Congress in America with full power to bind the colonies, for the repeal of the (remnants of the) Townshend, Boston Port, Massachusetts Government, and Administration of Justice Acts, and for a general pardon of all those who had in any way supported the colonists' cause. Complete text is in PH, XVIII, 978-82, and Almon, III, 182-86.

multitudes of his Majesty's subjects, who have cultivated and improved the same for the most part at their own charges, to the great increase of the commerce and naval strength of this kingdom, and have also, of their own free gift, made provision for the support of the civil government within their said plantations, have maintained many expensive wars against the Indian nations, and have at sundry times granted large sums of money, and other very considerable aids to his Majesty, and his royal predecessors, to support them against the enemies of this kingdom, notwithstanding which the inhabitants of the said colonies have been made liable to several taxes given and granted in parliament for the purpose of raising a revenue, when they have had no knights or burgesses, or others of their own chusing, to represent them in parliament; and from the great distance of the said colonies from this land, and other impediments, are not able conveniently to send representatives to the said parliament, whereby the said inhabitants of the British colonies have conceived themselves to be much aggrieved, and thereby great troubles have arisen, and are likely to continue, if a fitting remedy be not provided. Wherefore, we pray your Majesty that it may be enacted and declared, and it is hereby enacted and declared, by, &c. &c. &c.

"That no aid, subsidy, tax, duty, loan, benevolence, or any other burthen or imposition whatsoever, shall be granted, laid, assessed, levied, or collected upon the inhabitants of any colony or plantation in America, by the authority, or in virtue of any act of parliament, or in any other manner, or by any other authority, than the voluntary grant of the general assembly, or general court of each colony or plantation, and which shall be assented to by his Majesty's governor, and otherwise confirmed according to the usage of each province respectively, any law, statute, custom, right, prerogative, or any other matter whatsoever to the contrary notwithstanding. Saving to his Majesty, his heirs, and successors, his right of reserving and collecting quit-rents, and other his ancient dues and revenues, and all other duties and taxes by this Act not repealed, and saving and reserving to all proprietors and charter companies, their ancient rights, privileges, and possessions.

"Provided always, that nothing in this Act shall extend, or be construed to extend, to restrain the future imposition, and levy of duties and taxes for the regulation of trade and commerce in all the dominions to the imperial crown of this realm belonging.

"And in order to remove all doubt and uneasiness from the minds of his Majesty's subjects in the colonies, it is hereby further enacted, that if any act of parliament shall be hereafter made for the purpose of such regulation or trade, the produce of the duties thereby laid, shall be held by the collectors, or receivers of his Majesty's customs, for the disposal of the general assemblies, as if the same had been levied by the authority of the several general assemblies in the said colonies."

8

SPEECH IN SUPPORT OF
LORD JOHN CAVENDISH'S MOTION
FOR THE REVISAL OF
ALL THE LAWS AGGRIEVING
THE AMERICANS

NOVEMBER 6, 1776[1]

The Americans had declared their independence and were at war with England. The Rockinghams had exhausted every suggested method for persuading Parliament to reconsider but one. They now decided to adopt Burke's idea and secede from Parliament—in protest—shortly after it reconvened in the fall of 1776. The following speech was Burke's last before he joined the exodus.

REJOICED I am, Sir, that the learned gentleman[2] has regained, if not his talent, at least his voice; that as he would not, or could not, reply the other night to my hon. friend, charmed as he must have been with the powerful reasoning of that eloquent speech, he had the grace to be silent. On that memorable occasion he lay, like Milton's devil, prostrate "on the oblivious pool," confounded and astounded, though called upon by the whole Satanic host. He lay prostrate, dumbfounded, and unable to utter a single syllable, and suffered the goads of the two noble lords to prick him till he scarcely betrayed a single sign of animal or mental sensibility. Why, Sir, would he not be silent now—instead of attempting to answer what in truth was unanswerable? But the learned gentleman has now called to his assistance the bayonets of 12,000 Hessians; and as he thinks it absurd to reason at present with the Americans, he tells us that by the healing, sooth-

---

[1] *PH*, XVIII, 1441-45; *Middlesex Journal*, November 7, 1776, p. 4.
[2] Solicitor General Wedderburn.

ing, merciful measures of foreign swords, at the breasts of those unhappy people, their understandings would be enlightened and they would be enabled to comprehend the subtleties of his logic. It was well said, on another occasion, that your speech demands an army!—and I may say, that the learned gentleman demands blood. Reasoning he says is vain: the *sword* must *convince* America and clear up their clouded apprehensions. The learned gentleman's abilities surely desert him if he is obliged to call such a coarse argument as an army to his assistance; not that I mean anything reflecting on his parts. I always esteem, and sometimes dread, his talents. But has he told you why commissioners were not sent sooner to America? Has he explained that essential point? Not a jot. Why, after the Act passed for them, were they delayed full seven months and not permitted to sail till May; and why was the commission appointing them delayed till the 6th of that month? Answer this. The blood and devastation that followed was owing to this delay; upon your conscience it ought to lay a heavy load. If the measure was right and necessary in order for conciliation, as the King declared in his speech at the opening of that session, why was it not executed at a time in which it could be effectual instead of being *purposely deferred* to one when it could not possibly answer any end but that of adding hypocrisy to treachery and insult and mockery to cruelty and oppression? By this delay you drove them into the declaration of independency, *not* as a *matter of choice*, but *necessity*. And now [that] they have declared it, you bring it as an argument to prove that there can be no other reasoning used with them but the sword. What is this but declaring that you were originally determined not to *prevent* but to *punish* rebellion, not to use conciliation but an army, *not* to *convince* but to *destroy*! Such were the effects of those seven months cruelly lost, to which every mischief that has happened since must be attributed.

But still the learned gentleman persists, that nothing but the commissioners can give peace to America—[that] it is beyond the power of this House. What was the result of the conference with the delegates from the Congress? Why, we are told that they met in order to be convinced that taxation is no grievance—"no tyranny" used to be the phrase; but that is out of fashion now. Then, Sir, what an insult to all America was it to send as commissioners none but the commanders of the fleet and army to negotiate peace! Did it not shew how much you were determined that the only arguments you meant to use were your broadswords and broadsides. Let me assert, Sir, that the doctrines to be laid down in America would not have been too trivial an occasion, even for the reasoning abilities of the learned gentleman himself. But, Sir, you may think to carry these doctrines into execution—and be mistaken too; the battle is not yet fought. But if it was fought and the wreath of victory adorned your brow, still is not that continent conquered. Witness the behaviour of one miserable woman who, with her single arm, did that which an army of a hundred thousand men could not do—arrested your progress in the moment of your success. This miserable being was found in a cellar, with her visage besmeared and smutted over, with every mark of rage, despair, resolution, and the most *exalted heroism, buried* in combustibles, in order to fire New York and perish in its *ashes.* She was brought forth and, knowing that she would be condemned to die, upon being asked her purpose, said, "to fire the city!" and was determined to omit no opportunity of doing what her country called for. Her train was laid and fired; and it is worthy of your attention how Providence was pleased to make use of those humble means to serve the American cause, when open force was used in vain. In order to bring things to this unhappy situation, did not you pave the way, by a succession of acts of tyranny? For this you shut up their ports, cut off their fishery, annihilated their charter, and governed them by an army. Sir, the recollection of these things, being the evident causes of what we have seen, is more than what *ought* to be *endured.* This it is that has *burnt* the noble city of New York, that has planted the bayonet in the bosoms of my principals—in the bosom of the city where alone your wretched government once boasted the only friends she could number in America. If this was not the only succession of events you determined, and therefore looked for, why was America left without any power in it, to give security to the persons and property of those who were and wished to be loyal— this was essential to government. You did not, and might therefore be well said to have abdicated the government.

. . . Gods! Sir, shall we be told that you cannot analyze grievances?—that you can have no communication with rebels because they have declared for independency?—Shall you be told this when the tyrant Philip did it after the same circumstance in the Netherlands. By edict he allowed their ships to enter their ports and suffered them to depart in peace; he treated with them; made them propositions; and positively declared that he would redress all their grievances. And James II, when he was sailing from France at the head of a formidable force, assisted like you by foreign troops, and having a great party in the kingdom, still offered specific terms—while his exceptions of pardon were few, amongst the rest my hon. friend's ancestor, Sir Stephen Fox. But you will offer none. You simply tell them to lay down their arms and then you will do just as you please. Could the most cruel conqueror say less? Had you conquered the devil himself in hell, could you be less liberal? No! Sir, you would offer no terms. You meant to drive them to the declaration of independency; and even after it was issued, ought by your offers to have reversed the effect. You would not receive the remonstrance which I brought you from New York because it denied your rights to certain powers;[3] yet the late king of France received the remonstrances from his parliaments that expressly denied his right to the powers he was in the constant exercise of, answered them, and even redressed some of the grievances which those very remonstrances complained of, though he refused to grant what he thought more peculiarly entrenched upon his own authority.

In this situation, Sir, shocking to say, are we called upon by another proclamation to go to the altar of the Almighty, with war and vengeance in our hearts, instead of the peace of our blessed Saviour. He said, "My peace I give you." But we are, on this fast, to have war only in our hearts and mouths, war against our brethren. Till our churches are purified from this abominable service, I shall consider them, not as the temples of the Almighty, but the synagogues of Satan. An act not more *infamous*, respecting its political purposes, than *blasphemous* and *profane* as a pretended act of national devotion, when the people are called upon, in the most solemn and awful manner, to repair to church, to partake of a sacrament, and, at the foot of the altar, to commit sacrilege, to perjure themselves publicly by charging their American brethren with the horrid crime of rebellion, with propagating "specious falsehoods," when either the charge must be *notoriously false*, or those who make it, not knowing it to be true, call Almighty God to witness—not a *specious* but—a most *audacious* and *blasphemous* falsehood.

[3] Burke presented this on May 15, 1775, but it was not received, despite its affections of loyalty, because one passage questioned Parliament's power of taxation. See *PH*, XVIII, 643-55.

(The House groaned at this point of the speech, and some called out, "Order," "Order.") He said he rejoiced to hear such an involuntary burst of approbation of his remarks. He then repeated them, and, after urging the expediency of our ending the dispute with America, gave his hearty assent to Lord John's motion.

9

A LETTER TO THE
MARQUIS OF ROCKINGHAM
ACCOMPANIED BY AN ADDESS TO
THE KING AND AN ADDRESS
TO THE BRITISH COLONISTS IN
NORTH AMERICA

JANUARY 6, 1777[1]

Secession from Parliament by such a prominent minority as the Rock-inghams aroused a furor. Burke, as the group's leading writer and speaker, set out to explain the position, policy, and objectives of the Rockinghams. What follows is Burke's letter to Rockingham covering the manuscripts of two addresses that follow it. Burke observes that, under the circumstances then prevailing, there is an element of danger in their actions; it is probably because of those dangers that neither address was published at that time.

M Y DEAR LORD—I am afraid that I ought rather to beg your pardon for troubling you at all in this season of repose, than to apologise for having been so long silent on the approaching business. It comes upon us, not indeed in the most agreeable manner; but it does come upon us: and, I believe, your friends in general are in expectation of finding your Lordship resolved in what way you are to meet it. The deliberation is full of difficulties; but the determination is necessary.

The affairs of America seem to be drawing towards a crisis. The Howes are at this time in possession of, or are able to awe, the whole middle coast of America, from Delaware to the western boundary of Massachusetts Bay: the naval barrier on the side of Canada is broken; a great tract of country is open for the supply

[1] *Works*, II, 187-245.

of the troops; the river Hudson opens a way into the heart of the provinces; and nothing can, in all probability, prevent an early and offensive campaign. What the Americans *have* done is, in their circumstances, truly astonishing; it is, indeed, infinitely more than I expected from them. But having done so much, for some short time I began to entertain an opinion that they might do more. It is now, however, evident that they cannot look standing armies in the face. They are inferior in everything, even in numbers; I mean in the number of those whom they keep in constant duty and in regular pay. There seem, by the best accounts, not to be above 10,000 or 12,000 men, at most, in their grand army. The rest are militia, and not wonderfully well composed or disciplined. They decline a general engagement, prudently enough, if their object had been to make the war attend upon a treaty of good terms of subjection: but when they look further, this will not do. An army that is obliged at all times, and in all situations, to decline an engagement, may delay their ruin, but can never defend their country. Foreign assistance they have little, or none, nor are likely soon to have more. France, in effect, has no king, nor any minister accredited enough, either with the court or nation, to undertake a design of great magnitude.

In this state of things, I persuade myself, Franklin is come to Paris to draw from that court a definitive and satisfactory answer concerning the support of the colonies. If he cannot get such an answer, (and I am of opinion that at present he cannot,) then it is to be presumed he is authorised to negotiate with Lord Stormont on the basis of dependence on the Crown. This I take to be his errand: for I never can believe that he is come thither as a fugitive from his cause in the hour of its distress, or that he is going to conclude a long life, which has brightened every hour it has continued, with so foul and dishonourable a flight. On this supposition, I thought it not wholly impossible that the Whig party might be made a sort of mediators of the peace. It is unnatural to suppose that, in making an accommodation, the Americans should not choose rather to give credit to those who all along have opposed the measure of ministers, than to throw themselves wholly on the mercy of their bitter, uniform, and systematic enemies. It is indeed the victorious enemy that has the terms to offer; the vanquished party and their friends are, both of them, reduced in their power; and it is certain that those who are utterly broken and subdued have no option. But, as this is hardly yet the case of the Americans, in this middle state of their affairs, (much impaired, but not perfectly ruined,) one would think it must be their interest to provide, if possible, some further security for the terms which they may obtain from their enemies. If the Congress could be brought to declare in favour of those terms, for which 100 members of the House of Commons voted last year, with some civility to the party which held out those terms, it would undoubtedly have an effect to revive the cause of our liberties in England, and to give the colonies some sort of mooring and anchorage in this country. It seemed to me, that Franklin might be made to feel the propriety of such a step; and as I have an acquaintance with him, I had a strong desire of taking a turn to Paris. Everything else failing, one might obtain a better knowledge of the general aspect of affairs abroad, than, I believe, any of us possess at present. The Duke of Portland approved the idea. But when I had conversed with the very few of your Lordship's friends who were in town, and considered a little more maturely the constant temper and standing maxims of the party, I laid aside the design; not being desirous of risking the displeasure of those for whose sake alone I wished to take that fatiguing journey at this severe season of the year.

The Duke of Portland has taken with him some heads of deliberation, which were the result of a discourse with his Grace and Mr. Montagu at Burlington House. It seems essential to the cause, that your Lordship meet your friends with some settled plan either of action or inaction. Your friends will certainly require such a plan, and I am sure the state of affairs requires it, whether they call for it or not. As to the measure of a secession with reasons, after rolling the matter in my head a good deal, and turning it a hundred ways, I confess I still think it the most advisable, notwithstanding the serious objections that lie against it, and indeed the extreme uncertainty of all political measures, especially at this time. It provides for your honour. I know of nothing else that can so well do this: it is something, perhaps all, that can be done in our present situation. Some precaution, in this respect, is not without its motives. That very estimation, for which you have sacrificed everything else, is in some danger of suffering in the general wreck;[2] and perhaps it is likely to suffer

---

[2] In this paragraph Burke has been discussing the problems growing out of their secession from Parliament in November, 1776. He is trying to persuade Rockingham to act more positively and expresses his

the more, because you have hitherto confided more than was quite prudent in the clearness of your intentions, and in the solidity of the popular judgment upon them. The former, indeed, is out of the power of events; the latter is full of levity, and the very creature of fortune. However, such as it is, (and for one I do not think I am inclined to overvalue it,) both our interest and our duty make it necessary for us to attend to it very carefully, so long as we act a part in public. The measure you take for this purpose may produce no immediate effect; but with regard to the party, and the principles for whose sake the party exists, all hope of their preservation or recovery depends upon your preserving your reputation.

By the conversation of some friends, it seemed as if they were willing to fall in with this design, because it promised to emancipate them from the servitude of irksome business, and to afford them an opportunity of retiring to ease and tranquillity. If that be their object in the secession and addresses proposed, there surely never were means worse chosen to gain their end; and if this be any part of their project, it were a thousand times better it were never undertaken.—The measure is not only unusual, and as such critical, but it is in its own nature strong and vehement in a high degree. The propriety, therefore, of adopting it depends entirely upon the spirit with which it is supported and followed. To pursue violent measures with languor and irresolution is not very consistent in speculation, and not more reputable or safe in practice. If your Lordship's friends do not go to this business with their whole hearts, if they do not feel themselves uneasy without it, if they do not undertake it with a certain degree of zeal, and even with warmth and indignation, it had better be removed wholly out of our thoughts. A measure of less strength, and more in the beaten circle of affairs, if supported with spirit and industry, would be, on all accounts, infinitely more eligible.—We have to consider what it is, that, in this undertaking, we have against us: we have the weight of King, Lords, and Commons, in the other scale: we have against us, within a trifle, the whole body of the law: we oppose the more considerable part of the landed and mercantile interests: we contend, in a manner, against the whole

---

own support of a public explanation of their secession, which is one reason why he wrote the addresses that follow this letter. Burke is, however, concerned about the danger to Rockingham as a result of their actions.

church: we set our faces against great armies flushed with victory, and navies who have tasted of civil spoil, and have a strong appetite for more: our strength, whatever it is, must depend, for a good part of its effect, upon events not very probable. In such a situation, such a step requires, not only great magnanimity, but unwearied activity and perseverance, with a good deal, too, of dexterity and management, to improve every accident in our favour.

The delivery of this paper may have very important consequences. It is true that the court may pass it over in silence, with a real or effected contempt. But this I do not think so likely. If they do take notice of it, the mildest course will be such an address from parliament as the House of Commons made to the king on the London remonstrance in the year 1769. This address will be followed by addresses of a similar tendency from all parts of the kingdom, in order to overpower you with what they will endeavour to pass as the united voice and sense of the nation. But if they intend to proceed further, and to take steps of a more decisive nature, you are then to consider, not what they may legally and justly do, but what a parliament, omnipotent in power, influenced with party rage and personal resentment, operating under the implicit military obedience of court discipline, is capable of. Though they have made some successful experiments on juries, they will hardly trust enough to them to order a prosecution for a supposed libel. They may proceed in two ways, either by an *impeachment*, in which the Tories may retort on the Whigs (but with better success, though in a worse cause) the proceedings in the case of Sacheverel[1], or they may, without this form, proceed, as against the Bishop of Rochester, by a bill of pains and penalties more or less grievous. The similarity of the cases, or the justice, is (as I said) out of the question. The mode of proceeding has several very ancient, and very recent, precedents. None of these methods is impossible. The court may select three or four of the most distinguished among you for their victims; and therefore nothing is more remote from the tendency of the proposed act than any idea of retirement or repose. On the contrary, you have all of you, as principals or auxiliaries, a much better and more desperate conflict, in all probability, to undergo than any you have been yet engaged in. The only question is, whether the risk ought to be run for the chance (and it is no more) of recalling the people of England to their ancient principles, and to that personal interest which formerly they took in all public affairs? At any rate, I am sure it is right, if we take this step, to take it with a full view of the consequences; and with minds and measures in a state of preparation to meet them. It is not becoming that your boldness should arise from a want of foresight. It is more reputable, and certainly it is more safe, too, that it should be grounded on the evident necessity of encountering the dangers which you foresee.

Your Lordship will have the goodness to excuse me, if I state in strong terms the difficulties attending a measure, which on the whole I heartily concur in. But as, from my want of importance, I can be personally little subject to the most trying part of the consequences, it is as little my desire to urge others to dangers in which I am myself to have so inconsiderable a share.

If this measure should be thought too great for our strength, or the dispositions of the times, then the point will be to consider what is to be done in Parliament. A weak, irregular, desultory, peevish opposition there will be as much too little as the other may be too big. Our scheme ought to be such, as to have in it a succession of measures; else it is impossible to secure anything like a regular attendance; opposition will otherwise always carry a disreputable air; either will it be possible, without that attendance, to persuade the people that we are in earnest. Above all, a motion should be well digested for the first day. There is one thing in particular I wish to recommend to your Lordship's consideration; that is, the opening of the doors of the House of Commons. Without this, I am clearly convinced, it will be in the power of ministry to make our opposition appear without doors just in what light they please. To obtain a gallery is the easiest thing in the world, if we are satisfied to cultivate the esteem of our adversaries by the resolution and energy with which we act against them: but if their satisfaction and good humour be any part of our object, the attempt, I admit, is idle.

I had some conversation, before I left town, with the D. of M. He is of opinion, that, if you adhere to your resolution of seceding, you ought not to appear on the first day of the meeting. He thinks it can have no effect, except to break the continuity of your conduct, and thereby to weaken and fritter away the impression of it. It certainly will seem odd to give solemn reasons for a discontinuance of your attendance in parliament, after having two or three times returned to it, and immediately after a vigorous act of opposition. As to trials of the temper of the House, there have been of that sort so many already, that I see no reason for making another that would not hold equally good for another after that; particularly, as nothing has happened in the least calculated to alter the disposition of the House. If the secession were to be general, such an attendance, followed by such an act, would have force; but being in its nature incomplete and broken, to break it further by retreats and returns to the chase must entirely destroy its effect. I confess I am quite of the D. of M.'s opinion in this point. . . .[3]

AN ADDRESS TO THE KING

WE, your Majesty's most dutiful and loyal subjects, several of the peers of the realm, and several members of the House of Commons chosen by the people to represent them in parliament, do in our individual capacity, but with hearts filled with a warm affection to your Majesty, with a strong attachment to your royal house, and with the most unfeigned devotion to your true interest, beg leave, at this crisis of your affairs, in all humility to approach your royal presence.

Whilst we lament the measures adopted by the public councils of the kingdom, we do not mean to question the legal validity of their proceedings. We do not desire to appeal from them to any person whatsoever. We do not dispute the conclusive authority of the bodies in which we have a place over all their members. We know that it is our ordinary duty to submit ourselves to the determinations of the majority in everything except what regards the just defence of our honour and reputation. But the situation into which the British empire has been brought, and the conduct to which we are reluctantly driven in that situation, we hold ourselves bound by the relation in which we stand both to the Crown and the people clearly to explain to your Majesty and our country.

We have been called upon in the speech from the throne at the opening of this session of parliament, in a manner peculiarly marked, singularly emphatical, and from a place from whence anything implying censure falls with no common weight, to concur in unanimous approbation of those measures which have

---

[3] Burke concludes by mentioning that the following Addresses had been passed around among the party leaders.

produced our present distresses, and threaten us in future with others far more grievous. We trust, therefore, that we shall stand justified in offering to our sovereign and the public our reasons for persevering inflexibly in our uniform dissent from every part of those measures. We lament them from an experience of their mischief, as we originally opposed them from a sure foresight of their unhappy and inevitable tendency.

We see nothing in the present events in the least degree sufficient to warrant an alteration in our opinion. We were always steadily averse to this civil war—not because we thought it impossible that it should be attended with victory; but because we were fully persuaded that in such a contest victory would only vary the mode of our ruin; and, by making it less immediately sensible, would render it the more lasting and the more irretrievable. Experience had but too fully instructed us in the possibility of the reduction of a free people to slavery by foreign mercenary armies. But we had an horror of becoming the instruments in a design of which, in our turn, we might become the victims. Knowing the inestimable value of peace, and the contemptible value of what was sought by war, we wished to compose the distractions of our country, not by the use of foreign arms, but by prudent regulations in our own domestic policy. We deplored, as your Majesty has done in your speech from the throne, the disorders which prevail in your empire: but we are convinced that the disorders of the people, in the present time and in the present place, are owing to the usual and natural cause of such disorders at all times, and in all places, where such have prevailed—the misconduct of government; that they are owing to plans laid in error, pursued with obstinacy, and conducted without wisdom.

We cannot attribute so much to the power of faction, at the expense of human nature, as to suppose, that in any part of the world a combination of men, few in number, not considerable in rank, of no natural hereditary dependencies, should be able, by the efforts of their policy alone, or the mere exertion of any talents, to bring the people of your American dominions into the disposition which has produced the present troubles. We cannot conceive that, without some powerful concurring cause, any management should prevail on some millions of people, dispersed over an whole continent, in thirteen provinces, not only unconnected, but in many particulars of religion, manners, government, and local interest totally different and adverse, voluntarily to submit themselves to a suspension of all the profits of industry and all the comforts of civil life, added to all the evils of an unequal war carried on with circumstances of the greatest asperity and rigour. This, Sir, we conceive, could never have happened but from a general sense of some grievance, so radical in its nature, and so spreading in its effects, as to poison all the ordinary satisfactions of life, to discompose the frame of society, and to convert into fear and hatred that habitual reverence ever paid by mankind to an ancient and venerable government.

That grievance is as simple in its nature, and as level to the most ordinary understanding, as it is powerful in affecting the most languid passions; it is

"AN ATTEMPT MADE TO DISPOSE OF THE PROPERTY OF A WHOLE PEOPLE WITHOUT THEIR CONSENT."

Your Majesty's English subjects in the colonies, possessing the ordinary faculties of mankind, know, that to live under such a plan of government is not to live in a state of freedom. Your English subjects in the colonies, still impressed with the ancient feelings of the people from whom they are derived, cannot live under a government which does not establish freedom as its basis.

This scheme, being therefore set up in direct opposition to the rooted and confirmed sentiments and habits of thinking of an whole people, has produced the effects which ever must result from such a collision of power and opinion. For we beg leave, with all duty and humility, to represent to your Majesty (what we fear has been industriously concealed from you), that it is not merely the opinion of a very great number, or even of the majority, but the universal sense of the whole body of the people in those provinces, that the practice of taxing in the mode, and on the principles which have been lately contended for and enforced, is subversive of all their rights.

This sense has been declared, as we understand on good information, by the unanimous voice of all their assemblies; each assembly also, on this point, is perfectly unanimous within itself. It has been declared as fully by the actual voice of the people without these assemblies as by the constructive voice within them; as well by those in that country who addressed as by those who remonstrated; and it is as much the avowed opinion of those who have hazarded their all rather than take up arms against your Majesty's forces, as of those who have run the same risk to oppose them. The difference among them is, not on the grievance, but on the mode of redress; and we are sorry to say, that they who have conceived hopes from the placability of the ministers, who influence the public councils of this kingdom, disappear in the multitude of those who conceive that passive compliance only confirms and emboldens oppression.

The sense of a whole people, most gracious sovereign, never ought to be contemned by wise and beneficent rulers; whatever may be the abstract claims, or even rights, of *the supreme power*. We have been too early instructed, and too long habituated to believe that the only firm seat of all authority is in the minds, affections, and interests of the people, to change our opinions on the theoretic reasonings of speculative men, or for the convenience of a mere temporary arrangement of state. It is not consistent with equity or wisdom to set at defiance the general feelings of great communities, and of all the orders which compose them. Much power is tolerated, and passes unquestioned, where much is yielded to opinion. All is disputed where everything is enforced.

... We assure your Majesty, that, on our parts, we should think ourselves unjustifiable as good citizens, and not influenced by the true spirit of Englishmen, if, with any effectual means of prevention in our hands, we were to submit to taxes to which we did not consent, either directly, or by a representation of the people, securing to us the substantial benefit of an absolutely free disposition of our own property in that important case. And we add, Sir, if fortune, instead of blessing us with a situation where we may have daily access to the propitious presence of a gracious prince, had fixed us in settlements on the remotest part of the globe, we must carry these sentiments with us, as part of our being; persuaded, that the distance of situation would render this privilege in the disposal of property but the more necessary. If no provision had been made for it, such provision ought to be made or permitted. Abuses of subordinate authority increase, and all means of redress lessen, as the distance of the subject removes him from the seat of the supreme power. What, in those circumstances, can save him from the last extremes of indignity and oppression but something left in his own hands, which may enable him to conciliate the favour and control the excesses of government? When no means of power to awe or to oblige are possessed, the strongest ties which connect mankind in every relation, social and civil, and which teach them mutually to respect each other, are broken. Independency, from that moment, virtually exists. Its formal declaration will quickly follow. Such must be our feelings for ourselves; we are not in possession of another rule for our brethren.

When the late attempt practically to annihilate that inestimable privilege was made, great disorders and tumults very unhappily and very naturally arose from it. In this state of things we were of opinion that satisfaction ought instantly to be given; or that, at least, the punishment of the disorder ought to be attended with the redress of the grievance. We were of opinion, that if our dependencies had so outgrown the positive institutions made for the preservation of liberty in this kingdom that the operation of their powers was become rather a pressure than a relief to the subjects in the colonies, wisdom dictated that the spirit of the constitution should rather be applied to their circumstances, than its authority enforced with violence in those very parts where its reason became wholly inapplicable.

Other methods were then recommended, and followed, as infallible means of restoring peace and order. We looked upon them to be, what they have since proved to be, the cause of inflaming discontent into disobedience, and resistance into revolt. The subversion of solemn fundamental charters, on a suggestion of abuse, without citation, evidence, or hearing: the total suspension of the commerce of a great maritime city, the capital of a great maritime province, during the pleasure of the Crown: the establishment of a military force, not accountable to the ordinary tribunals of the country in which it was kept up—these and other proceedings at that time, if no previous cause of dissension had subsisted, were sufficient to produce great troubles: unjust at all times, they were then irrational.

We could not conceive, when disorders had arisen from the complaint of one violated right, that to violate every other was the proper means of quieting an exasperated people. It seemed to us absurd and preposterous to hold out, as the means of calming a people in a state of extreme inflammation, and ready to take up arms, the austere law which a rigid conqueror would impose, as the sequel of the most decisive victories.

Recourse, indeed, was at the same time had to force; and we saw a force sent out, enough to menace liberty, but not to awe opposition; tending to bring odium on the civil power, and contempt on the military; at once to provoke and encourage resistance. Force was sent out not sufficient to hold one town; laws were passed to inflame thirteen provinces.

This mode of proceeding by harsh laws and feeble armies could not be defended on the principle of mercy and forbearance. For mercy, as we conceive, consists, not in the weakness of the means, but in the benignity of the ends. We apprehend that mild measures may be powerfully enforced; and that acts of extreme rigour and injustice may be attended with as much feebleness in the execution as severity in the formation.

In consequence of these terrors, which, falling upon some, threatened all, the colonies made a common cause with the sufferers; and proceeded, on their part, to acts of resistance. In that alarming situation, we besought your Majesty's ministers to entertain some distrust of the operation of coercive measures, and to profit of their experience. Experience had no effect. The modes of legislative rigour were construed, not to have been erroneous in their policy, but too limited in their extent. New severities were adopted. The fisheries of your people in America followed their charters; and their mutual combination to defend what they thought their common rights, brought on a total prohibition of their mutual commercial intercourse. No distinction of persons or merits was observed—the peaceable and the mutinous, friends and foes, were alike involved, as if the rigour of the laws had a certain tendency to recommend the authority of the legislator.

Whilst the penal laws increased in rigour, and extended in application over all the colonies, the direct force was applied but to one part. Had the great fleet and foreign army since employed been at that time called for, the greatness of the preparation would have declared the magnitude of the danger. The nation would have been alarmed, and taught the necessity of some means of reconciliation with our countrymen in America, who, whenever they are provoked to resistance, demand a force to reduce them to obedience full as destructive to us as to them. But parliament and the people, by a premeditated concealment of their real situation, were drawn into perplexities which furnished excuses for further armaments; and whilst they were taught to believe themselves called to suppress a riot, they found themselves involved in a mighty war.

At length British blood was spilled by British hands—a fatal era, which we must ever deplore, because your empire will for ever feel it. Your Majesty was touched with a sense of so great a disaster. Your paternal breast was affected with the sufferings of your English subjects in America. In your speech from the throne, in the beginning of the session of 1775, you were graciously pleased to declare yourself inclined to relieve their distresses, and to pardon their errors. You felt their sufferings under the late penal acts of parliament. But your ministry felt differently. Not discouraged by the pernicious effects of all they had hitherto advised, and notwithstanding the gracious declaration of your Majesty, they obtained another act of parliament, in which the rigours of all the former were consolidated, and embittered by circumstances of additional severity and outrage. The whole trading property of America (even unoffending shipping in port) was indiscriminately and irrecoverably given, as the plunder of foreign enemies, to the sailors of your navy. This property was put out of the reach of your mercy. Your people were despoiled; and your navy, by a new, dangerous, and prolific example, corrupted with the plunder of their countrymen. Your people in that part of your dominions were put, in their general and political as well as their personal capacity, wholly out of the protection of your government.

Though unwilling to dwell on all the improper modes of carrying on this unnatural and ruinous war, and which have led directly to the present unhappy separation of Great Britain and its colonies, we must beg leave to represent two particulars, which we are sure must have been entirely contrary to your Majesty's order or approbation. Every course of action in hostility, however that hostility may be just or merited, is not justifiable or excusable. It is the duty of those who claim to rule over others not to provoke them beyond the necessity of the case; nor to leave stings in their minds which must long rankle, even when the appearance of tranquillity is restored.—We therefore assure your Majesty, that it is with shame and sorrow we have seen several acts of hostility, which could have no other tendency than incurably to alienate the minds of your American subjects. To excite, by a proclamation issued by your Majesty's governor, a universal insurrection of negro slaves in any of the colonies, is a measure full of complicated horrors; absolutely illegal; suitable neither to the practice of war nor to the laws of peace. Of the same quality we look upon all attempts to bring down on your subjects an irruption of those fierce and cruel tribes of savages and cannibals, in whom the vestiges of human nature are nearly effaced by ignorance and barbarity. They are not fit allies for your Majesty in a war with your people. They are not fit instruments of an English government. These, and many other acts, we disclaim as having advised or approved when done; and we clear ourselves to your Majesty, and to all civilised nations, from any participation whatever, before or after the fact, in such unjustifiable and horrid proceedings.

But there is one weighty circumstance which we lament equally with the causes of war, and with the modes of carrying it on— that no disposition whatsoever towards peace or reconciliation has ever been shown by those who have directed the public councils of this kingdom, either before the breaking out of these hostilities, or during the unhappy continuance of them. Every proposition made in your parliament to remove the original cause of these troubles, by taking off taxes, obnoxious for their principle or their design, has been overruled: every bill, brought in for quiet, rejected even on the first proposition. The petitions of the colonies have not been admitted even to a hearing. The very possibility of public agency, by which such petitions could authentically arrive at parliament, has been evaded and chicaned away. All the public declarations which indicate anything resembling a disposition to reconciliation, seem to us loose, general, equivocal, capable of various meanings, or of none; and they are accordingly construed differently, at different times, by those on whose recommendation they have been made; being wholly unlike the precision and stability of public faith; and bearing no mark of that ingenuous simplicity, and native candour and integrity, which formerly characterised the English nation.

Instead of any relaxation of the claim of taxing at the discretion of parliament, your ministers have devised a new mode of enforcing that claim, much more effectual for the oppression of the colonies, though not for your Majesty's service, both as to the quantity and application, than any of the former methods; and their mode has been expressly held out by ministers, as a plan not to be departed from by the House of Commons, and as the very condition on which the legislature is to accept the dependence of the colonies.

At length, when, after repeated refusals to hear or to conciliate, an act, dissolving your government by putting your people in America out of your protection, was passed, your ministers suffered several months to elapse without affording to them, or to any community, or any individual amongst them, the means of entering into that protection even on unconditional submission, contrary to your Majesty's gracious declaration from the throne, and in direct violation of the public faith.

We cannot, therefore, agree to unite in new severities against the brethren of our blood for their asserting an independency, to which, we know in our conscience, they have been necessitated by the conduct of those very persons who now make use of that argument to provoke us to a continuance and repetition of the acts, which in a regular series have led to this great misfortune.

The reasons, dread Sir, which have been used to justify this perseverance in a refusal to hear or conciliate, have been reduced into a sort of parliamentary maxims which we do not approve. The first of these maxims is, "that the two Houses ought not to receive (as they have hitherto refused to receive) petitions containing matter derogatory to any part of the authority they claim." We conceive this maxim, and the consequent practice, to be unjustifiable by reason or the practice of other sovereign powers, and that it must be productive, if adhered to, of a total separation between this kingdom and its dependencies. The supreme power, being in ordinary cases the ultimate judge, can, as we conceive, suffer nothing in having any part of his rights excepted to, or even discussed, before himself. We know that sovereigns in other countries, where the assertion of absolute regal power is as high as the assertion of absolute power in any politic body can possibly be here, have received many petitions in direct opposition to many of their claims of prerogative; have listened to them; condescended to discuss and to give answers to them. This refusal to admit even the discussion of any part of an undefined prerogative will naturally tend to annihilate any privilege that can be claimed by every inferior dependent community, and every subordinate order in the state.

The next maxim, which has been put as a bar to any plan of accommodation, is, "that no offer of terms of peace ought to be made before parliament is assured that these terms will be accepted." On this we beg leave to represent to your Majesty, that if in all events the policy of this kingdom is to govern the people in your colonies as a free people, no mischief can possibly happen from a declaration to them, and to the world, of the manner and form in which parliament proposes that they shall enjoy the freedom it protects. . . . The glory and propriety of offered mercy is neither tarnished nor weakened by the folly of those who refuse to take advantage of it.

We cannot think that the declaration of independency makes any natural difference in the reason and policy of the offer. No prince out of the possession of his dominions, and become a sovereign *de jure* only, ever thought it derogatory to his rights or his interests to hold out to his former subjects a distinct prospect of the advantages to be derived from his readmission, and a security for some of the most fundamental of those popular privileges in vindication of which he had been deposed. On the contrary, such offers have been almost uniformly made under similar circumstances. Besides, as your Majesty has been graciously pleased, in your speech from the throne, to declare your intention of restoring your people in the colonies to a state of law and liberty, no objection can possibly lie against defining what that law and liberty are; because those who offer and those who are to receive terms frequently differ most widely, and most materially, in the signification of these words, and in the objects to which they apply.

To say that we do not know, at this day, what the grievances of the colonies are (be they real or pretended), would be unworthy of us. But whilst we are thus waiting to be informed of what we perfectly know, we weaken the powers of the commissioners; we delay, perhaps we lose, the happy hour of peace; we are wasting the substance of both countries; we are continuing the effusion of human, of Christian, of English blood.

We are sure that we must have your Majesty's heart along with us, when we declare in favour of mixing something conciliatory with our force. Sir, we abhor the idea of making a conquest of our countrymen. We wish that they may yield to well ascertained, well authenticated, and well secured terms of reconciliation; not that your Majesty should owe the recovery of your dominions to their total waste and destruction. Humanity will not permit us to entertain such a desire; nor will the reverence we bear to the civil rights of mankind make us even wish that questions of great difficulty, of the last importance, and lying deep in the vital principles of the British constitution, should be solved by the arms of foreign mercenary soldiers.

It is not, Sir, from a want of the most inviolable duty to your Majesty, not from a want of a partial and passionate regard to that part of your empire in which we reside, and which we wish to be supreme, that we have hitherto withstood all attempts to render the supremacy of one part of your dominions inconsistent with the liberty and safety of all the rest. The motives of our opposition are found in those very sentiments which we are supposed to violate. For we are convinced beyond a doubt that a system of dependence, which leaves no security to the people for any part of their freedom in their own hands, cannot be established in any inferior member of the British empire, without consequentially destroying the freedom of that very body in favour of whose boundless pretensions such a scheme is adopted. We know and feel that arbitrary power over distant regions is not within the competence, nor to be exercised agreeably to the forms, or consistently with the spirit, of great popular assemblies. If such assemblies are called to a nominal share in the exercise of such power, in order to screen, under general participation, the guilt of desperate measures, it tends only the more deeply to corrupt the deliberative character of those assemblies, in training them to blind obedience; in habituating them to proceed upon grounds of fact, with which they can rarely be sufficiently acquainted, and in rendering them executive instruments of designs, the bottom of which they cannot possibly fathom.

To leave any real freedom to parliament, freedom must be left to the colonies. A military government is the only substitute for civil liberty. That the establishment of such a power in America will utterly ruin our finances (though its certain effect) is the smallest part of our concern. It will become an apt, powerful, and certain engine for the destruction of our freedom here. Great bodies of armed men, trained to a contempt of popular assemblies representative of an English people; kept up for the purpose of exacting impositions without their consent, and maintained by that exaction; instruments in subverting, without any process of law, great ancient establishments and respected forms of governments; set free from, and therefore above, the ordinary English tribunals of the country where they serve;—these men cannot so transform themselves, merely by crossing the sea, as to behold with love and reverence, and submit with profound obedience to the very same things in Great Britain which in America they had been taught to despise, and had been accustomed to awe and humble. All your Majesty's troops, in the rotation of service, will pass through this discipline, and contract these habits. If we could flatter ourselves that this would not happen, we must be the weakest of men: we must be the worst, if we were indifferent whether it happened or not. What, gracious sovereign, is the empire of America to us, or the empire of the world, if we lose our own liberties? We deprecate this last of evils. We deprecate the effect of the doctrines which must support and countenance the government over conquered Englishmen.

As it will be impossible long to resist the powerful and equitable arguments in favour of the freedom of these unhappy people that are to be drawn from the principle of our own liberty, attempts will be made, attempts have been made, to ridicule and to argue away this principle; and to inculcate into the minds of your people other maxims of government and other grounds of obedience, than those which have prevailed at and since the glorious revolution. By degrees, these doctrines, by being convenient, may grow prevalent. The consequence is not certain; but a general change of principles rarely happens among a people without leading to a change of government.

Sir, your throne cannot stand secure upon the principles of unconditional submission and passive obedience; on powers exercised without the concurrence of the people to be governed; on acts made in defiance of their prejudices and habits; on acquiescence procured by foreign mercenary troops, and secured by standing armies. These may possibly be the foundation of other thrones: they must be the subversion of yours. It was not to passive principles in our ancestors that we owe the honour of appearing before a sovereign who cannot feel that he is a prince without knowing that we ought to be free. The revolution is a departure from the ancient course of the descent of this monarchy. The people at that time re-entered into their original rights; and it was not because a positive law authorised what was then done, but because the freedom and safety of the subject, the origin and cause of all laws, required a proceeding paramount and superior to them. At that ever-memorable and instructive period, the letter of the law was superseded in favour of the substance of liberty. To the free choice, therefore, of the people, without either king or parliament, we owe that happy establishment, out of which both king and parliament were regenerated. From that great principle of liberty have originated the statutes, confirming and ratifying the establishment from which your Majesty derives your right to rule over us. Those statutes have not given us our liberties; our liberties have produced them. Every hour of your Majesty's reign your title stands upon the very same foundation on which it was at first laid; and we do not know a better on which it can possibly be placed.

Convinced, Sir, that you cannot have different rights and a different security in different parts of your dominions, we wish to lay an even platform for your throne; and to give it an unmovable stability, by laying it on the general freedom of your people; and by securing to your Majesty that confidence and affection in all parts of your dominions which makes your best security and dearest title in this the chief seat of your empire.

Such, Sir, being amongst us the foundation of monarchy itself, much more clearly and much more peculiarly is it the ground of all parliamentary power. Parliament is a security provided for the protection of freedom, and not a subtile fiction contrived to amuse the people in its place. The authority of both Houses can still less than that of the Crown be supported upon different principles in different places; so as to be for one part of your subjects a protector of liberty, and for another a fund of despotism, through which prerogative is extended by occasional powers, whenever an arbitrary will finds itself straitened by the restrictions of law. Had it seemed good to parliament to consider itself as the indulgent guardian and strong protector of the freedom of the subordinate popular assemblies, instead of exercising its powers to their annihilation, there is no doubt that it never could have been their inclination, because not their interest, to raise questions on the extent of parliamentary rights, or to enfeeble privileges which were the security of their own. Powers, evident from necessity, and not suspicious from an alarming mode or purpose in the exertion, would, as formerly they were, be cheerfully submitted to; and these would have been fully sufficient for conservation of unity in the empire, and for directing its wealth to one common centre. Another use has produced other consequences; and a power which refuses to be limited by moderation must either be lost, or find other more distinct and satisfactory limitations.

As for us, a supposed, or, if it could be, a real, participation in arbitrary power would never reconcile our minds to its establishment. We should be ashamed to stand before your Majesty boldly asserting, in our own favour, inherent rights which bind and regulate the Crown itself, and yet insisting on the exercise, in our own persons, of a more arbitrary sway over our fellow-citizens and fellow-freemen.

These, gracious sovereign, are the sentiments which we consider ourselves as bound, in justification of our present conduct, in the most serious and solemn manner to lay at your Majesty's

feet. We have been called by your Majesty's writs and proclamations, and we have been authorised, either by hereditary privilege, or the choice of your people, to confer and treat with your
Majesty, in your highest councils, upon the arduous affairs of
your kingdom. We are sensible of the whole importance of the
duty which this constitutional summons implies. We know the religious punctuality of attendance which, in the ordinary course, it
demands. It is no light cause which, even for a time, could persuade us to relax in any part of that attendance. The British
empire is in convulsions which threaten its dissolution. Those
particular proceedings which cause and inflame this disorder, after
many years' incessant struggle, we find ourselves wholly unable to
oppose, and unwilling to behold. All our endeavours having proved
fruitless, we are fearful at this time of irritating, by contention,
those passions which we have found it impracticable to compose
by reason. We cannot permit ourselves to countenance, by the
appearance of a silent assent, proceedings fatal to the liberty and
unity of the empire; proceedings which exhaust the strength of
all your Majesty's dominions, destroy all trust and dependence
of our allies, and leave us both at home and abroad exposed to the
suspicious mercy and uncertain inclinations of our neighbour and
rival powers; to whom, by this desperate course, we are driving
our countrymen for protection, and with whom we have forced
them into connexions, and may bind them by habits and by interest—an evil which no victories that may be obtained, no severities
which may be exercised, ever will or can remove.

If but the smallest hope should from any circumstances appear
of a return to the ancient maxims and true policy of this kingdom,
we shall with joy and readiness return to our attendance, in order
to give our hearty support to whatever means may be left for
alleviating the complicated evils which oppress this nation.

If this should not happen, we have discharged our consciences
by this faithful representation to your Majesty and our country;
and, however few in number, or however we may be overborne by
practices, whose operation is but too powerful, by the revival of
dangerous, exploded principles, or by the misguided zeal of such
arbitrary factions as formerly prevailed in this kingdom, and
always to its detriment and disgrace, we have the satisfaction of
standing forth and recording our names in assertion of those
principles whose operation hath, in better times, made your Majesty a great prince, and the British dominions a mighty empire.

ADDRESS TO THE BRITISH COLONISTS
IN NORTH AMERICA

THE very dangerous crisis, into which the British empire is brought, as it accounts for, so it justifies, the unusual step we take in addressing ourselves to you.

The distempers of the state are grown to such a degree of violence and malignity as to render all ordinary remedies vain and frivolous. In such a deplorable situation an adherence to the common forms of business appears to us rather as an apology to cover a supine neglect of duty, than the means of performing it in a manner adequate to the exigency that presses upon us. The common means we have already tried, and tried to no purpose. As our last resource, we turn ourselves to you. We address you merely in our private capacity; vested with no other authority than what will naturally attend those, in whose declarations of benevolence you have no reason to apprehend any mixture of dissimulation or design.

We have this title to your attention: we call upon it in a moment of the utmost importance to us all. We find, with infinite concern, that arguments are used to persuade you of the necessity of separating yourselves from your ancient connection with your parent country, grounded on a supposition that a general principle of alienation and enmity to you had pervaded the whole of this kingdom; and that there does no longer subsist between you and us any common and kindred principles, upon which we can possibly unite consistently with those ideas of liberty in which you have justly placed your whole happiness.

If this fact were true, the inference drawn from it would be irresistible. But nothing is less founded. We admit, indeed, that violent addresses have been procured with uncommon pains by wicked and designing men, purporting to the genuine voice of the whole people of England; that they have been published by authority here; and made known to you by proclamations; in order, by despair and resentment, incurably to poison your minds against the origin of your race, and to render all cordial reconciliation between us utterly impracticable. The same wicked men, for the same bad purposes, have so far surprised the justice of parliament, as to cut off all communication betwixt us, except what is to go in their own fallacious and hostile channel.

But we conjure you by the invaluable pledges, which have hitherto united, and which we trust will hereafter lastingly unite us, that you do not suffer yourselves to be persuaded, or provoked, into an opinion, that you are at war with this nation. Do not think, that the whole, or even the uninfluenced majority, of Englishmen in this island are enemies to their own blood on the American continent. Much delusion has been practised; much corrupt influence treacherously employed. But still a large, and we trust the largest and soundest, part of this kingdom perseveres in the most perfect unity of sentiments, principles, and affections, with you. It spreads out a large and liberal platform of common liberty, upon which we may all unite for ever. It abhors the hostilities which have been carried on against you, as much as you who feel the cruel effect of them. It has disclaimed, in the most solemn manner, at the foot of the throne itself, the addresses, which tended to irritate your sovereign against his colonies. We are persuaded that even many of those who unadvisedly have put their hands to such intemperate and inflammatory addresses, have not at all apprehended to what such proceedings naturally lead; and would sooner die, than afford them the least countenance, if they were sensible of their fatal effects on the union and liberty of the empire.

For ourselves, we faithfully assure you that we have ever considered you as rational creatures; as free agents; as men willing to pursue, and able to discern, your own true interest. We have wished to continue united with you, in order that a people of one origin and one character should be directed to the rational objects of government by joint counsels, and protected in them by a common force. Other subordination in you we require none. We have never pressed that argument of general union to the extinction of your local, natural, and just privileges. Sensible of what is due both to the dignity and weakness of man, we have never wished to place over you any government, over which, in great fundamental points, you should have no sort of check or control in your own hands, or which should be repugnant to your situation, principles, and character.

No circumstances of fortune, you may be assured, will ever induce us to form, or tolerate, any such design. If the disposition of Providence (which we deprecate) should even prostrate you at our feet, broken in power and in spirit, it would be our duty and inclination to revive, by every practical means, that free energy of mind, which a fortune unsuitable to your virtue had damped and dejected; and to put you voluntarily in possession of those very privileges which you had in vain attempted to assert by arms. For we solemnly declare, that although we should look upon a separation from you as a heavy calamity (and the heavier, because we know you must have your full share in it), yet we had much rather see you totally independent of this Crown and kingdom, than joined to it by so unnatural a conjunction as that of freedom with servitude—a conjunction which, if it were at all practicable, could not fail in the end of being more mischievous to the peace, prosperity, greatness, and power of this nation, than beneficial, by an enlargement of the bounds of nominal empire.

But because, brethren, these professions are general, and such as even enemies may make, when they reserve to themselves the construction of what servitude and what liberty are, we inform you, that we adopt your own standard of the blessing of free government. We are of opinion that you ought to enjoy the sole and exclusive right of freely granting, and applying to the support of your administration, what God has freely granted as a reward to your industry. And we do not confine this immunity from exterior coercion in this great point solely to what regards your local establishment, but also to what may be thought proper for the maintenance of the whole empire. In this resource we cheerfully trust and acquiesce: satisfied by evident reason that no other expectation of revenue can possibly be given by free men; and knowing, from an experience uniform both on yours and on our side of the ocean, that such an expectation has never yet been disappointed. We know of no road to your coffers but through your affections.

To manifest our sentiments the more clearly to you and to the world on this subject; we declare our opinion, that if no revenue at all, which, however, we are far from supposing, were to be obtained from you to this kingdom, yet as long as it is our happiness to be joined with you in bonds of fraternal charity and freedom, with an open and flowing commerce between us, one principle of enmity and friendship pervading, and one right of war and peace directing, the strength of the whole empire, we are likely to be at least as powerful as any nation, or as any combination of nations, which in the course of human events may be formed against us. We are sensible that a very large proportion of the wealth and power of every empire must necessarily be thrown upon the presiding state. We are sensible that such a state ever has borne, and ever must bear, the greatest part, and sometimes the whole, of the public expenses: and we think her well indemnified for that (rather apparent than real) inequality of charge, in the dignity and pre-eminence she enjoys, and in the superior opulence which, after all charges defrayed, must necessarily remain at the centre of affairs. Of this principle we are not without evidence in our remembrance (not yet effaced) of the glorious and happy days of this empire. We are, therefore, incapable of that prevaricating style, by which, when taxes without your consent are to be extorted from you, this nation is represented as in the lowest state of impoverishment and public distress; but when we are called upon to oppress you by force of arms, it is painted as scarcely feeling its impositions, abounding with wealth, and inexhaustible in its resources.

We also reason and feel as you do on the invasion of your charters. Because the charters comprehend the essential forms by which you enjoy your liberties, we regard them as most sacred, and by no means to be taken away or altered without process, without examination, and without hearing, as they have lately been. We even think that they ought by no means to be altered at all but at the desire of the greater part of the people who live under them. We cannot look upon men as delinquents in the mass; much less are we desirous of lording over our brethren, insulting their honest pride, and wantonly overturning establishments judged to be just and convenient by the public wisdom of this nation at their institution; and which long and inveterate use has taught you to look up to with affection and reverence. As we disapproved of the proceedings with regard to the forms of your constitution, so we are equally tender of every leading principle of free government. We never could think with approbation of putting the military power out of the coercion of the civil justice in the country where it acts.

We disclaim also any sort of share in that other measure which has been used to alienate your affections from this country, namely, the introduction of foreign mercenaries. We saw their employment with shame and regret, especially in numbers so far exceeding the English forces as in effect to constitute vassals who have no sense of freedom, and strangers who have no common interest or feelings, as the arbiters of our unhappy domestic quarrel.

We likewise saw with shame the African slaves, who had been sold to you on public faith, and under the sanction of acts of parliament, to be your servants and your guards, employed to cut the throats of their masters.

You will not, we trust, believe that, born in a civilised country, formed to gentle manners, trained in a merciful religion, and living in enlightened and polished times where even foreign hostility is softened from its original sternness, we could have thought of letting loose upon you, our late beloved brethren, these fierce tribes of savages and cannibals, in whom the traces of human nature are effaced by ignorance and barbarity. We rather wished to have joined with you in bringing gradually that unhappy part of mankind into civility, order, piety, and virtuous discipline, than to have confirmed their evil habits, and increased their natural ferocity, by fleshing them in the slaughter of you, whom our wiser and better ancestors had sent into the wilderness, with the express view of introducing, along with our holy religion, its humane and charitable manners. We do not hold that all things are lawful in war. We should think that every barbarity, in fire, in wasting, in murders, in tortures, and other cruelties too horrible, and too full of turpitude, for Christian mouths to utter, or ears to hear, if done at our instigation by those who we know will make war thus if they make it at all, to be to all intents and purposes as if done by ourselves. We clear ourselves to you our brethren, to the present age, and to future generations, to our king and our country, and to Europe, which as a spectator beholds this tragic scene, of every part or share in adding this last and worst of evils to the inevitable mischiefs of a civil war.

We do not call you rebels and traitors. We do not call for the vengeance of the Crown against you. We do not know how to qualify millions of our countrymen, contending with one heart for an admission to privileges which we have ever thought our own happiness and honour, by odious and unworthy names. On the contrary, we highly revere the principles on which you act, though we lament some of their effects. Armed as you are, we embrace you as our friends, and as our brethren, by the best and dearest ties of relation.

We view the establishment of the English colonies on principles of liberty as that which is to render this kingdom venerable to future ages. In comparison of this we regard all the victories and conquests of our warlike ancestors, or of our own times, as bar-

barous, vulgar distinctions, in which many nations, whom we look upon with little respect or value, have equalled if not far exceeded us. This is the peculiar and appropriated glory of England. Those who *have and who hold* to that foundation of common liberty, whether on this or on your side of the ocean, we consider as the true, and the only true, Englishmen. Those who depart from it, whether there or here, are attainted, corrupted in blood, and wholly fallen from their original rank and value. They are the real rebels to the fair constitution and just supremacy of England.

We exhort you, therefore, to cleave for ever to those principles, as being the true bond of union in this empire; and to show, by a manly perseverance, that the sentiments of honour, and the rights of mankind, are not held by the uncertain events of war, as you have hitherto shown a glorious and affecting example to the world that they are not dependent on the ordinary conveniences and satisfactions of life.

Knowing no other arguments to be used to men of liberal minds, it is upon these very principles, and these alone, we hope and trust that no flattering and no alarming circumstances shall permit you to listen to the seductions of those who would alienate you from your dependence on the Crown and parliament of this kingdom. That very liberty, which you so justly prize above all things, originated here: and it may be very doubtful whether, without being constantly fed from the original fountain, it can be at all perpetuated or preserved in its native purity and perfection. Untried forms of government may, to unstable minds, recommend themselves even by their novelty. But you will do well to remember that England has been great and happy under the present limited monarchy (subsisting in more or less vigour and purity) for several hundred years. None but England can communicate to you the benefits of such a constitution. We apprehend you are not now, nor for ages are likely to be, capable of that form of constitution in an independent state. Besides, let us suggest to you our apprehensions that your present union (in which we rejoice, and which we wish long to subsist) cannot always subsist without the authority and weight of this great and long-respected body, to equipoise, and to preserve you amongst yourselves in a just and fair equality. It may not even be impossible that a long course of war with the administration of this country may be but a prelude to a series of wars and contentions among yourselves, to end, at length (as such scenes have too often ended), in a species of humiliating repose, which nothing but the preceding calamities would reconcile to the dispirited few who survived them. We allow that even this evil is worth the risk to men of honour, when rational liberty is at stake, as in the present case we confess and lament that it is. But if ever a real security, by parliament, is given against the terror or the abuse of unlimited power, and after such security given you should persevere in resistance, we leave you to consider whether the risk is not incurred without an object; or incurred for an object infinitely diminished by such concessions in its importance nad value.

As to other points of discussion, when these grand fundamentals of your grants and charters are once settled and ratified by clear parliamentary authority, as the ground for peace and forgiveness on our side, and for a manly and liberal obedience on yours, treaty, and a spirit of reconciliation, will easily and securely adjust whatever may remain. Of this we give you our word, that so far as we are at present concerned, and if by any event we should become more concerned hereafter, you may rest assured, upon the pledges of honour not forfeited, faith not violated, and uniformity of character and profession not yet broken, we at least, on these grounds, will never fail you.

Respecting your wisdom, and valuing your safety, we do not call upon you to trust your existence to your enemies. We do not advise you to an unconditional submission. With satisfaction we assure you that almost all in both Houses (however unhappily they have been deluded, so as not to give any immediate effect to their opinion) disclaim that idea. You can have no friends in whom you cannot rationally confide. But parliament is your friend from the moment in which, removing its confidence from those who have constantly deceived its good intentions, it adopts the sentiments of those who have made sacrifices (inferior indeed to yours), but have, however, sacrificed enough to demonstrate the sincerity of their regard and value for your liberty and prosperity.

Arguments may be used to weaken your confidence in that public security; because, from some unpleasant appearances, there is a suspicion that parliament itself is somewhat fallen from its independent spirit. How far this supposition may be founded in fact we are unwilling to determine. But we are well assured from experience, that even if all were true that is contended for, and in the extent, too, in which it is argued, yet as long as the solid and well-disposed forms of this constitution remain, there ever is within parliament itself a power of renovating its principles, and effecting a self-reformation, which no other plan of government has ever contained. This constitution has therefore admitted innumerable improvements, either for the correction of the original scheme, or for removing corruptions, or for bringing its principles better to suit those changes which have successively happened in the circumstances of the nation, or in the manners of the people.

We feel that the growth of the colonies is such a change of circumstances; and that our present dispute is an exigency as pressing as any which ever demanded a revision of our government. Public troubles have often called upon this country to look into its constitution. It has ever been bettered by such a revision. . . . If we set about this great work, on both sides, with the same conciliatory turn of mind, we may now, as in former times, owe even to our mutual mistakes, contentions, and animosities, the lasting concord, freedom, happiness, and glory of this empire.

Gentlemen, the distance between us, with other obstructions, has caused much misrepresentation of our mutual sentiments. We, therefore, to obviate them as well as we are able, take this method of assuring you of our thorough detestation of the whole war; and particularly the mercenary and savage war carried on or attempted against you: our thorough abhorrence of all addresses adverse to you, whether public or private; our assurances of an invariable affection towards you; our constant regard to your privileges and liberties; and our opinion of the solid security you ought to enjoy for them, under the paternal care and nurture of a protecting parliament.

Though many of us have earnestly wished that the authority of that august and venerable body, so necessary in many respects to the union of the whole, should be rather limited by its own equity and discretion, than by any bounds described by positive laws and public compacts; and though we felt the extreme difficulty, by any theoretical limitations, of qualifying that authority so as to preserve one part and deny another; and though you (as we gratefully acknowledge) had acquiesced most cheerfully under that prudent reserve of the constitution, at that happy moment, when neither you nor we apprehended a further return of the exercise of invidious powers, we are now as fully persuaded as you can be, by the malice, inconstancy, and perverse inquietude of many men, and by the incessant endeavours of an arbitrary faction, now too powerful, that our common necessities do require a full explanation and ratified security for your liberties and our quiet.

Although his Majesty's condescension in committing the direction of his affairs into the hands of the known friends of his family, and of the liberties of all his people, would, we admit, be a great means of giving repose to your minds, as it must give infinite facility to reconciliation, yet we assure you, that we think, with such a security as we recommend, adopted from necessity, and not choice, even by the unhappy authors and instruments of the public misfortunes, that the terms of reconciliation, if once accepted by parliament, would not be broken. We also pledge ourselves to you, that we should give, even to those unhappy persons, a hearty support in effectuating the peace of the empire; and every opposition in an attempt to cast it again into disorder.

When that happy hour shall arrive, let us in all affection recommend to you the wisdom of continuing, as in former times, or even in a more ample measure, the support of your government, and even to give to your administration some degree of reciprocal interest in your freedom. We earnestly wish you not to furnish your enemies, here or elsewhere, with any sort of pretexts for reviving quarrels by too reserved and severe or penurious an exercise of those sacred rights, which no pretended abuse in the exercise ought to impair, nor, by overstraining the principles of freedom, to make them less compatible with those haughty sentiments in others, which the very same principles may be apt to breed in minds not tempered with the utmost equity and justice.

The well-wishers of the liberty and union of this empire salute you, and recommend you most heartily to the Divine protection.

10

A LETTER TO JOHN FARR AND JOHN HARRIS, ESQUIRES, SHERIFFS OF BRISTOL, ON THE AFFAIRS OF AMERICA

APRIL, 1777[1]

Burke's recent behavior had alarmed many of his constituents and he took it upon himself to address a special open letter to Bristol explaining his actions and the reasons for them. The letter was written shortly after the two above addresses and the ideas expressed in it reflect and supplement many comments made in those addresses. Three days after completing this letter, Burke returned to his seat in Parliament; the secession had failed.

GENTLEMEN—I have the honour of sending you the two last Acts which have been passed with regard to the troubles in America. These Acts are similar to all the rest which have been made on the same subject. They operate by the same principle, and they are derived from the very same policy. I think they complete the number of this sort of statutes to nine. It affords no matter for very pleasing reflection to observe that our subjects diminish as our laws increase.

If I have the misfortune of differing with some of my fellow-citizens on this great and arduous subject, it is no small consolation to me that I do not differ from you. With you I am perfectly united. We are heartily agreed in our detestation of a civil war. We have ever expressed the most unqualified disapprobation of all the steps which have led to it, and of all those which tend to prolong it. And I have no doubt that we feel exactly the same

[1] *Works*, VI, 149-97.

emotions of grief and shame in all its miserable consequences; whether they appear, on the one side or the other, in the shape of victories or defeats, of captures made from the English on the continent, or from the English in these islands, of legislative regulations which subvert the liberties of our brethren, or which undermine our own.

Of the first of these statutes (that for the letter of marque) I shall say little. Exceptionable as it may be, and as I think it is in some particulars, it seems the natural, perhaps necessary, result of the measures we have taken and the situation we are in. The other (for a partial suspension of the Habeas Corpus) appears to me of a much deeper malignity.[2] During its progress through the House of Commons it has been amended, so as to express, more distinctly than at first it did, the avowed sentiments of those who framed it; and the main ground of my exception to it is because it does express, and does carry into execution, purposes which appear to me so contradictory to all the principles, not only of the constitutional policy of Great Britain, but even of that species of hostile justice which no asperity of war wholly extinguishes in the minds of a civilised people.

It seems to have in view two capital objects—the first to enable administration to confine, as long as it shall think proper, those whom that Act is pleased to qualify by the name of pirates. Those so qualified I understand to be the commanders and mariners of such privateers and ships of war belonging to the colonies as in the course of this unhappy contest may fall into the hands of the crown. They are therefore to be detained in prison, under the criminal description of piracy, to a future trial and ignominious punishment, whenever circumstances shall make it convenient to execute vengeance on them under the colour of that odious and infamous offence.

To this first purpose of the law I have no small dislike, because the Act does not (as all laws and all equitable transactions ought to do) fairly describe its object. The persons who make a naval war upon us in consequence of the present troubles may be rebels, but to call and treat them as pirates is confounding not only the natural distinction of things, but the order of crimes, which, whether by putting them from a higher part of the scale to the lower, or from the lower to the higher, is never done without dan-

---

[2] It affected North America and ships on the high seas.

gerously disordering the whole frame of jurisprudence. Though piracy may be, in the eye of the law, a *less* offence than treason, yet as both are in effect punished with the same death, the same forfeiture, and the same corruption of blood, I never would take from any fellow-creature whatever any sort of advantage which he may derive to his safety from the pity of mankind, or to his reputation from their general feelings, by degrading his offence when I cannot soften his punishment. The general sense of mankind tells me that those offences which may possibly arise from mistaken virtue are not in the class of infamous actions. . . .

Besides, I must honestly tell you that I could not vote for, or countenance in any way, a statute which stigmatises with the crime of piracy these men whom an Act of Parliament had previously put out of the protection of the law. When the legislature of this kingdom had ordered all their ships and goods, for the mere new-created offence of exercising trade, to be divided as a spoil among the seamen of the navy, to consider the necessary reprisal of an unhappy, proscribed, interdicted people as the crime of piracy would have appeared, in any other legislature than ours, a strain of the most insulting and most unnatural cruelty and injustice. I assure you I never remember to have heard of anything like it in any time or country.

The second professed purpose of the Act is to detain in England for trial those who shall commit high treason in America.

That you may be enabled to enter into the true spirit of the present law it is necessary, gentlemen, to apprise you that there is an Act, made so long ago as in the reign of Henry the Eighth, before the existence or thought of any English colonies in America, for the trial in this kingdom of treasons committed out of the realm. In the year 1769 Parliament thought proper to acquaint the crown with their construction of that Act in a formal address, wherein they entreated his Majesty to cause persons charged with high treason in America to be brought into this kingdom for trial. By this Act of Henry the Eighth, *so construed and so applied*, almost all that is substantial and beneficial in a trial by jury is taken away from the subject in the colonies. This is however saying too little, for to try a man under that Act is, in effect, to condemn him unheard. A person is brought hither in the dungeon of a ship's hold, thence he is vomited into a dungeon on land, loaded with irons, unfurnished with money, unsupported by friends, three thousand miles from all means of calling upon or confronting evidence, where no one local circumstance that tends to detect perjury can possibly be judged of—such a person may be executed according to form, but he can never be tried according to justice.

I therefore could never reconcile myself to the bill I send you, which is expressly provided to remove all inconveniences from the establishment of a mode of trial which has ever appeared to me most unjust and most unconstitutional. Far from removing the difficulties which impede the execution of so mischievous a project, I would heap new difficulties upon it if it were in my power. All the ancient, honest, juridical principles and institutions of England are so many clogs to check and retard the headlong course of violence and oppression. They were invented for this one good purpose, that what was not just should not be convenient. Convinced of this I would leave things as I found them. The old, cool-headed, general law is as good as any deviation dictated by present heat.

I could see no fair, justifiable expedience pleaded to favour this new suspension of the liberty of the subject. If the English in the colonies can support the independency to which they have been unfortunately driven, I suppose nobody has such a fanatical zeal for the criminal justice of Henry the Eighth that he will contend for executions which must be retaliated tenfold on his own friends, or who has conceived so strange an idea of English dignity as to think the defeats in America compensated by the triumphs at Tyburn. If, on the contrary, the colonies are reduced to the obedience of the crown, there must be, under that authority, tribunals in the country itself fully competent to administer justice on all offenders. But if there are not, and that we must suppose a thing so humiliating to our Government as that all this vast continent should unanimously concur in thinking that no ill fortune can convert resistance to the royal authority into a criminal act, we may call the effect of our victory peace, or obedience, or what we will; but the war is not ended, the hostile mind continues in full vigour, and it continues under a worse form. If your peace be nothing more than a sullen pause from arms, if their quiet be nothing but the meditation of revenge, where smitten pride smarting from its wounds festers into new rancour, neither the Act of Henry the Eighth, nor its handmaid of this reign, will answer any wise end of policy or justice. For if the bloody fields which they saw and felt are not sufficient to subdue the reason of

America (to use the expressive phrase of a great lord in office), it is not the judicial slaughter which is made in another hemisphere against their universal sense of justice that will ever reconcile them to the British Government.

I take it for granted, gentlemen, that we sympathise in a proper horror of all punishment further than as it serves for an example. To whom then does the example of an execution in England for this American rebellion apply? Remember, you are told every day, that the present is a contest between the two countries, and that we in England are at war for *our own* dignity against our rebellious children. Is this true? If it be, it is surely among such rebellious children that examples for disobedience should be made, to be in any degree instructive; for whoever thought of teaching parents their duty by an example from the punishment of an undutiful son? As well might the execution of a fugitive negro in the plantations be considered as a lesson to teach masters humanity to their slaves. Such executions may indeed satiate our revenge, they may harden our hearts, and puff us up with pride and arrogance. Alas! this is not instruction!

If anything can be drawn from such examples by a parity of the case, it is to show how deep their crime and how heavy their punishment will be who shall at any time dare to resist a distant power actually disposing of their property, without their voice or consent to the disposition, and overturning their franchises without charge or hearing. God forbid that England should ever read this lesson written in the blood of *any* of her offspring!

War is at present carried on between the king's natural and foreign troops on one side and the English in America on the other, upon the usual footing of other wars; and accordingly an exchange of prisoners has been regularly made from the beginning. If notwithstanding this hitherto equal procedure, upon some prospect of ending the war with success (which, however, may be delusive), administration prepares to act against those as *traitors* who remain in their hands at the end of the troubles, in my opinion we shall exhibit to the world as indecent a piece of injustice as ever civil fury has produced. If the prisoners, who have been exchanged, have not by that exchange been *virtually pardoned*, the cartel (whether avowed or understood) is a cruel fraud; for you have received the life of a man, and you ought to return a life for it, or there is no parity of fairness in the transaction.

If, on the other hand, we admit that they who are actually

exchanged are pardoned, but contend that you may justly reserve for vengeance those who remain unexchanged, then this unpleasant and unhandsome consequence will follow: that you judge of the delinquency of men merely by the time of their guilt, and not by the heinousness of it; and you make fortune and accidents, and not the moral qualities of human action, the rule of your justice.

These strange incongruities must ever perplex those who confound the unhappiness of civil dissensions with the crime of treason. . . .[3]

This Act, proceeding on these principles, that is, preparing to end the present troubles by a trial of one sort of hostility under the name of piracy, and of another by the name of treason, and executing the Act of Henry the Eighth according to a new and unconstitutional interpretation, I have thought evil and dangerous, even though the instruments of effecting such purposes had been merely of a neutral quality.

But it really appears to me, that the means which this Act employs are, at least, as exceptionable as the end. Permit me to open myself a little upon this subject, because it is of importance to me, when I am obliged to submit to the power without acquiescing in the reason of an Act of legislature, that I should justify my dissent by such arguments as may be supposed to have weight with a sober man.

The main operative regulation of the Act is to suspend the common law, and the statute *Habeas Corpus* (the sole securities either for liberty or justice), with regard to all those who have been out of the realm, or on the high seas, within a given time. The rest of the people, as I understand, are to continue as they stood before.

I confess, gentlemen, that this appears to me as bad in the principle, and far worse in its consequence, than an universal suspension of the *Habeas Corpus* Act; and the limiting qualification, instead of taking out the sting, does in my humble opinion sharpen and envenom it to a greater degree. Liberty, if I under-

[3] Burke then elaborated on this confusion and quickly arrived at two conclusions. First, that if Americans are only rebels, then the generals have no power to release captives. Second, that, although lawyers may not see the distinction between rebel and pirate, legislators, who are guided in England by "reason and equity," do and they, therefore, should remedy the unjust treatment of Americans resulting from the unwarranted application of 35 Henry VIII to America.

stand it at all, is a *general* principle, and the clear right of all the subjects within the realm or of none. Partial freedom seems to me a most invidious mode of slavery. But, unfortunately, it is the kind of slavery the most easily admitted in times of civil discord; for parties are but too apt to forget their own future safety in their desire of sacrificing their enemies. . . .

This Act, therefore, has this distinguished evil in it, that it is the first *partial* suspension of the *Habeas Corpus* that has been made. The precedent, which is always of very great importance, is now established. For the first time a distinction is made among the people within this realm. Before this Act, every man putting his foot on English ground, every stranger owing only a local and temporary allegiance, even negro slaves who had been sold in the colonies and under an Act of Parliament, became as free as every other man who breathed the same air with them. Now a line is drawn, which may be advanced farther and farther at pleasure on the same argument of mere expedience on which it was first described. There is no equality among us; we are not fellow-citizens, if the mariner who lands on the quay does not rest on as firm legal ground as the merchant who sits in his counting-house. Other laws may injure the community, this dissolves it. As things now stand, every man in the West Indies, every one inhabitant of three unoffending provinces on the continent, every person coming from the East Indies, every gentleman who has travelled for his health or education, every mariner who has navigated the seas, is, for no other offence, under a temporary proscription. Let any of these facts (now become presumptions of guilt) be proved against him, and the bare suspicion of the crown puts him out of the law. It is even by no means clear to me whether the negative proof does not lie upon the person apprehended on suspicion to the subversion of all justice.

I have not debated against this bill in its progress through the House, because it would have been vain to oppose and impossible to correct it. It is some time since I have been clearly convinced that in the present state of things all opposition to any measures proposed by ministers, where the name of America appears, is vain and frivolous. You may be sure that I do not speak of my opposition, which in all circumstances must be so, but that of men of the greatest wisdom and authority in the nation. Everything proposed against America is supposed of course to be in favour of Great Britain. Good and ill success are equally admitted as reasons for preserving in the present methods. Several very prudent and very well-intentioned persons were of opinion that during the prevalence of such dispositions, all struggle rather inflamed than lessened the distemper of the public councils. Finding such resistance to be considered as factious by most within-doors, and by very many without, I cannot conscientiously support what is against my opinion, nor prudently contend with what I know is irresistible. Preserving my principles unshaken, I reserve my activity for rational endeavours; and I hope that my past conduct has given sufficient evidence that if I am a single day from my place, it is not owing to indolence or love of dissipation. The slightest hope of doing good is sufficient to recall me to what I quitted with regret. In declining for some time my usual strict attendance, I do not in the least condemn the spirit of those gentlemen who, with a just confidence in their abilities (in which I claim a sort of share from my love and admiration of them), were of opinion that their exertions in this desperate case might be of some service. They thought that by contracting the sphere of its application they might lessen the malignity of an evil principle. Perhaps they were in the right. But when my opinion was so very clearly to the contrary, for the reasons I have just stated, I am sure *my* attendance would have been ridiculous.

I must add in further explanation of my conduct that, far from softening the features of such a principle, and thereby removing any part of the popular odium or natural terrors attending it, I should be sorry that anything framed in contradiction to the spirit of our constitution did not instantly produce, in fact, the grossest of the evils with which it was pregnant in its nature. It is by lying dormant a long time, or being at first very rarely exercised, that arbitrary power steals upon a people. On the next unconstitutional Act, all the fashionable world will be ready to say—Your prophecies are ridiculous, your fears are vain, you see how little of the mischiefs which you formerly foreboded are come to pass. Thus, by degrees, that artful softening of all arbitrary power, the alleged infrequency or narrow extent of its operation, will be received as a sort of aphorism—and Mr. *Hume* will not be singular in telling us that the felicity of mankind is no more disturbed by it than by earthquakes or thunder or the other more unusual accidents of nature.

The Act of which I speak is among the fruits of the American war; a war in my humble opinion productive of many mischiefs of a kind which distinguish it from all others. Not only our policy is deranged, and our empire distracted, but our laws and our legislative spirit appear to have been totally perverted by it. We have made war on our colonies, not by arms only, but by laws. As hostility and law are not very concordant ideas, every step we have taken in this business has been made by trampling on some maxim of justice, or some capital principle of wise government. What precedents were established, and what principles overturned (I will not say of English privilege, but of general justice), in the Boston Port, the Massachusetts Charter, the Military Bill, and all that long array of hostile Acts of Parliament by which the war with America has been begun and supported! Had the principles of any of these Acts been first exerted on English ground they would probably have expired as soon as they touched it. But by being removed from our persons they have rooted in our laws, and the latest posterity will taste the fruits of them.

Nor is it the worst effect of this unnatural contention, that our *laws* are corrupted. Whilst *manners* remain entire, they will correct the vices of law, and soften it at length to their own temper. But we have to lament that in most of the late proceedings we see very few traces of that generosity, humanity, and dignity of mind which formerly characterised this nation. War suspends the rules of moral obligation, and what is long suspended is in danger of being totally abrogated. Civil wars strike deepest of all into the manners of the people. They vitiate their politics, they corrupt their morals, they pervert even the natural taste and relish of equity and justice. By teaching us to consider our fellow-citizens in a hostile light, the whole body of our nation becomes gradually less dear to us. The very names of affection and kindred, which were the bond of charity whilst we agreed, become new incentives to hatred and rage, when the communion of our country is dissolved. We may flatter ourselves that we shall not fall into this misfortune. But we have no charter of exemption that I know of from the ordinary frailties of our nature.

What but that blindness of heart which arises from the frenzy of civil contention could have made any persons conceive the present situation of the British affairs as an object of triumph to themselves, or of congratulation to their sovereign? Nothing surely could be more lamentable to those who remember the flourishing days of this kingdom than to see the insane joy of several unhappy people, amidst the sad spectacle which our affairs and conduct exhibit to the scorn of Europe. We behold (and it seems some people rejoice in beholding) our native land, which used to sit the envied arbiter of all her neighbours, reduced to a servile dependence on their mercy, acquiescing in assurances of friendship which she does not trust, complaining of hostilities which she dares not resent, deficient to her allies, lofty to her subjects, and submissive to her enemies; whilst the liberal Government of this free nation is supported by the hireling sword of German boors and vassals; and three millions of the subjects of Great Britain are seeking for protection to English privileges in the arms of France. . . .[4]

There are many circumstances in the zeal shown for civil war which seem to discover but little of real magnanimity. The addressers offer their own persons, and they are satisfied with hiring Germans. They promise their private fortunes, and they mortgage their country. They have all the merit of volunteers, without risk of person or charge of contribution; and when the unfeeling arm of a foreign soldiery pours out their kindred blood like water, they exult and triumph as if they themselves had performed some notable exploit. I am really ashamed of the fashionable language which has been held for some time past, which, to say the best of it, is full of levity. You know that I allude to the general cry against the cowardice of the Americans, as if we despised them for not making the king's soldiery purchase the advantage they have obtained at a dearer rate. It is not, gentlemen, it is not to respect the dispensations of Providence, nor to provide any decent retreat in the mutability of human affairs. It leaves no medium between insolent victory and infamous defeat. It tends to alienate our minds farther and farther from our natural regards, and to make an eternal rent and schism in the British nation. Those who do not wish for such a separation would not dissolve that cement

[4] Burke now proceeded with a long lamentation on the wretched state of affairs, the death of dear ones and those well known, the danger from other powers, and the failure to realize any substantial success in America:

As yet ["those gentlemen who have prayed for war"], and their German allies of twenty hireling states, have contended only with the unprepared strength of our own infant colonies. But America is not subdued. Not one unattacked village which was originally adverse throughout that vast continent has yet submitted from love or terror. You have the ground you encamp on, and you have no more.

of reciprocal esteem and regard which can alone bind together the parts of this great fabric. It ought to be our wish, as it is our duty, not only to forbear this style of outrage ourselves, but to make every one as sensible as we can of the impropriety and unworthiness of the tempers which give rise to it, and which designing men are labouring with such malignant industry to diffuse amongst us. It is our business to counteract them if possible; if possible to awake our natural regards, and to revive the old partiality to the English name. Without something of this kind I do not see how it is ever practicable really to reconcile with those whose affection, after all, must be the surest hold of our government; and which is a thousand times more worth to us than the mercenary zeal of all the circles of Germany.

I can well conceive a country completely overrun, and miserably wasted, without approaching in the least to settlement. In my apprehension, as long as English government is attempted to be supported over Englishmen by the sword alone, things will thus continue. I anticipate in my mind the moment of the final triumph of foreign military force. When that hour arrives (for it may arrive), then it is that all this mass of weakness and violence will appear in its full light. If we should be expelled from America, the delusion of the partisans of military government might still continue. They might still feed their imaginations with the possible good consequences which might have attended success. Nobody could prove the contrary by facts. But in case the sword should do all that the sword can do, the success of their arms and the defeat of their policy will be one and the same thing. You will never see any revenue from America. Some increase of the means of corruption, without ease of the public burthens, is the very best that can happen. Is it for this that we are at war—and in such a war?

As to the difficulties of laying once more the foundations of that government which, for the sake of conquering what was our own, has been voluntarily and wantonly pulled down by a court faction here, I tremble to look at them. Has any of these gentlemen, who are so eager to govern all mankind, showed himself possessed of the first qualification towards government, some knowledge of the object and of the difficulties which occur in the task they have undertaken?

I assure you that, on the most prosperous issue of your arms, you will not be where you stood, when you called in war to supply the defects of your political establishment. Nor would any disorder or disobedience to government which could arise from the most abject concession on our part ever equal those which will be felt after the most triumphant violence. You have got all the intermediate evils of war into the bargain.

I think I know America. If I do not my ignorance is incurable, for I have spared no pains to understand it; and I do most solemnly assure those of my constituents who put any sort of confidence in my industry and integrity, that everything that has been done there has arisen from a total misconception of the object; that our means of originally holding America, that our means of reconciling with it after quarrel, of recovering it after separation, of keeping it after victory, did depend and must depend in their several stages and periods, upon a total renunciation of that unconditional submission, which has taken such possession of the minds of violent men. The whole of those maxims upon which we have made and continued this war must be abandoned. Nothing indeed (for I would not deceive you) can place us in our former situation. That hope must be laid aside. But there is a difference between bad and the worst of all. Terms relative to the cause of the war ought to be offered by the authority of Parliament. An arrangement at home promising some security for them ought to be made. By doing this, without the least impairing of our strength, we add to the credit of our moderation, which in itself is always strength more or less.

I know many have been taught to think that moderation in a case like this is a sort of treason, and that all arguments for it are sufficiently answered by railing at rebels and rebellion and by charging all the present or future miseries which we may suffer on the resistance of our brethren. But I would wish them in this grave matter, and if peace is not wholly removed from their hearts, to consider seriously, first, that to criminate and recriminate never yet was the road to reconciliation in any difference amongst men. In the next place, it would be right to reflect that the American English (whom they may abuse if they think it honourable to revile the absent) can, as things now stand, neither be provoked at our railing nor bettered by our instruction. All communication is cut off between us, but this we know with certainty that, though we cannot reclaim them, we may reform ourselves. If measures of peace are necessary, they must begin somewhere, and a conciliatory temper must precede and prepare every plan of reconciliation. Nor do I conceive that we suffer anything by thus regulating our own minds. We are not disarmed by being disencumbered of our passions. Declaiming on rebellion never added a bayonet or a charge of powder to your military force, but I am afraid that it has been the means of taking up many muskets against you.

This outrageous language, which has been encouraged and kept alive by every art, has already done incredible mischief. For a long time, even amidst the desolations of war and the insults of hostile laws daily accumulated on one another, the American leaders seem to have had the greatest difficulty in bringing up their people to a declaration of total independence. But the court gazette accomplished what the abettors of independence had attempted in vain. When that disingenuous compilation and strange medley of railing and flattery was adduced as a proof of the united sentiments of the people of Great Britain, there was a great change throughout all America. The tide of popular affection, which had still set towards the parent country, began immediately to turn, and to flow with great rapidity in a contrary course. Far from concealing these wild declarations of enmity, the author of the celebrated pamphlet,[5] which prepared the minds of the people for independence, insists largely on the multitude and the spirit of these addresses; and he draws an argument from them which (if the fact was as he supposes) must be irresistible. For I never knew a writer on the theory of government so partial to authority as not to allow that the hostile mind of the rulers to their people did fully justify a change of government; nor can any reason whatever be given why one people should voluntarily yield any degree of pre-eminence to another but on a supposition of great affection and benevolence towards them. Unfortunately your rulers, trusting to other things, took no notice of this great principle of connection. From the beginning of this affair they have done all they could to alienate your minds from your own kindred; and if they could excite hatred enough in one of the parties towards the other, they seemed to be of opinion that they had gone half the way towards reconciling the quarrel.

I know it is said that your kindness is only alienated on account of their resistance; and therefore, if the colonies surrender at discretion, all sort of regard and even much indulgence is meant

---

[5] Referring to Thomas Paine, author of "Common Sense."

towards them in future. But can those who are partisans for continuing a war to enforce such a surrender be responsible (after all that has passed) for such a future use of a power that is bound by no compacts and restrained by no terror? Will they tell us what they call indulgences? Do they not at this instant call the present war and all its horrors a lenient and merciful proceeding?

No conqueror that I ever heard of has *professed* to make a cruel, harsh, and insolent use of his conquest. No! The man of the most declared pride scarcely dares to trust his own heart with this dreadful secret of ambition. But it will appear in its time; and no man who professes to reduce another to the insolent mercy of a foreign arm ever had any sort of goodwill towards him. The profession of kindness with that sword in his hand and that demand of surrender is one of the most provoking acts of his hostility. I shall be told that all this is lenient as against rebellious adversaries. But are the leaders of their faction more lenient to those who submit? Lord Howe and General Howe have powers under an Act of Parliament to restore to the king's peace and to free trade any men or district which shall submit. Is this done? We have been over and over informed by the authorised gazette that the city of New York and the countries of Staten and Long Island have submitted voluntarily and cheerfully, and that many are very full of zeal to the cause of administration. Were they instantly restored to trade? Are they yet restored to it? Is not the benignity of two commissioners, naturally most humane and generous men, some way fettered by instructions equally against their dispositions and spirit of parliamentary faith, when Mr. Tryon, vaunting of the fidelity of the city in which he is governor, is obliged to apply to Ministry for leave to protect the king's loyal subjects, and to grant to them (not the disputed rights and privileges of freedom) but the common rights of men by the name of *graces*? Why do not the commissioners restore them on the spot? Were they not named as commissioners for that express purpose? But we see well enough to what the whole leads. The trade of America is to be dealt out in *private indulgences and graces*; that is, in jobs to recompense the incendiaries of war. They will be informed of the proper time in which to send out their merchandise. From a national the American trade is to be turned into a personal monopoly; and one set of merchants are to be rewarded for the pretended zeal of which another set are the dupes, and thus between craft and credulity the voice of reason is stifled, and all the misconduct, all the calamities of the war are covered and continued.

If I had not lived long enough to be little surprised at anything, I should have been in some degree astonished at the continued rage of several gentlemen who, not satisfied with carrying fire and sword into America, are animated nearly with the same fury against those neighbours of theirs whose only crime it is that they have charitably and humanely wished them to entertain more reasonable sentiments, and not always to sacrifice their interest to their passion. All this rage against unresisting dissent convinces me that at bottom they are far from satisfied they are in the right. For what is it they would have? A war? They certainly have at this moment the blessing of something that is very like one, and if the war they enjoy at present be not sufficiently hot and extensive, they may shortly have it as warm and as spreading as their hearts can desire. Is it the force of the kingdom they call for? They have it already; and if they choose to fight their battles in their own person, nobody prevents their setting sail to America in the next transports. Do they think that the service is stinted for want of liberal supplies? Indeed they complain without reason. The table of the House of Commons will glut them let their appetite for expense be never so keen. And I assure them further that those who think with them in the House of Commons are full as easy in the control as they are liberal in the vote of these expenses. If this be not supply or confidence sufficient, let them open their own private purse-strings and give from what is left to them as largely and with as little care as they think proper.

Tolerated in their passions, let them learn not to persecute the moderation of their fellow-citizens. If all the world joined them in a full cry against rebellion, and were as hotly inflamed against the whole theory and enjoyment of freedom as those who are the most factious for servitude, it could not in my opinion answer any one end whatsoever in this contest. The leaders of this war could not hire (to gratify their friends) one German more than they do, or inspire him with less feeling for the persons or less value for the privileges of their revolted brethren. If we all adopted their sentiments to a man, their allies, the savage Indians, could not be more ferocious than they are; they could not murder one more helpless woman or child, or with more exquisite refinements of cruelty torment to death one more of their English

flesh and blood than they do already. The public money is given to
purchase this alliance—and they have their bargain.

They are continually boasting of unanimity, or calling for it.
But before this unanimity can be matter either of wish or congratulation we ought to be pretty sure that we are engaged in a
rational pursuit. Frenzy does not become a slighter distemper
on account of the number of those who may be infected with it.
Delusion and weakness produce not one mischief the less because
they are universal. I declare that I cannot discern the least advantage which could accrue to us if we were able to persuade our
colonies that they had not a single friend in Great Britain. On
the contrary, if the affections and opinions of mankind be not
exploded as principles of connection, I conceive it would be happy
for us if they were taught to believe that there was even a
formed American party in England to whom they could always
look for support! Happy would it be for us if, in all tempers, they
might turn their eyes to the parent state, so that their very turbu-
lence and sedition should find vent in no other place than this. I
believe there is not a man (except those who prefer the interest
of some paltry faction to the very being of their country) who
would not wish that the Americans should from time to time carry
many points, and even some of them not quite reasonable, by the
aid of any denomination of men here rather than they should
be driven to seek for protection against the fury of foreign mercenaries and the waste of savages in the arms of France.

When any community is subordinately connected with another,
the great danger of the connection is the extreme pride and self-
complacency of the superior, which in all matters of controversy
will probably decide in its own favour. It is a powerful corrective
to such a very rational cause of fear if the inferior body can be
made to believe that the party inclination, or political views, of
several in the principal state will induce them in some degree
to counteract this blind and tyrannical partiality. There is no
danger that any one acquiring consideration or power in the presiding state should carry this leaning to the inferior too far. The
fault of human nature is not of that sort. Power, in whatever
hands, is rarely guilty of too strict limitations on itself. But one
great advantage to the support of authority attends such an amicable and protecting connection, that those who have conferred
favours obtain influence, and from the foresight of future events
can persuade men who have received obligations sometimes to

return them. Thus, by the mediation of those healing principles (call them good or evil), troublesome discussions are brought to some sort of adjustment, and every hot controversy is not a civil war.

But if the colonies (to bring the general matter home to us) could see that, in Great Britain, the mass of the people are melted into its Government, and that every dispute with the Ministry must of necessity be always a quarrel with the nation, they can stand no longer in the equal and friendly relations of fellow-citizens to the subjects of this kingdom. Humble as this relation may appear to some, when it is once broken a strong tie is dissolved. Other sort of connections will be sought. For there are very few in the world who will not prefer a useful ally to an insolent master.

Such discord has been the effect of the unanimity into which so many have of late been seduced or bullied, or into the appearance of which they have sunk through mere despair. They have been told that their dissent from violent measures is an encouragement to rebellion. Men of great presumption and little knowledge will hold a language which is contradicted by the whole course of history. *General* rebellions and revolts of a whole people never were *encouraged*, now or at any time. They are always *provoked*. But if this unheard-of doctrine of the encouragement of rebellion were true, if it were true that an assurance of the friendship of numbers in this country towards the colonies could become an encouragement to them to break off all connection with it, what is the inference? Does anybody seriously maintain that, charged with my share of the public councils, I am obliged not to resist projects which I think mischievous lest men who suffer should be encouraged to resist? The very tendency of such projects to produce rebellion is one of the chief reasons against them. Shall that reason not be given? Is it then a rule that no man in this nation shall open his mouth in favour of the colonies, shall defend their rights, or complain of their sufferings? Or, when war finally breaks out, no man shall express his desires of peace? Has this been the law of our past, or is it to be the terms of our future connection? . . .

But the rebels looked for assistance from this country. They did so in the beginning of this controversy most certainly; and they sought it by earnest supplications to Government, which dignity rejected, and by a suspension of commerce, which the wealth of this nation enabled you to despise. When they found that neither prayers nor menaces had any sort of weight, but that a firm resolution was taken to reduce them to unconditional obedience by a military force, they came to the last extremity. Despairing of us, they trusted in themselves. Not strong enough themselves, they sought succour in France. In proportion as all encouragement here lessened, their distance from this country increased. The encouragement is over; the alienation is complete.

In order to produce this favourite unanimity in delusion, and to prevent all possibility of a return to our ancient happy concord, arguments for our continuance in this course are drawn from the wretched situation itself into which we have been betrayed. It is said that, being at war with the colonies, whatever our sentiments might have been before all ties between us are now dissolved, and all the policy we have left is to strengthen the hands of Government to reduce them. On the principle of this argument, the more mischiefs we suffer from any administration, the more our trust in it is to be confirmed. Let them but once get us into a war, and then their power is safe, and an Act of oblivion passed for all their misconduct.

But is it really true, that Government is always to be strengthened with the instruments of war, but never furnished with the means of peace? In former times ministers, I allow, have been sometimes driven by the popular voice to assert by arms the national honour against foreign powers. But the wisdom of the nation has been far more clear when those ministers have been compelled to consult its interests by treaty. We all know that the sense of the nation obliged the court of King Charles the Second to abandon the *Dutch war*; a war, next to the present, the most impolitic which we ever carried on. . . . The people of England were then, as they are now, called upon to make Government strong. They thought it a great deal better to make it wise and honest.

When I was amongst my constituents at the last summer assizes, I remember that men of all descriptions did then express a very strong desire for peace, and no slight hopes of attaining it from the commission sent out by my Lord Howe. And it is not a little remarkable that, in proportion as every person showed a zeal for the court measures, he was then earnest in circulating an opinion of the extent of the supposed powers of that commission. When I told them that Lord Howe had no powers to treat, or to promise satisfaction on any point whatsoever of the controversy, I was hardly credited, so strong and general was the desire of terminating this war by the method of accommodation. As far as I could discover, this was the temper then prevalent through the kingdom. The king's forces, it must be observed, had at that time been obliged to evacuate Boston. The superiority of the former campaign rested wholly with the colonists. If such powers of treaty were to be wished whilst success was very doubtful, how came they to be less so since his Majesty's arms have been crowned with many considerable advantages? Have these successes induced us to alter our mind; as thinking the season of victory not the time for treating with honour or advantage? Whatever changes have happened in the national character, it can scarcely be our wish that terms of accommodation never should be proposed to our enemy, except when they must be attributed solely to our fears. It has happened, let me say unfortunately, that we read of his Majesty's commission for making peace and his troops evacuating his last town in the thirteen colonies at the same hour and in the same gazette. It was still more unfortunate that no commission went to America to settle the troubles there until several months after an Act had been passed to put the colonies out of the protection of this Government, and to divide their trading property, without a possibility of restitution, as spoil among the seamen of the navy. The most abject submission on the part of the colonies could not redeem them. There was no man on that whole continent, or within three thousand miles of it, qualified by law to follow allegiance with protection or submission with pardon. A proceeding of this kind has no example in history. Independency, and independency with an enmity (which, putting ourselves out of the question, would be called natural and much provoked), was the inevitable consequence. How this came to pass the nation may be one day in a humour to inquire.

All the attempts made this session to give fuller powers of peace to the commanders in America were stifled by the fatal confidence of victory, and the wild hopes of unconditional submission. There was a moment favourable to the king's arms, when if any powers of concession had existed on the other side of the Atlantic, even after all our errors, peace in all probability might have been restored. But calamity is unhappily the usual season of reflection, and the pride of men will not often suffer reason to have any scope until it can be no longer of service.

I have always wished that, as the dispute had its apparent origin from things done in Parliament, and as the Acts passed there had provoked the war, that the foundations of peace should be laid in Parliament also. I have been astonished to find that those whose zeal for the dignity of our body was so hot as to light up the flames of civil war should even publicly declare that these delicate points ought to be wholly left to the crown. Poorly as I may be thought affected to the authority of Parliament, I shall never admit that our constitutional rights can ever become a matter of ministerial negotiation.

I am charged with being an American. If warm affection towards those over whom I claim any share of authority be a crime, I am guilty of this charge. But I do assure you (and they who know me publicly and privately will bear witness to me), that if ever one man lived more zealous than another for the supremacy of Parliament and the rights of this imperial crown, it was myself. Many others, indeed, might be more knowing in the extent of the foundation of these rights. I do not pretend to be an antiquary, a lawyer, or qualified for the chair of professor in metaphysics. I never ventured to put your solid interests upon speculative grounds. My having constantly declined to do so has been attributed to my incapacity for such disquisitions; and I am inclined to believe it is partly the cause. I never shall be ashamed to confess that where I am ignorant I am diffident. I am indeed not very solicitous to clear myself of this imputed incapacity, because men, even less conversant than I am in this kind of subtleties, and placed in stations to which I ought not to aspire, have, by the mere force of civil discretion, often conducted the affairs of great nations with distinguished felicity and glory.

When I first came into a public trust, I found your Parliament in possession of an unlimited legislative power over the colonies. I could not open the statute book without seeing the actual exercise of it, more or less, in all cases whatsoever. This possession passed with me for a title. It does so in all human affairs. No man examines into the defects of his title to his paternal estate, or to his established Government. Indeed common sense taught me that a legislative authority, not actually limited by the express terms of its foundation, or by its own subsequent acts, cannot have its powers parcelled out by argumentative distinctions, so as to enable us to say that here they can, and there they cannot, bind. Nobody was so obliging as to produce to me any record of such distinctions, by compact or otherwise, either at the successive formation of the several colonies, or during the existence of any of them. If any gentlemen[6] were able to see how one power could be given up (merely on abstract reasoning) without giving up the rest, I can only say that they saw farther than I could; nor did I ever presume to condemn any one for being clear-sighted when I was blind. I praise the penetration and learning, and hope that their practice has been correspondent to their theory.

I had indeed very earnest wishes to keep the whole body of this authority perfect and entire as I found it; and to keep it so, not for our advantage solely, but principally for the sake of those on whose account all just authority exists—I mean the people to be governed. For I thought I saw that many cases might well happen in which the exercise of every power comprehended in the broadest idea of legislature might become, in its time and circumstances, not a little expedient for the peace and union of the colonies amongst themselves, as well as for their perfect harmony with Great Britain. Thinking so (perhaps erroneously), but being honestly of that opinion, I was at the same time very sure that the authority, of which I was so jealous, could not under the actual circumstances of our plantations be at all preserved in any of its members but by the greatest reserve in its application, particularly in those delicate points in which the feelings of mankind are the most irritable. They who thought otherwise have found a few more difficulties in their work than, I hope, they were thoroughly aware of when they undertook the present business. I must beg leave to observe that it is not only the invidious branch of taxation that will be resisted, but that no other given part of legislative rights can be exercised without regard to the general opinion of those who are to be governed. That general opinion is the vehicle and organ of legislative omnipotence. Without this it may be a theory to entertain the mind, but it is nothing in the direction of affairs. The completeness of the legislative authority of Parliament *over this kingdom* is not questioned; and yet many things indubitably included in the abstract idea of that power, and which carry no absolute injustice in themselves, yet being contrary to the opinions and feelings of the people, can as little be exercised as if Parliament in that case had been possessed of no right at all. . . .[7] In effect, to follow not to force the public inclination, to give a direction, a form, a technical dress, and a

---

[6] The reference here is to Chatham.

[7] Burke gives as examples the revival of the Star-chamber and the alteration of the established religion.

specific sanction to the general sense of the community, is the true end of legislature.

. . . So truly has prudence (constituted as the god of this lower world) the entire dominion over every exercise of power committed into its hands; and yet I have lived to see prudence and conformity to circumstances wholly set at nought in our late controversies, and treated as if they were the most contemptible and irrational of all things. I have heard it a hundred times very gravely alleged that, in order to keep power in mind, it was necessary, by preference, to exert it in those very points in which it was most likely to be resisted and the least likely to be productive of any advantage.

These were the considerations, gentlemen, which led me early to think that, in the comprehensive dominion which the Divine Providence had put into our hands, instead of troubling our understandings with speculations concerning the unity of empire, and the identity or distinction of legislative powers, and inflaming our passions with the heat and pride of controversy, it was our duty, in all soberness, to conform our government to the character and circumstances of the several people who composed this mighty and strangely diversified mass. I never was wild enough to conceive that one method would serve for the whole; that the natives of Hindostan and those of Virginia could be ordered in the same manner, or that the Cutchery court and the grand jury of Salem could be regulated on a similar plan. I was persuaded that government was a practical thing, made for the happiness of mankind, and not to furnish out a spectacle of uniformity to gratify the schemes of visionary politicians. Our business was to rule, not to wrangle; and it would have been a poor compensation that we had triumphed in a dispute, whilst we lost an empire.

If there be one fact in the world perfectly clear it is this: "That the disposition of the people of America is wholly averse to any other than a free government;" and this is indication enough to any honest statesman how he ought to adapt whatever power he finds in his hands to their case. If any ask me what a free government is, I answer that, for any practical purpose, it is what the people think so; and that they, and not I, are the natural, lawful, and competent judges of this matter. If they practically allow me a greater degree of authority over them than is consistent with any correct ideas of perfect freedom, I ought to thank them for so great a trust and not to endeavour to prove from thence that they have reasoned amiss, and that, having gone so far, by analogy, they must hereafter have no enjoyment but by my pleasure.

If we had seen this done by any others, we should have concluded them far gone in madness. It is melancholy as well as ridiculous to observe the kind of reasoning with which the public has been amused, in order to divert our minds from the common sense of our American policy. There are people who have split and anatomised the doctrine of free government as if it were an abstract question concerning metaphysical liberty and necessity, and not a matter of moral prudence and natural feeling. They have disputed whether liberty be a positive or a negative idea; whether it does not consist in being governed by laws without considering what are the laws or who are the makers; whether man has any rights by nature; and whether all the property he enjoys be not the alms of his government, and his life itself their favour and indulgence. Others, corrupting religion as these have perverted philosophy, contend that Christians are redeemed into captivity, and the blood of the Saviour of mankind has been shed to make them the slaves of a few proud and insolent sinners. These shocking extremes provoking to extremes of another kind, speculations are let loose as destructive to all authority as the former are to all freedom; and every government is called tyranny and usurpation which is not formed on their fancies. In this manner the stirrers-up of this contention, not satisfied with distracting our dependencies and filling them with blood and slaughter, are corrupting our understandings; they are endeavouring to tear up, along with practical liberty, all the foundations of human society, all equity and justice, religion, and order.

Civil freedom, gentlemen, is not, as many have endeavoured to persuade you, a thing that lies hid in the depth of abstruse science. It is a blessing and a benefit, not an abstract speculation; and all the just reasoning that can be upon it is of so coarse a texture as perfectly to suit the ordinary capacities of those who are to enjoy, and of those who are to defend it. Far from any resemblance to those propositions in geometry and metaphysics, which admit no medium, but must be true or false in all their latitude, social and civil freedom, like all other things in common life, are variously mixed and modified, enjoyed in very different degrees, and shaped into an infinite diversity of forms, according to the temper and circumstances of every community. The *extreme* of liberty (which is its abstract perfection, but its real fault) obtains nowhere, nor ought to obtain anywhere. Because extremes, as we all know, in every point which relates either to our duties or satisfactions in life, are destructive both to virtue and enjoyment. Liberty too must be limited in order to be possessed. The degree of restraint it is impossible in any case to settle precisely. But it ought to be the constant aim of every wise public council to find out, by cautious experiments and rational, cool endeavours, with how little, not how much, of this restraint the community can subsist. For liberty is a good to be improved, and not an evil to be lessened. It is not only a private blessing of the first order, but the vital spring and energy of the state itself, which has just so much life and vigour as there is liberty in it. But whether liberty be advantageous or not (for I know it is a fashion to decry the very principle) none will dispute that peace is a blessing; and peace must in the course of human affairs be frequently bought by some indulgence and toleration at least to liberty. For as the Sabbath (though of Divine institution) was made for man, not man for the Sabbath, government, which can claim no higher origin or authority, in its exercise at least, ought to conform to the exigencies of the time and the temper and character of the people with whom it is concerned, and not always to attempt violently to bend the people to their theories of subjection. The bulk of mankind on their part are not excessively curious concerning any theories, whilst they are really happy; and one sure symptom of an ill-conducted state is the propensity of the people to resort to them.

But when subjects, by a long course of such ill conduct, are once thoroughly inflamed, and the state itself violently distempered, the people must have some satisfaction to their feelings more solid than a sophistical speculation on law and government. Such was our situation, and such a satisfaction was necessary to prevent recourse to arms; it was necessary towards laying them down: it will be necessary to prevent the taking them up again and again. Of what nature this satisfaction ought to be I wish it had been the disposition of Parliament seriously to consider. It was certainly a deliberation that called for the exertion of all their wisdom.

I am, and ever have been, deeply sensible of the difficulty of reconciling the strong presiding power, that is so useful towards the conservation of a vast, disconnected, infinitely diversified empire, with that liberty and safety of the provinces, which they must enjoy (in opinion and practice at least) or they will not be provinces at all. I know, and have long felt, the difficulty of reconciling the unwieldly haughtiness of a great ruling nation, habituated to command, pampered by enormous wealth, and confident from a long course of prosperity and victory, to the high spirit of free dependencies, animated with the first glow and activity of juvenile heat, and assuming to themselves as their birthright some part of that very pride which oppresses them. They who perceive no difficulty in reconciling these tempers (which however to make peace must some way or other be reconciled), are much above my capacity or much below the magnitude of the business. Of one thing I am perfectly clear, that it is not by deciding the suit, but by compromising the difference that peace can be restored or kept. They who would put an end to such quarrels, by declaring roundly in favour of the whole demands of either party, have mistaken, in my humble opinion, the office of a mediator.

The war is now of full two years' standing; the controversy, of many more. In different periods of the dispute, different methods of reconciliation were to be pursued. I mean to trouble you with a short state of things at the most important of these periods, in order to give you a more distinct idea of our policy with regard to this most delicate of all objects. The colonies were from the beginning subject to the legislature of Great Britain, on principles which they never examined; and we permitted to them many local privileges, without asking how they agreed with that legislative authority. Modes of administration were formed in an insensible and very unsystematic manner. But they gradually adapted themselves to the varying condition of things: what was first a single kingdom, stretched into an empire; and an imperial superintendency, of some kind or other, became necessary. Parliament, from a mere representative of the people, and a guardian of popular privileges for its own immediate constituents, grew into a mighty sovereign. Instead of being a control on the crown on its own behalf, it communicated a sort of strength to the royal authority; which was wanted for the conservation of a new object, but which could not be safely trusted to the crown alone. On the other hand, the colonies, advancing by equal steps and governed by the same necessity, had formed within themselves, either by royal instruction or royal charter, assemblies so exceedingly resembling a parliament in all their forms, functions, and powers, that it was impossible they should not imbibe some opinion of a similar authority.

At the first designation of these assemblies they were probably not intended for anything more (nor perhaps did they think themselves much higher) than the municipal corporations within this island, to which some at present love to compare them. But nothing in progression can rest on its original plan. We may as well think of rocking a grown man in the cradle of an infant. Therefore, as the colonies prospered and increased to a numerous and mighty people, spreading over a very great tract of the globe, it was natural that they should attribute to assemblies, so respectable in their formal constitution, some part of the dignity of the great nations which they represented. No longer tied to bye-laws these assemblies made Acts of all sorts and in all cases whatsoever. They levied money, not for parochial purposes, but upon regular grants to the crown, following all the rules and principles of a parliament, to which they approached every day more and more nearly. Those who think themselves wiser than Providence and stronger than the course of nature may complain of all this variation on the one side or the other, as their several humours and prejudices may lead them. But things could not be otherwise, and English colonies must be had on these terms or not had at all. In the meantime neither party felt any inconvenience from this double legislature, to which they had been formed by imperceptible habits and old custom, the great support of all the governments in the world. Though these two legislatures were sometimes found perhaps performing the very same functions, they did not very grossly or systematically clash. In all likelihood this arose from mere neglect, possibly from the natural operation of things which, left to themselves, generally fall into their proper order. But whatever was the cause, it is certain that a regular revenue, by the authority of Parliament, for the support of civil and military establishments, seems not to have been thought of until the colonies were too proud to submit, too strong to be forced, too enlightened not to see all the consequences which must arise from such a system.

If ever this scheme of taxation was to be pushed against the inclinations of the people, it was evident that discussions must arise which would let loose all the elements that composed this double constitution, would show how much each of their members had departed from its original principles, and would discover contradictions in each legislature, as well to its own first principles as to its relation to the other, very difficult, if not absolutely impossible, to be reconciled.

Therefore at the first fatal opening of this contest, the wisest course seemed to be to put an end as soon as possible to the immediate causes of the dispute, and to quiet a discussion, not easily settled upon clear principles, and arising from claims which pride would permit neither party to abandon, by resorting as nearly as possible to the old, successful course. A mere repeal of the obnoxious tax, with a declaration of the legislative authority of this kingdom, was then fully sufficient to procure peace to *both sides.* Man is a creature of habit, and the first breach being of very short continuance, the colonies fell back exactly into their ancient state. The congress has used an expression with regard to this pacification which appears to me truly significant. After the repeal of the Stamp Act, "the colonies fell," says this assembly, "into their ancient state of *unsuspecting confidence in the mother-country.*" This unsuspecting confidence is the true centre of gravity amongst mankind, about which all the parts are at rest. It is this *unsuspecting confidence* that removes all difficulties and reconciles all the contradictions which occur in the complexity of all ancient, puzzled, political establishments. Happy are the rulers which have the secret of preserving it!

The whole empire has reason to remember with eternal gratitude, the wisdom and temper of that man[8] and his excellent associates, who, to recover this confidence, forged a plan of pacification in 1766. That plan, being built upon the nature of man and the circumstances and habits of the two countries, and not on any visionary speculations, perfectly answered its end as long as it was thought proper to adhere to it. Without giving a rude shock to the dignity (well or ill understood) of this Parliament, they gave perfect content to our dependencies. Had it not been for the mediatorial spirit and talents of that great man, between such clashing pretensions and passions, we should then have rushed headlong (I know what I say) into the calamities of that civil war in which, by departing from his system, we are at length involved; and we should have been precipitated into that war at a time when circumstances both at home and abroad were far, very far, more unfavourable unto us than they were at the breaking out of the present troubles.

I had the happiness of giving my first votes in Parliament for

[8] His mentor, the Marquis of Rockingham, who directed the repeal of the Stamp Act, March 1766, as leader of the Ministry at that time.

their pacification. I was one of those almost unanimous members who, in the necessary concessions of Parliament, would as much as possible have preserved its authority and respected its honour. I could not at once tear from my heart prejudices which were dear to me, and which bore a resemblance to virtue. I had then and I have still my partialities. What Parliament gave up I wished to be given as of grace and favour and affection, and not as a restitution of stolen goods. High dignity relented as it was soothed, and a benignity from old acknowledged greatness had its full effect on our dependencies. Our unlimited declaration of legislative authority produced not a single murmur. If this undefined power has become odious since that time and full of horror to the colonies, it is because the *unsuspicious confidence* is lost, and the parental affection, in the bosom of whose boundless authority they reposed their privileges, is become estranged and hostile.

It will be asked, if such was then my opinion of the mode of pacification, how I came to be the very person who moved, not only for a repeal of all the late coercive statutes, but for mutilating, by a positive law, the entireness of the legislative power of Parliament, and cutting off from it the whole right of taxation? I answer, because a different state of things requires a different conduct. When the dispute had gone to these last extremities (which no man laboured more to prevent than I did) the concessions which had satisfied in the beginning could satisfy no longer, because the violation of tacit faith required explicit security. The same cause which has introduced all formal compacts and covenants among men made it necessary. I mean habits of soreness, jealousy, and distrust. I parted with it as with a limb, but as a limb to save the body; and I would have parted with more if more had been necessary, anything rather than a fruitless, hopeless, unnatural civil war. This mode of yielding would, it is said, give way to independency without a war. I am persuaded from the nature of things and from every information that it would have had a directly contrary effect. But if it had this effect I confess that I should prefer independency without war to independency with it, and I have so much trust in the inclinations and prejudices of mankind and so little in anything else that I should expect ten times more benefit to this kingdom from the affection of America, though under a separate establishment, than from her perfect submission to the crown and Parliament, accompanied with her terror, disgust, and abhorrence. Bodies tied together by so unnatural a bond of union as mutual hatred are only connected to their ruin.

One hundred and ten respectable members of Parliament voted for that concession. Many not present when the motion was made were of the sentiments of those who voted. I knew it would then have made peace. I am not without hopes that it would do so at present if it were adopted. No benefit, no revenue could be lost by it, something might possibly be gained by its consequences. For be fully assured that of all the phantoms that ever deluded the fond hopes of a credulous world a parliamentary revenue in the colonies is the most perfectly chimerical. Your breaking them to any subjection, far from relieving your burthens (the pretext for this war) will never pay that military force which will be kept up to the destruction of their liberties and yours. I risk nothing in this prophecy.

Gentlemen, you have my opinion on the present state of public affairs. Mean as they may be in themselves, your partiality has made them of some importance. Without troubling myself to inquire whether I am under a formal obligation to it, I have a pleasure in accounting for my conduct to my constituents. I feel warmly on this subject, and I express myself as I feel. . . .[9]

There never, gentlemen, was a period in which the steadfastness of some men has been put to so sore a trial. It is not very difficult for well-formed minds to abandon their interest, but the separation of fame and virtue is a harsh divorce. Liberty is in danger of being made unpopular to Englishmen. Contending for an imaginary power we begin to acquire the spirit of domination and to lose the relish of honest equality. The principles of our forefathers become suspected to us, because we see them animating the present opposition of our children. The faults which grow out of the luxuriance of freedom appear much more shocking to us than the base vices which are generated from the rankness of servitude. Accordingly the least resistance to power appears more inexcusable in our eyes than the greatest abuses of authority. All dread of a standing military force is looked upon as a supersti-

[9] At this point Burke goes into a very lengthy defense of his party allegiance and party politicking, describing them as honorable pursuits and not corrupt, as "the court party" would have people think. In addition, he asserts that his efforts here have been directed only towards the preservation of the English race and the English constitution through "a firm and lasting union" of the English peoples.

tious panic. All shame of calling in foreigners and savages in a civil contest is worn off. We grow indifferent to the consequences inevitable to ourselves from the plan of ruling half the empire by a mercenary sword. We are taught to believe that a desire of domineering over our countrymen is love to our country, that those who hate civil war abate rebellion, and that the amiable and conciliatory virtues of lenity, moderation, and tenderness to the privileges of those who depend on this kingdom are a sort of treason to the state.

It is impossible that we should remain long in a situation which breeds such notions and dispositions without some great alteration in the national character. Those ingenuous and feeling minds who are so fortified against all other things, and so unarmed to whatever approaches in the shape of disgrace, finding these principles, which they considered as sure means of honour, to be grown into disrepute, will retire disheartened and disgusted. Those of a more robust make, the bold, able, ambitious men who pay some of their court to power through the people, and substitute the voice of transient opinion in the place of true glory, will give in to the general mode; and those superior understandings which ought to correct vulgar prejudice will confirm and aggravate its errors. Many things have been long operating towards a gradual change in our principles. But this American war has done more in a very few years than all the other causes could have effected in a century. It is therefore not on its own separate account, but because of its attendant circumstances that I consider its continuance or its ending in any way but that of an honourable and liberal accommodation as the greatest evils which can befall us. For that reason I have troubled you with this long letter. For that reason I entreat you again and again neither to be persuaded, shamed, or frighted out of the principles that have hitherto led so many of you to abhor the war, its cause, and its consequences. Let us not be among the first who renounce the maxims of our forefathers.

I have the honour to be, gentlemen, your most obedient and faithful humble servant,

EDMUND BURKE.

BEACONSFIELD, *April 3, 1777.*

P.S.—You may communicate this letter in any manner you think proper to my constituents.

11

SPEECH DURING THE DEBATES
ON MR. CHARLES FOX'S MOTION
FOR AN ENQUIRY INTO
THE STATE OF THE NATION

DECEMBER 2, 1777[1]

News and rumors had begun to reach London by December 1, 1777, about the disastrous defeats inflicted upon British troops in America. There was talk that General John Burgoyne had been overwhelmed, and Burke could not help mixing in some gloating with his regrets over the turn of events. Despite the rumors, Parliament would not receive official notification of Burgoyne's defeat at Saratoga from Lord Germain until Wednesday, December 3, 1777. However, Burke seized the opportunity on Tuesday, during the debate on Fox's planned motion for a general inquiry into the state of American affairs, to castigate the ministry for its unrealistic policy and behavior.

MR. BURKE observed, that he never knew the noble lord [North] to behave with so much candour, generosity, and spirit, as today. He had agreed to every title of his hon. friend's request; he had published a bond wherein he granted all; but in the end was inserted a little defeasance, with a power of revocation, by which he preserved himself from the execution of every grant he had made. His conduct reminded him of a certain governor,[2] who, when he arrived at his place of appointment, sat down to a table covered with every dainty and delicacy that art, nature, and a provident steward could furnish; but a pigmy physi-

[1]*PH*, XIX, 515-17.
[2] *The London Packet*, December 3, 1777, p. 2, reports that Burke's reference here is to the incident in Cervantes' *Don Quixote* when Sancho Pancha becomes governor of Barataria.

cian, who watched over the health of the governor, excepted to
one dish, because it was disagreeable, to another, because it was
hard of digestion, to a third, because it was unhealthy; and in
this progressive mode robbed the governor of every dish on the
table and left him without a dinner. He exposed the folly of the
idea that we must not negotiate with the Americans until they
had renounced their claim of independence. Are they not, he observed, in possession? Are they not independent *de facto*? They
possess the whole country of America. What we have, we have
gained by arms. If we have a government in America, it is
founded upon conquest since they set up their independence; and
as they enjoy the right *de facto* and we alone *de jure*, we must
and ought to treat with them on the terms of a *foederal union*. He
instanced the supposition of a treaty with France. The king of
Great Britain enjoys the right *de jure* to the kingdom of France;
the French king enjoys it *de facto*. He is merely a congress
usurper; and yet would it be argued that no treaty of peace
could take place with him until he had renounced his claim. He
wished the House to consider the effects that would arise from a
renunciation of their independence. By renouncing their independence, the Americans acknowledged their rebellion; by ac-
knowledging their rebellion, they acknowledged their crime; by
their crime they were deprived of their rights and obnoxious
to punishment. In such case, no treaty could be made consistent
with the honour of the British name; so that terms of negotiation
must be entered into during their independence. He said that the
Act on which Lord and Sir W[illiam] Howe were vested with
their commissions proposed two methods to be prosecuted to
bring about a peace; the one by force of arms, the other by terms
of conciliation. It would be necessary to inquire if both these
methods had been practised; the first, he was sensible had been
indeed tried, but he was afraid the second had not, else why were
not New York, Staten and Long Islands, with any other territory
we are in possession of, restored to the King's peace? Governor
Tryon had written to General Howe for the purpose of restoring
New York to the King's peace. General Howe answered that he
could not do it without the concurrence of the Secretary of State;
and there it stopped. This, he hoped, would be particularly en-
quired into. He supported the propriety of his hon. friend's
motion on several other grounds equally able and pointed and
hoped he would not depart from a tittle of his proposition.

12

SPEECH DURING THE DEBATE
ON THE DEFEAT OF
BURGOYNE'S ARMY AT SARATOGA

DECEMBER 3, 1777[1]

Secretary of State for the Colonies, Lord Germain, confirmed the rumors of Burgoyne's defeat at Saratoga, and, during the ensuing heated debate, Burke assaulted the mistakes of the military and the ministry.

M R. BURKE thanked the two hon. gentlemen[2] who had spoken before him for having afforded him some time to calm the tumult and perturbation in his breast, occasioned by the information given to the House by the noble lord. A whole army compelled to lay down their arms and receive laws from their enemies was a matter so new that he doubted if such another instance could be found in the annals of our history. The effrontery with which it was told excited no less astonishment than indignation. Ignorance had stamped every step taken during the course of the expedition; but it was the ignorance of the minister for the American department and not to be imputed to General Burgoyne, of whose good conduct, bravery, and skill, he did not entertain even the shadow of a doubt. The noble lord would perhaps urge in his defence that he had not had proper information and that his accounts had led him into error; but would the House admit such an excuse as an explanation of his offence? An offence which carried with it the most fatal consequences to

---

[1] *Lloyd's Evening Post*, XLI, 538.
[2] Lord Germain and James Luttrell.

the honour and interests of the nation. The noble lord said, if there was any blame to be laid—If there was any blame? Could an entire army be reduced to the painful necessity of laying down their arms and becoming prisoners of war without supposing that there was subject for blame somewhere? With the general and his troops, he was persuaded, there was no fault to be found; it could be traced nowhere but to the noble lord, whose ignorance was not brought as an extenuation but as a justification of his crime.

The Americans had, he observed, been always represented as cowards. This was far from being true; and he appealed to the conduct of Arnold and Gates towards General Burgoyne, as a striking proof of their bravery. Our army was totally at their mercy. We had employed the savages to butcher them, their wives, their aged parents, and their children; and yet, generous to the last degree, they gave our men leave to depart on their parole, never more to bear arms against North America. Bravery and cowardice could never inhabit the same bosom; generosity, valour, and humanity are ever inseparable. Poor, indeed, the Americans were, but in that consists their greatest strength. Sixty thousand men had fallen at the feet of their magnanimous, because voluntary, poverty. They had not yet lost all regard for the country from whence they sprung; anxious still for our home-defence, they had sent us back our troops and left their hands free to fight against every enemy of Great Britain but themselves. He reproached the noble lord for his misconduct and foolish credulity. He said he was astonished at him. In the beginning of last year, the noble lord informed them that the enemy were cowardly and our army superior in number. On what did he ground this information? On report, mere idle report, to which the noble lord was always an implicit slave. He said that the information on which ministers confided should be precise and certain, that misinformation was no palliation for their errors, and he did not imagine that the House would admit it as such. The intended measure was a conjunction between Howe and Burgoyne, but it was to be produced in the strangest manner he had ever heard of. The armies were to meet—yes; Howe was travelling southwards, and Burgoyne in the very same direction! The advocates for administration, he said, had delighted in representing America in an abject situation—as being without salt, without shoes, without a rag on their back, without stockings, &c. If the House had applied to him in the beginning of the war, he could have told them of many more wants than all those together under which the Americans laboured, but he could also have informed them that men fighting for liberty were not influenced by such particulars, that these only affected the body, but that the souls of the Americans were unreduced.

An enquiry ought to take place immediately into the causes of the failure of the expedition; nor should the vote for a further supply of troops be passed until the enquiry had been made, otherwise it would be only enabling Lord George Germain to send them over to America to be slaughtered, or made prisoners.[3]

[3] This last paragraph is not in Almon (VIII, 101-02) or in Hansard (XIX, 537-39)—which reprinted Almon—or in *Gentleman's Magazine*, (XLVIII, 294-95)—which is a condensation from the same source as the latter two. For another version, though of questionable accuracy, see *The London Chronicle*, (December 4, 1777) XLII, 549. *The London Packet* for December 3-5, 1777 (p. 3), incidentally, has an account almost identical to that in *The Lloyd's Evening Post*, but adds at the end: "It were impossible, in the narrow limits of a few columns of a newspaper, to give the reader any more than the mere outlines of Mr. Burke's speech which lasted a long time, and was no less remarkable for the soundness of reasoning it contained than the very moving and pathetic manner in which he delivered it, particularly his excordum." Most accounts only say that "He concluded with a few words on the Solicitor General, whom he called the counsel to the noble lord."

13

EXCERPTS FROM A SPEECH
AT GUILDHALL, BRISTOL,
PREVIOUS TO THE ELECTION

SEPTEMBER 6, 1780[1]

Burke's day of reckoning had come; he had to stand for reelection at Bristol. For some time he had known that the opposition to and criticism of him was quite powerful there. He chose this opportunity to defend his actions during the previous six years. The following includes his remarks on America. Unfortunately they were delivered at a time when conditions in America were very discouraging to Englishmen. Three days later, realizing he would probably be defeated, Burke withdrew his name and was soon elected by another constituency.

To OPEN my whole heart to you on this subject, I do confess, however, that there were other times, besides the two years, in which I did visit you, when I was not wholly without leisure for repeating that mark of my respect. But I could not bring my mind to see you. You remember that in the beginning of this American war (that era of calamity, disgrace, and downfall, an era which no feeling mind will ever mention without a tear for England) you were greatly divided; and a very strong body, if not the strongest, opposed itself to the madness which every art and every power were employed to render popular, in order that the errors of the rulers might be lost in the general blindness of the nation. This opposition continued until after our great, but most unfortunate, victory at Long Island. Then all the mounds and banks of our constancy were borne down at once,

---

[1] *Works*, VI, 374-76, 380-82, 402-03, 416-17, 418.

and the frenzy of the American war broke in upon us like a deluge. This victory, which seemed to put an immediate end to all difficulties, perfected us in that spirit of domination which our unparalleled prosperity had but too long nurtured. We had been so very powerful, and so very prosperous, that even the humblest of us were degraded into the vices and follies of kings. We lost all measure between means and ends; and our headlong desires became our politics and our morals. All men who wished for peace, or retained any sentiments of moderation, were overborne or silenced; and this city was led by every artifice (and probably with the more management because I was one of your members) to distinguish itself by its zeal for that fatal cause. In this temper of yours and of my mind, I should sooner have fled to the extremities of the earth than have shown myself here. I, who saw in every American victory (for you have had a long series of these misfortunes) the germ and seed of the naval power of France and Spain, which all our heat and warmth against America was only hatching into life—I should not have been a welcome visitant, with the brow and the language of such feelings. . . . But time at length has made us all of one opinion, and we have all opened our eyes on the true nature of the American war, to the true nature of all its successes and all its failures.

*   *   *   *

I was an Irishman in the Irish business, just as much as I was an American, when, on the same principles, I wished you to concede to America at a time when she prayed concession at our feet. Just as much was I an American when I wished Parliament to offer terms in victory and not to wait the well chosen hour of defeat for making good by weakness and by supplication a claim of prerogative, preeminence, and authority.

Instead of requiring it from me, as a point of duty, to kindle with your passions, had you all been as cool as I was, you would have been saved disgraces and distresses that are unutterable. Do you remember our commission? We sent out a solemn embassy across the Atlantic Ocean, to lay the crown, the peerage, the commons of Great Britain at the feet of the American Congress. That our disgrace might want no sort of brightening and burnishing, observe who they were that composed this famous embassy. My Lord Carlisle is among the first ranks of our nobility.

He is the identical man who, but two years before, had been put forward, at the opening of a session, in the House of Lords, as the mover of an haughty and rigorous address against America. He was put in the front of the embassy of submission. Mr. Eden was taken from the office of Lord Suffolk, to whom he was then Under-Secretary of State—from the office of that Lord Suffolk who but a few weeks before, in his place in parliament, did not deign to inquire where a congress of vagrants was to be found. This Lord Suffolk sent Mr. Eden to find these vagrants, without knowing where his king's generals were to be found who were joined in the same commission of supplicating those whom they were sent to subdue. They enter the capital of America only to abandon it; and these assertors and representatives of the dignity of England, at the tail of a flying army, let fly their Parthian shafts of memorials and remonstrances at random behind them. Their promises and their offers, their flatteries and their menaces, were all despised; and we were saved the disgrace of their formal reception only because the Congress scorned to receive them, while the state-house of independent Philadelphia opened her doors to the public entry of the ambassador of France. From war and blood we went to submission, and from submission plunged back again to war and blood, to desolate and be desolated, without measure, hope, or end. I am a Royalist: I blushed for this degradation of the crown. I am a Whig: I blushed for the dishonor of Parliament. I am a true Englishman: I felt to the quick for the disgrace of England. I am a man: I felt for the melancholy reverse of human affairs in the fall of the first power in the world.

*   *   *   *

. . . I confess to you freely, that the sufferings and distresses of the people of America in this cruel war have at times affected me more deeply than I can express. I felt every gazette of triumph as a blow upon my heart, which has an hundred times sunk and fainted within me at all the mischiefs brought upon those who bear the whole brunt of war in the heart of their country. Yet the Americans are utter strangers to me; a nation among whom I am not sure that I have a single acquaintance. Was I to suffer my mind to be so unaccountably warped, was I to keep such iniquitous weights and measures of temper and of reason, as to sympathize with those who are in open rebellion against an authority which

I respect, at war with a country which by every title ought to be, and is, most dear to me, and yet to have no feeling at all for the hardships and indignities suffered by men who by their very vicinity are bound up in a nearer relation to us,[2] who contribute their share, and more than their share, to the common prosperity, who perform the common offices of social life, and who obey the laws, to the full as well as I do?

*   *   *   *

. . . It is but too true, that the love, and even the very idea, of genuine liberty is extremely rare. It is but too true that there are many whose whole scheme of freedom is made up of pride, perverseness, and insolence. They feel themselves in a state of thraldom, they imagine that their souls are cooped and cabined in, unless they have some man or some body of men dependent on their mercy. This desire of having some one below them descends to those who are the very lowest of all; and a Protestant cobbler, debased by his poverty, but exalted by his share of the ruling church, feels a pride in knowing it is by his generosity alone that the peer whose footman's instep he measures is able to keep his chaplain from a jail. This disposition is the true source of the passion which many men in a very humble life have taken to the American war. *Our* subjects in America; *our* colonies; *our* dependants. This lust of party power is the liberty they hunger and thirst for; and this Siren song of ambition has charmed ears that one would have thought were never organized to that sort of music.

This way of *proscribing the citizens by denominations and general descriptions*, dignified by the name of reason of state, and security for constitutions and commonwealths, is nothing better at bottom than the miserable invention of an ungenerous ambition which would fain hold the sacred trust of power, without any of the virtues or any of the energies that give a title to it—a receipt of policy, made up of a detestable compound of malice, cowardice, and sloth.

. . . Crimes are the acts of individuals, and not of denominations; and therefore arbitrarily to class men under general descriptions, in order to proscribe and punish them in the lump for a presumed delinquency, of which perhaps but a part, perhaps

[2] Referring to the Irish.

none at all, are guilty, is indeed a compendious method, and saves a world of trouble about proof. But such a method, instead of being law, is an act of unnatural rebellion against the legal dominion of reason and justice; and this vice, in any constitution that entertains it, at one time or other will certainly bring on its ruin.

14

SPEECH SECONDING AN
AMENDMENT BY LORD NORTH
TO THE ADDRESS SUPPORTING
THE PRELIMINARY ARTICLES
OF PEACE

FEBRUARY 17, 1783[1]

The English had lost the war; Cornwallis had surrendered at York-town in October, 1781; and Lord North had resigned in February, 1782. Rockingham had finally returned to power in March only to die and be succeeded by Lord Shelburne in July. Shelburne had a vision of a new union of Great Britain and the United States, with the latter to open up and exploit the interior of America, and England to serve as the focal point of trade for America. To expedite this, Shelburne was eager to regain American confidence and friendship; and so he acceded to an extremely liberal treaty. But fearing that Parliament would not understand his purposes, he tried to justify the treaty to them by minimizing the concessions given to America and her allies. The crucial debates took place on this day and the opposition to the treaty's provisions contributed to Shelburne's downfall one week later.

M<small>R</small>. B<small>URKE</small> was very pleasant in his remarks on the modesty of the address. At the beginning of the session ministers had been very verbose because when men design to perform little, they promise a great deal. Now that Ministers had given way to the enemies of this country immense possessions, few words were judged to be wisest. But, perhaps, the country would deem the verbose address less exceptionable than that which was defended on the ground of its modesty; at least, he was sure the country would less feel the consequences of the one than of the other; but

[1] *PH*, XXIII, 466-69; *London Chronicle*, LIII, 165.

the right honourable Secretary[2] had adopted a style of reasoning fit for the defence of such conduct. In the first place he says this country was in a very bad state—its finances exhausted and its people adverse to the continuance of the war; and he gave it as a reason why we should accede to the terms of our enemies, while in the same breath he contradicts himself and asserts that "True, the peace is a bad one, but could you have made a better? Much has been given to the enemy, but, thank God, that much is a heap of rubbish." France has obtained Tobago and St. Lucie in the West Indies, a dangerous extent of fishery, all the forts and islands in Africa, and a district in the East Indies, which cannot fail to render France a formidable enemy, whenever war shall again break out. To Spain we have ceded East Florida, and guaranteed West Florida and Minorca. To America we had given an unlimited extent of territory, part of the province of Canada, a right of fishery, and other extraordinary cessions; and yet the right honourable Secretary tells the House that what we have conceded is of little worth to us and, in effect, a heap of rubbish. The right honourable Secretary forgot that this depreciation of what we had ceded to France, to Spain, and to America but ill agreed with this other, and indeed his chief argument in defence of the peace, namely, that being triumphant at the end of the last war, we insisted on terms humiliating to the House of Bourbon and that now the House of Bourbon, having the turn of the scale in the fortune of war, had a right to dictate terms of peace to us; and it was natural to expect, that they should insist on having those humiliating terms reversed. Is France then so moderate in the hour of her triumph that she is contented with a mere nominal cession? Does a heap of rubbish gratify her ambition? Modest House of Bourbon! Humble in prosperity, self-denying, when she could best feed her vanity and her interest! . . .

. . . He [then] came to a consideration of the Treaty with the United States, a treaty which in its preamble declared reciprocal advantage and mutual convenience to be its basis, but which was full of the most important concessions on our part, without the smallest balance or equipoise to support that reciprocity it so much boasted. Had he been worthy to advise ministers in making that treaty, he said, he would have advised them not to mention such a word as reciprocity. If the terms, from the necessity of

[2] Thomas Townshend.

our situation, were obliged to be such as were replete with disgraceful concession, to talk of reciprocity was adding insult to injury. In like manner, if what this country owed the Loyalists could not be obtained, (and why it could not, he was at a loss to imagine) he would not have said one syllable about those most unhappy men. Better to have left the whole to future negotiation and to have been totally silent upon the subject in the treaty, than to have consented to have set our hands to a gross libel on the national character, and in one flagitious article plunged the dagger into the hearts of the Loyalists and manifested our own impotency, ingratitude, and disgrace.[3] Mr. Burke said there were some of the Loyalists whose conduct he never had approved because he had been persuaded it led to mischief and ruin; but he had no right to say that even such of them as he had described might not be influenced by motives of purity and, looking at affairs through the medium of prejudice, instil into others those erroneous notions which they themselves had imbibed and which they firmly believed. At any rate, it must be agreed on all hands that a vast number of the Loyalists had been deluded by this country and had risked everything in our cause. To such men the nation owed protection, and its honour was pledged for their security at all hazards. How far any description of the refugees merited the titles of Vipers and Traitors bestowed on them by the honourable gentleman who moved the address, he would leave the world to imagine. He saw no use, however, in abusing and villifying those whom we had shamefully abandoned. . . .[4]

After creating some laughter at the expence of the present administration, he reverted to his original argument, that the peace was disadvantageous and disgraceful. In answer to Mr.

[3] Burke is here referring to the clause in the treaty wherein Congress agreed only to "earnestly recommend" to the states the restoration of confiscated royalist estates.

[4] This view of American Loyalists should be compared with that in his speech on June 6, 1788, below pp. 218-220. In addition, on February 22, 1782 (*PH*, XXII, 1038-39), Burke had launched a verbal attack against the then new Secretary of State for the Colonies, Welbore Ellis, while speaking in behalf of Gen. Conway's motion to end the American War. In it Burke criticized the former's opinion of American Loyalists, and his own comments there offer an interesting contrast to his views expressed in the speech above and in that of June 6, 1788:

The fact was plain, the right hon. gentleman was already in possession of all the noble lord's refugees; 72,000£. worth of refugees had

Powys's declaration, that the noble lord in the blue ribband was the cause of it, he said it by no means followed that we must submit to any terms because the war had been calamitous and unfortunate. The success of the last campaign gave us advantage ground, and we had a right either to have conceded less, or to have obtained more.

He concluded with seconding the amendment.

---

come to him as part of the inheritance. Oh! that we could only come to the happy moment when ministers would be pleased charitably to forbear the name of our friends in America. It was our friends in America that had done all the mischief. Every calamity of the war had arisen from our friends; and if such were to be our friends, he wished to God that we might hear of them no more. When exhausted and famishing, had our friends assisted us? Had they brought us a single bullock, a single bushel of Indian corn? Had they assisted us in any one shape or way? No! they had drawn us in the north to Saratoga, and in the south to Yorktown. What did the right hon. gentleman mean by his holding out the delusion of more friends? . . .

15

SPEECH BEFORE
THE HOUSE OF COMMONS
IN SUPPORT OF THE
AMERICAN INTERCOURSE BILL

MARCH 7, 1783[1]

Shelburne had informed few people of the scope of his American scheme. It is apparent here that Burke did not understand his intention, which was to link the United States and England by new, loose—but strong—ties of commerce. The bill before Parliament was designed to implement Shelburne's peace treaty by placing American shipping on an equal footing with English shipping, the hope being that America would devote itself to opening the continent while relying on British goods and trade. Burke and many others were highly critical of this bill—as they had been a month before of the preliminary peace treaty—for mercantilism still had many followers in 1783. Nevertheless, Burke's support of the bill brings us full circle to his first and basic evaluation of Anglo-American relations as primarily and most desirably commercial.

M R. BURKE laid at the door of ministers all the mischiefs that were apprehended and might arise from the Bill. They were to be all ascribed to their neglect. And it was astonishing, indeed, that in the course of seven months negotiation with the American commissioners at Paris, not one commercial regulation to form an intercourse between the two countries had ever been so much as talked of. The interregnum which had now actually shown itself, he feared, had taken place many months ago. At least there had been, it was obvious, an interregnum of all attention to duty and all regard for the first and most important

[1] Debrett, John, *The Parliamentary Register,* XXVI, 441-43 (Debrett took over the *Register* from Almon in 1781). See also, *London Chronicle,* LIII, 231.

interests of the country when the provisional treaty was negotiated at Paris. To that interregnum, he in his conscience believed, were owing the difficulties the House laboured under at
that moment. Had not his Majesty's ministers been guilty of the
fatal neglect of not preparing and providing an article for the
future regulation of the commerce of this country and America
when they negotiated the treaty with America, the House would
not then have felt itself embarrassed as it did [over the problem
of] how to proceed with the present Bill.

The provisional treaty proved the talents of the negotiators as
Geographers, but no one would ever have suspected commercial
men had been engaged in it. A very able gentleman indeed (Mr.
Oswald), who was possessed of as great commercial knowledge as
any man, was employed in the negotiation; but by a strange provision of departments, he was sent into the woods of Canada to find
out and ascertain the boundaries. Another gentleman, who was his
assistant, and capable of giving the clearest lights on the subject
of trade was also sent rambling into the woods. That noble lord,
instead of applying to those persons who could have given him
some information about the fisheries, Mr. Holdsworth and Mr.
Brett, had sent merchants into the woods, who could give him no
assistance. The two negotiators, having passed seven months without having done anything for the commerce of this country, put
him in mind of two Irishmen. One of them being asked what he
was doing, answered—nothing; and the other having been asked
the same question, replied—I am helping him; so that it looked
like the cross-readings (alluding to Mr. Whitford's propensity and
talents), which nature designed for one line of business, employed
in another, for which nature had not qualified them. This surely
was singular conduct in ministers, but this was not all; for the
provisional treaty, such as it was, was signed on the 23d of November, and yet no plan, no system of commercial intercourse,
had since been formed. But in the month of March, a crude and
undigested Bill was brought to parliament, without any previous
communication with the Americans. However, such as it was,
considering the necessity of the times, he would support the
principle of the Bill, though he disliked the clauses. Mr. Burke
displayed a great deal of humour in comparing this country and
America to a man and a woman courting. The present Bill was
somewhat like a courtship, if any were to take place between
himself and a lady, where the natural order of things would be
reversed and the lady would have much to give, he little or noth-

ing to return. So, in the instance of the Bill before the House, Great Britain was extremely fond in her wooing and, in her love-fit, was ready to give largely; whereas, to his knowledge, America had nothing to give in return.

A right hon. member, who had displayed an uncommon degree of commercial knowledge,[2] was afraid that we should lose our manufactures by the emigration of our working tools. As to the latter, it was really not worth mentioning. It was one of the puerilities of our laws to forbid the exportation of manufacturing tools; but this was a farce. We might as well attempt to prevent the making of hay in America by forbidding the exportation of scythes. As to the emigration of artificers, he did not think it possible to prevent it; nor indeed would it be very wise to attempt it. But still he saw little danger from this of our losing our manufactures. It was very well known that before the war 8,000 persons used to emigrate in a year from the north of Ireland to America, and yet there never was a linen manufacture set up there. The reason was obvious; these persons betook themselves immediately to agriculture and the grazing of cattle. The cheapness of land and, above all, the idleness which necessarily attended upon the cheapness, and which was the great and principal boon that America held out to emigrants, naturally prevented men from thinking of manufactures. And while there was an immense extent of territory, of nearly 900,000 square miles, to attract the attention of the inhabitants to agriculture, we had no reason to apprehend that they would be able, for a very long time indeed, to rival us in manufactures. As to the provision trade, the Americans had it always, for they supplied the islands for years back with provisions. The loss of the sugar trade, indeed, would be a heavy one, and perhaps it must be lost one time or other, but he did not apprehend that the loss was near at hand.

. . . The principle that he wished to lay down, with respect to America, would be not to treat her subjects as aliens. He would still treat them as fellow-subjects, as far as he could, and establish his regulations rather by an improvement of the old commercial system than by an introduction of a new one. By the old laws, it was necessary that the American ships should be registered and bring their certificates with them; now he would have all prohibitory acts, and all those relative to the registering, repealed, and leave the American vessels in every respect as they were before, in point of trade.

[2] William Eden.

16

SPEECH BEFORE
THE HOUSE OF COMMONS
IN SUPPORT OF A BILL
TO COMPENSATE AMERICAN
LOYALISTS

JUNE 6, 1788[1]

The war was over and peace had been made. Many other issues had arisen to occupy Burke's time and thought. Nevertheless, not all of the problems arising out of the Revolution had been resolved, and one in particular concerned the sizeable number of American Loyalists who had lost their property and, in many cases, had had to leave America. Many had been ruined financially because of their loyalty to England, and although many Loyalists were welcomed back in America in the late 1780's, relatively few received any compensation and their grievances thus remained unsatisfied. The motion now proposed to compensate American Loyalists, and Burke, who had had reservations about the Loyalists (see above, pp. 213-214, n.4), nevertheless now declared that England was bound by promises to aid them. This is Burke's last speech on American affairs.

M R. BURKE said that he felt extreme concern at discovering that an hon. gentleman[2] of so enlightened a mind, and of the purity of whose intentions, on all occasions, no man could make the smallest question, had any doubts or objections to the present motion. He never gave a vote with more satisfaction than he should give his vote for the present motion because, though the Loyalists had no claim upon the House founded in strict right—which must necessarily be arbitrary, and could admit of no modification whatever, but must be fully satisfied to its utmost extent,

---

[1] Debrett, XLI, 55-56.
[2] William Hussey.

whatever that might be—yet the House was bound in honour and justice to take their claims into consideration. Mr. Burke assured the Committee that such a mode of compensating the claims of the Loyalists would do the country the highest credit. It was a new and a noble instance of national bounty and generosity. At the Restoration, he remembered the case had been widely different. There the poor bishops, who had been so long deprived of their sees, were deemed well [enough?] off to obtain their sees again, and the sum of 80,000£. was all that the House had voted for the King to distribute among the Loyalists, though it was a well-known fact that the Marquis of Worcester alone had lost an estate of 300,000£.

Mr. Burke descanted on these historical facts and said it was a solid satisfaction to his mind that he had uniformly voted against every question that led to the consequences that laid the Committee under the necessity of coming to the vote then proposed. He should, nevertheless, cheerfully vote any sum however large, upon the account stated because, though the American war had been carried on by the voice of a majority, all were involved in the promises of that majority; and the Loyalists had certainly been assured from the first authority in the state that if they left their property and joined the King's army, or came to England, they should receive protection and support. That pledge was sacred and ought to be faithfully fulfilled. With regard to the proposed mode of making the compensation, he thought it both liberal and prudent, neither too large on the one hand, nor too small on the other; and he gave the right hon. gentleman credit for having made the divisions, and distinguished the deductions to be taken from the claims of the different classes of Loyalists. It did this country honour, inasmuch as it showed our attention to the different extent and force of the claims of the several claimants; and it would not have done them honour had they expected to have been paid the full amount of those claims because it would have proved that they had no real principle of loyalty to inspire their conduct, but that they had joined the side that they had joined, under a certain expectation of running no risk whatever but of receiving back the whole of their property.

After observations on the good effect of such a liberal line of conduct—upon which he founded hopes that, if anything would, *that* [referring to compensation by Great Britain], at one day or other, might effect a renewal of ancient amity and connection between America and Great Britain—and after rejoicing that America had not the honour of compensating the Loyalists for their losses, which would have been a wise way of settling up in the world for themselves, Mr. Burke concluded with giving his assent to the motion.